Heterographies

Heterographies

Sexual Difference in French Autobiography

Alex Hughes

Oxford • New York

First published in 1999 by
Berg
Editorial offices:
150 Cowley Road, Oxford, OX4 1JJ, UK
70 Washington Square South, New York, NY 10012, USA

© Alex Hughes, 1999

Berg is the imprint of Oxford International Publishers Ltd.

Library of Congress Cataloging-in-Publication Data

A catalogue record for this book is available from the Library of Congress. ·

British Library Cataloguing-in-Publication Data

A catalogue record for this book is available from the British Library.

ISBN 1 85973 320 4 (Cloth)

Typeset by JS Typesetting, Wellingborough, Northants.
Printed in the United Kingdom by WBC Book Manufacturers, Bridgend,
Mid Glamorgan.

Contents

Acknowledgements

I am most grateful to the editors of *Modern and Contemporary France* and *French Forum* for giving me permission to return, in Chapter 2 part I and Chapter 5 part II, to material first published in their journals and to rework and expand it as part of the comparative analysis offered here.

Introduction

The readings offered in the five chapters that make up the body of this volume reflect concerns that have constituted the focus of my research and teaching activities for a number of years. *Heterographies* derives its impetus, in other words, from my ongoing interest in issues of sexual and gender representation, and in the intersections of sexual difference and life-writing. Its title invokes the diversity of the texts its analyses target, the variety of theoretical perspectives that inform these analyses, and the manner in which, within them, a series of 'encounters' between specific instances of male- and female-authored narrative discourse are brought into being. The self-representational works with which *Heterographies* engages are narrative constructs that not only point up the central place accorded by autobiographical discourse in all its variant modalities to the articulation of sexed subjectivity but also attest to my personal fascination with a particular group of twentieth-century French autobiographical practitioners: Violette Leduc (1907–1972); Jean-Paul Sartre (1905–1980); Hervé Guibert (1955–1991); Marguerite Duras (1914–1996); André Gide (1869–1951); Marie Cardinal (1929–); Simone de Beauvoir (1908–1986); and Serge Doubrovsky (1928–). In Section III of this Introduction, I shall outline the ambit of the readings I make of a cluster of *récits de vie* published by these authors between 1926 and 1990, and establish the nature and scope of the project my readings promote. Before I do that, I shall use Section II to comment in general terms on the gender/sex/sexuality: autobiography interface and to survey critical literature concerned with the phenomenon of gendered self-representation. First, though, I want to talk about what life-writing 'is', in a contextualizing move that, inevitably, carries with it the risk of overschematization but has the virtue of familiarizing my readers, from the outset, with the discursive terrain to which *Heterographies* attends.

Autobiographical Paradigms

In 'Le pacte autobiographique' (1975),[1] Philippe Lejeune defines autobiography famously and centrally as a 'retrospective prose narrative written by a real person concerning his own existence, where the focus is his individual life, in particular the story of his personality'.[2] The autobiographical artefact his much-cited definition profiles and privileges may be qualified as the 'formal' or the 'canonical' or the 'classic' *récit autobiographique*. Key avatars of it include the *Confessions* of

St Augustine and Jean-Jacques Rousseau, both of which are usually taken as 'founding' works of the autobiographical genre. It typically favours a narrative organization characterized by chronological progression because, as the Lejeunian commentator Paul John Eakin affirms, an organization of this ilk coheres with the 'essential narrativity of human existence'.[3] Equally, through the narrative strategies it adopts, it makes a manifest commitment to sincerity and referentiality: that is, it flags the story it tells not only as (intentionally) veridical but as grounded in a reality that is extratextual.[4] In order, Lejeune proposes, to persuade us that what it offers for our scrutiny is an 'essentially referential account of [its author's] life, which represents as truthfully as possible that life on paper',[5] the *autoportrait classique*[6] includes narrative elements that initiate an autobiographical 'pact' and incite its readers to endorse it. The 'pact' in question – a key focus of Lejeune's metanarrative speculations – constitutes a contract of identity, in which the reader partakes and which s/he must accept.[7] Sealed, generally, by an intradiegetic deployment of the proper name, the autobiographical 'pact' is set up inside the (canonical) autobiographical *opus* as the emblem and guarantee of its autobiographical, non-fictional status. The elements that establish it function to encourage us to construe the text in which they feature as one whose author, narrator and protagonist share an identitarian connection; as one that is therefore an exercise in 'proper' self-representation; and as one that communicates, veraciously, some aspect of its creator's existence and essence.[8]

In practice, of course, as Lejeune himself signals, autobiographical writings of a 'contractual' stripe do not always fulfil each of the conditions his primary definition adumbrates absolutely.[9] Clearly, moreover, even the most orthodox of autobiographical essays cannot be relied on to live up, comprehensively, to the promise of referentiality and sincerity whose enunciation is peculiar to autobio-graphical – and biographical – discourse, and will rarely claim to do so completely. 'Pure' autobiographical truth/reference is fundamentally impossible because, as Liz Stanley observes, 'memory is necessarily limited, [. . .] fictive devices are always necessary in producing accounts of ourselves [and] the apparently referential and unique selves that auto/biographical accounts invoke are actually invocations of a cultural representation of what selves should be'.[10] It is an authorial (and cultural) fantasy, not an achievable goal: an object of autobiographical aspiration, rather than a desideratum that lends itself to realization. And, not unexpectedly, the majority of canonically-formatted autobiographies contain components that reveal this to be the case. They include, in other words, narrative indications or procedures that let us know, as Michael Sheringham pithily puts it, that the subject of auto-biography is a constructed *hybrid*, a 'fusion of past and present, self and other, document and desire, referential and textual'.[11] They posit themselves as proffering, finally, a *resemblance* of the truth and an *image* of the real, rather than strict verisimilitude.[12]

Narrative discourse, then, that respects the formal parameters of the 'traditional' autobiographical paradigm may be understood, broadly, as a discourse that both works to express individual identity/history in a would-be truthful, referential manner and exposes the activity it pursues as un- or only partially actualizable. The impossibility that inheres in autobiography helps us to see why individual authors, seduced by the life-writing enterprise, elect to step outside the bounds of the autobiographical model 'proper', and to pursue practices of self-representation that self-consciously problematize the factuality/sincerity of the self-reflexive narrative a(rtefa)ct, play with the fiction:autobiography divide, and thereby point up what Serge Doubrovsky conceives as the 'folly' intrinsic in the writerly attempt to sustain an autobiographical discourse of self- or existential truth.[13] These practices are commonly associated with postmodern autobiographers such as Roland Barthes – that is, with writers whose work evinces a mid-/late twentieth-century contestation of the concept of the coherent, stable, transcribable 'self' – and with women life-writers: however, they are certainly not exclusive to them, or exclusive to the autoreferential literature of the contemporary period.[14]

Self-reflexive narrative modalities that are excluded from the generic realm of 'formal' autobiography and call its pretensions and processes into question, or refuse to embrace them wholesale, include the autobiographical novel and *auto-fiction*. In the *roman autobiographique*, the literary practitioner produces a form of *écriture de soi* by drawing on the data of his/her lived reality, narratively and (re)creatively. At the same time, s/he eschews the autobiographical, 'contractual' act of self-identification/nomination, thwarting the reader's will to construe his/her story as referential or veridical.[15] The narrative enterprise that the autobiographical novelist pursues, and whose fictional grounding is habitually signalled in Francophone writing by a peritextual deployment of the generic tag *roman* (novel),[16] can be read as a kind of cop-out, a forfeiture of honesty. But, equally, we can understand it as a project that acknowledges and works with the ineluctable (self-)fabrication that autobiography 'proper' necessarily entails. The 'fictiveness' built into the autobiographical endeavour is exposed and engaged with more radically, however, in the narrative procedure that is *autofiction*. Practised most famously, in France, by Serge Doubrovsky, and theorized in his 1988 essay 'Autobiographie/vérité/psychanalyse',[17] autofictional discursivity involves the elaboration of a textual account that presents itself as novelistic (that is, as a *roman*) yet introduces us to a narrator/protagonist who is nominally identified with its author and shares his experiential history. Entrenched in generic ambiguity and a narrative 'undecidability' that hinders us from taking the tale it tells as either totally factual or totally invented, compelling us to perceive that tale as somehow (deliberately) 'true-and-untrue', *autofiction* draws our attention, dramatically, to the 'composante fictionnelle des récits de vie'.[18] Concomitantly, it 'puts the author in the text' in a way that the autobiographical novel does not, even as it prevents us from 'seeing' or identifying him/her within it with the (misguided) ease we bring to our reading of the *autoportrait classique*.[19]

Autobiography/Sexual Difference

As my foregoing remarks reveal, the life-writing enterprise – an enterprise to which literary practitioners habitually recur in order to achieve some measure of self-understanding or self-reconciliation[20] – embraces a variety of narrative forms, which do not engage identically with the referentiality/(re)creativity dynamic and are differently 'received' by the reader. In all its heterogeneous manifestations, however, *l'écriture de soi* tends, as a discourse of selfhood and experience, to incorporate representations of sexuality and sexual difference, to point up issues of gender and engenderment and, often, to privilege its rendering of sexed subjectivity – because, self-evidently, sex and gender (formation) constitute fundamental organizing components of human identity.[21] Allied to this phenomenon is a corpus of what Shirley Neuman qualifies as 'gender conscious' critical readings of autobiographical textuality.[22] The readings in question are contained, *inter alia*, in four edited collections of essays – Domna Stanton's *The Female Autograph* (1984);[23] Shari Benstock's *The Private Self* (1988);[24] *Life/Lines* (1988), compiled by Bella Brodzki and Celeste Schenck;[25] and Neuman's own *Autobiography and Questions of Gender* (1991) – and two single-authored works, Liz Stanley's *The Auto/biographical I* (1992) and Leigh Gilmore's *Autobiographics* (1994).[26] And I want, now, to comment briefly on what these studies do and do not do.

Informed by a variety of conceptual perspectives, and driven by diverse aims and intentions, all the critical texts cited above contribute to a historically contextual-izable feminist project of 'visibilization':[27] that is, to an exegetical endeavour that seeks to expose, delineate and/or flag up the exclusion of 'autogynographies' from the autobiographical canon (cf. Stanton); the lack of 'consecratory' attention accorded to them in key works of autobiographical analysis and literary history (cf. Stanton, Gilmore); the academic legitimacy of women's autobiography and of critical writings concerned with it (cf. Benstock); the procedures and paradigms women life-writers adopt to speak of themselves and for their (female) readership (cf. Benstock, Brodzski and Schenck); the communities within which women write (cf. Gilmore); and the reading 'maps' or interpretative strategies that allow us to situate women's life-writings and/in their relation to the variant discourses and cultural institutions with which they intersect (cf. Gilmore, Stanley). The visibilizing project that these studies sustain is, moreover, an important and laudable one. However, with the central exception of Neuman's *Autobiography and Questions of Gender*, they broadly neglect to engage consistently or productively with the fact that, as Elaine Showalter reminds us,[28] masculinities as well as femininities constitute valid objects of analytical inquiry and problematization, and must not be ignored by gender-oriented literary critical practice if gender criticism is to evolve beyond limits imposed by the doxas of patriarchy. In other words, their exclusively gynocentric orientation – born out of the discouraging androcentrism of much mid-twentieth-century autobiographical (and literary) scholarship, and, indubitably, legitimated by it – helps to *invisibilize* the value of 'speaking of gender', and of sexual difference, across a spectrum of male- as well as female-authored autobiographical narrative productions.[29]

In her Introduction to *Autobiography and Questions of Gender* – a collection devoted in the main to Anglophone life-writing – Shirley Neuman pertinently suggests that if work dedicated to the conceptualization of a poetics of gender in autobiography has not, hitherto, adequately addressed the category in relation to which 'genderic difference' is defined and constructed (that is, masculinity), this is in part because the gender ideology of Western culture posits men as the only, or the only visible/viable, sex category, and as one whose specificity needs neither to be represented nor theorized.[30] Further, in a move similar to that effected by Showalter in *Speaking of Gender* (and somewhat ironically, given that the majority of the essays her edited volume contains scrutinize women's narratives and autobiographical practice), she urges literary critics to make good the gaps in gender-and-autobiography studies, to read men's *and* women's self-histories in a gender-sensitive mode, and to acknowledge male- as well as female-authored autobiographies as sites of an expression of sexed subjecthood, of gendered representation. In this monograph, I have adopted Neuman's exhortation as a guiding principle. In so doing, I have elaborated a nexus of critical readings that illuminate the workings of sexual difference in/and autobiography (i) in relation, specifically, to twentieth-century French life-writing and (ii) in a very particularized fashion.

Heterographies

The best-known of the critical accounts that take French autobiographical discourse (as opposed to individual French autobiographers) as their focus do not prioritize a gender-conscious reading perspective. Concerned, above all, with questions of genre and narrative practice, Lejeune's *Le Pacte autobiographique* resolutely refuses to develop gender-focused analyses and, moreover, leaves the reader with the (mistaken) impression that women-authored French autobiographies, if not inexistent, must be a very rare breed indeed.[31] Sheringham's more recent *French Autobiography: Devices and Desires* (1993) neither ignores the autobiographical productions of France's *écrivaines* nor neglects to read them with an eye to their particularity, but is certainly not a study in which issues pertaining to sexual difference are treated extensively.[32] The same can be said of *L'Autobiographie* (1997), for all that its authors, Jacques Lecarme and Eliane Lecarme-Tabone, devote two of their twenty-four chapters to 'l'autobiographie des femmes'.[33] A preoccupation with sexual/gender inscription in/and Francophone life-writing does characterize Leah Hewitt's *Autobiographical Tightropes* (1991) and Raylene Ramsay's *The French New Autobiographies* (1996). Neither of these single-authored works, however, can be deemed to move the 'gender and autobiography' debate forward, by addressing sexual difference *comprehensively*.[34] The first of them, which attends, richly, to the contradictions and tensions encountered by Francophone women literary practitioners as they embrace the autobiographical endeavour, is exclusively gynocentric.[35] The second, while it is not, contains only one chapter in which male-authored autobiographical discourse (Robbe-Grillet's) is scrutinized in depth as a locus of gendered (self-) representation.

In contrast to the last-mentioned essays, *Heterographies* seeks to engage with the renditions of sexual difference proffered in or constituted by a number of modern French *récits de vie* in a manner that *is* consistently 'inclusive' – that is, that eschews a gynocentrism it is tempting, in the late 1990s, to qualify as slightly anachronistic, and treats of men's and women's writings in equal measure. Equally, though, it opts for an approach that is localized as well. My analyses, in other words, neither turn on an effort to produce universalizing generalizations about what men's and women's self-inscriptive discourse is 'like', nor aim to persuade the reader to elaborate such generalizations. Rather, my readings attend to particular differences – and parallels – that obtain between individual works of male- and female-authored French *écriture de soi*, as well as to the particular masculinities and femininities profiled within them.

All ten texts scrutinized in my study are narratives in which issues and experiences related to sexuality, desire and/or gendered or sexual identity are invoked. In the five chapters that make *Heterographies* up, these narratives are brought together in 'pairs', and subjected to a series of detailed explications that (i) approach them in a sustainedly gender-centred if methodologically eclectic manner and (ii) cast some of their similarities and dissimilarities into relief. My strategy, in short, privileges a practice of close, gender-oriented, comparative interpretation. An analogous exegetical procedure is productively employed in Denise Brahimi's *Appareillages* (1991), a monograph whose discussions target a cluster of predominantly fictional, second- and third-world (predominantly) Francophone texts.[36] Brahimi's project, however, rests on an attempt to evaluate the specificity of women's literary creativity ('l'apport spécifique des femmes à la création artistique'), in part by measuring it against a masculine yardstick.[37] My own purpose, in counterpoint, is to bring into conjunction self-representational *récits* drawn from the male and the female writing camps, and to read these *récits* in conjunction, in order that specific manifestations of sexual difference – a difference mobilized and articulated in the autobiographical discursive sphere – might emerge as objects of critical scrutiny. Relying as it does on the creation, and the dissection, of a matrix of male/female narrative 'meetings', my reading practice may strike some of my readers as overinvested in a masculine/feminine polarity promoted and naturalized by the gender ideology of heterosexual normalcy, and as therefore somehow heterosexist.[38] In view of this I want to signal, from the outset, that a key concern of my analyses – which seek to reflect on difference in as broad-ranging a fashion as possible, and treat, *inter alia*, of French-authored life-writings inscribed with a 'gay signature' (Gide's *Si le grain ne meurt*; Guibert's *A l'ami qui ne m'a pas sauvé la vie*; Leduc's *La Bâtarde*) – is the autobiographical transcription of same-sex relationality and desire.

What, then, do the readings that *Heterographies* comprises address? In Chapter 1, I consider the erasures and occlusions woven into two highly dissimilar *récits d'enfance*, Violette Leduc's *L'Asphyxie* (1946) and Jean-Paul Sartre's *Les Mots* (1964). Locating textual 'burial' as an obsessional narrative strategy, and as a strategy stimulated by anxiety and sexual investment alike, I discuss the diverse motivations subtending the maternally-related encryptments effected in the child-hood self-histories these particular authors produced. Chapter 2 takes as its focus a pair of more contemporary texts, Hervé Guibert's *L'Image fantôme* (1981) and Marguerite Duras's *L'Amant* (1984). Here, I situate the procedures of photographic writing and photographic fetishization inscribed in the autobiographically unorthodox discursive spaces these narratives constitute, illuminate the divergences and convergences that divide/connect the *photo/autoécriture* of their creators, and reflect on the ways in which the photo-writing of Guibert and Duras can be deemed to be driven by desire. In Chapters 1 and 2, amongst other things, I pinpoint a concern with the qualities of the maternal subject as a factor common to, and as one of the defining characteristics of, the life-writings I examine. In Chapters 3 and 4, I concentrate on the representations of space elaborated in self-inscriptive works by Gide, Cardinal, Guibert and Beauvoir. Chapter 3 foregrounds the different – but equally gender-inflected – visions of colonial North Africa adumbrated in Gide's *Si le grain ne meurt* (1926) and Cardinal's *Les Mots pour le dire* (1975), and dissects the degree to which these individual male/female-authored visions mesh with discursive paradigms associated with the colonialist literary field. Chapter 4 explores the treatments of the medical environment proffered in Guibert's autofictional *A l'ami qui ne m'a pas sauvé la vie* (1990) and Beauvoir's (auto)biographical *Une mort très douce* (1964), highlighting the manner in which, in both of these self-referential works, the activity of clinical narrative geographization seemingly enables the life-writing subject to (re)connect with the inaccessible, same-sex Other. Likewise, my fourth chapter focuses on the accounts Beauvoir and Guibert offer of the production/fabrication, in the medical milieu, of 'abject' identity. Finally, in Chapter 5, using the work of Judith Butler as my theoretical support, I turn my attention to the interimplicated articulations of 'queer' gender identity-performance elaborated in Serge Doubrovsky's second *autofiction*, *Un amour de soi* (1982) and Violette Leduc's more formally autobiographical *La Bâtarde* (1964). While each of my chapters, and the paired readings they provide, are self-contained, I have sought wherever possible to profile the manifold connections that bind the texts composing my corpus, and to encourage my readers to pick up on them.

Concluding Remarks

I want to draw my introductory discussion to a close by signalling some of the writing strategies I have chosen to adopt in *Heterographies*. And there are three key things that I want to say about them. First, although the interpretations I have elaborated are intended to reflect the complexities of the narratives they address, I have endeavoured throughout to write for a wide audience and to avoid being unnecessarily or wilfully obscure. Second, in talking about the *dramatis personae* invoked in the life-writings I scrutinize, I have sought to do so in a manner that acknowledges the fact that all these *personae* are *textual* creations/constructs, but also recognizes that particular modalities of autobiographical discourse invite us to speak in particular – and variant – ways about the narrativized, narrating selves they present for our inspection. Third, I am aware that some readers of this book may not be French speakers, but that many will be. In terms of quotation and reference, I have therefore proceeded as follows. I have kept titles of texts, whether primary or secondary, in French. Quotations from the French-authored primary works constituting my corpus are given in translation in my main text (I have provided my own translation if none exists), and in the original in the notes. Where I simply refer to particular parts of the French primary text under examination, I have included page references to it and to its published translation in the body of my discussion, using acronyms in order to do so. In the case of French-authored secondary or critical writings that have been translated into English, that are as well known in translation as they are in their original French and that feature prominently in my discussion, I have cited the English translation as well as the French original, on occasion (see Chapters 2 and 4) via the use of acronyms contained in the body of my text. When quoting from such writings, I have drawn on their English translations in my main discussion, citing or simply referencing the French original in my notes. French critical/secondary texts and essays that have Anglophone translations but that I do not refer to at length or in detail are referenced in the original: however, my Bibliography gives details of their English versions. On occasion, I quote from French-language essays that have not been translated into English. Here, I provide a translation of my own, citing the original text in my notes.

I could not have produced *Heterographies* without the help and support of a number of friends and colleagues. I should like to conclude my Introduction by expressing my heartfelt thanks to those people who read sections of my manuscript in its various stages, gave advice about the readings it pursues or provided me with material that enabled me to develop them further. They are: Jennifer Birkett; Jean-Pierre Boulé; Ceri Crossley; Serge Doubrovsky; Alison Fell; Sarah Fishwick; Owen Heathcote; Diana Holmes; Samantha Milton; Andrea Noble; Naomi Segal; Michael Sheringham; Judith Still; Ursula Tidd; James Williams and Anne Witz. *Heterographies* is dedicated to Andrea, Anne, Ceri and Nick Hammond – good companions in The Land That Time Forgot, and wise counsellors in times of trouble.

Notes

1. P. Lejeune (1975), 'Le pacte autobiographique', in *Le Pacte autobiographique*, Paris, pp. 13–46, translated as 'The Autobiographical Pact', trans. K. Leary, in P. Lejeune (1989), *On Autobiography*, Minneapolis, pp. 3–30.
2. 'récit rétrospectif en prose qu'une personne réelle fait de sa propre existence, lorsqu'elle met l'accent sur sa vie individuelle, en particulier sur l'histoire de sa personnalité'. See 'Le pacte autobiographique', p. 14; 'The Autobiographical Pact', p. 4.
3. See Paul John Eakin (1989), 'Foreword', in P. Lejeune, *On Autobiography*, pp. vii–xxvii, p. xii. Eakin explains here that Lejeune's theoretical work both privileges and devalues autobiographical 'linearity' and, ultimately, can be taken to underestimate the 'significance of chronology as a structure of reference in autobiography' (cf. p. xii), even though his key classification of what autobiography 'is' implicitly foregrounds the centrality of chronological patterning to autobiographical practice.
4. See 'Le pacte autobiographique', pp. 36–7; 'The Autobiographical Pact', p. 22. Useful also on the claims that 'classic' autobiography makes is M. Darrieussecq (1996), 'L'Autofiction, un genre pas sérieux', *Poétique*, no. 107, pp. 369–80, pp. 375–6. I invoke this latter piece in detail in Chapter 4.
5. L. Stanley (1992), *The Auto/biographical I: The Theory and Practice of Feminist Auto/biography*, Manchester and New York, pp. 60–1.
6. Serge Doubrovsky uses this term to denote 'canonical' autobiography, and I shall do likewise, even though Lejeune distinguishes between the *autobiographie* 'proper' and the *autoportrait*. See S. Doubrovsky (1988), 'Autobiographie/vérité/psychanalyse', in *Autobiographiques: de Corneille à Sartre*, Paris, pp. 61–79, translated as 'Autobiography/Truth/Psychoanalysis', trans. L. Whalen and J. Ireland, *Genre*, 1993, vol. XXVI, pp. 27–42.
7. See 'Le pacte autobiographique' pp. 26–7; 'The Autobiographical Pact', pp. 13–14.

8. See 'Le pacte autobiographique', p. 36; 'The Autobiographical Pact', p. 22.
9. See 'Le pacte autobiographique', pp. 14–15; 'The Autobiographical Pact', pp. 4–5.
10. *The Auto/biographical I*, p. 62.
11. M. Sheringham (1993), *French Autobiography: Devices and Desires*, Oxford, p. 21.
12. See 'Le pacte autobiographique', p. 36; 'The Autobiographical Pact, p. 22.
13. See 'Autobiographie/vérité/psychanalyse', p. 63; 'Autobiography/Truth/Psychoanalysis', pp. 28–9. I refer extensively to Doubrovsky's essay in Chapters 4 and 5.
14. On Barthes and his fellow 'postmodernist' autobiographers as life-writers whose work can be read in the context of a broader 'crisis of representation' and as inflected by post-structuralist deconstructive theories of the subject, see Shirley Neuman (1991), 'Autobiography and Questions of Gender: An Introduction', in S. Neuman (ed.), *Autobiography and Questions of Gender*, London and Portland, pp. 1–11, p. 1. On women's autobiography as the site of a deconstruction of the fiction/autobiography binary, see Stanley, *The Auto/biographical I*, pp. 64–5.
15. On the characteristics of the autobiographical novel and the 'fictional' pact it sets up, see 'Le pacte autobiographique', pp. 24–7; 'The Autobiographical Pact', pp. 12–15.
16. We should always bear in mind that generic 'tagging' may reflect a classificatory decision taken by a text's publisher rather than its author, as part of a marketing strategy intended to orient its reception in the interest of wider sales.
17. Other key essays in which *autofiction* is dissected in detail are Darrieussecq's 'L'Autofiction, un genre pas sérieux' and J. Lecarme and E. Lecarme-Tabone (1997), 'Autofictions', in *L'Autobiographie*, Paris, pp. 267–83. This latter piece is useful because it summarizes the range of theorizations/definitions of *autofiction* that French narratological commentators have produced, and lists French-language works of life-writing that may be deemed autofictional. These include Guibert's *A l'ami qui ne m'a pas sauvé la vie*, which I discuss in Chapter 4, and Doubrovsky's *Un amour de soi*, addressed in Chapter 5. The conceptualization of *autofiction* I am working with here in my Introduction, in brief and, in more detail, in Chapters 4 and 5 is that provided by Doubrovsky – who 'invented' the term in the first place to signal the ambiguous generic status of his self-narrative *Fils* (1977). Lecarme and Lecarme-Tabone label it, somewhat reprovingly, as a 'définition stricte': I see it rather as productively precise.
18. See H. Jaccomard (1993), *Lecteur et lecture dans l'autobiographie française contemporaine*, Geneva, p. 97. Various critics invoke the notion of generic and narrative 'undecidability' with regard to *autofiction*. In Chapter 4, I scrutinize the reader-response provoked by autofictional ambiguity in more detail.

19. Darrieussecq's 'L'Autofiction, un genre pas sérieux' (cf. pp. 378–9) addresses this aspect/function of *autofiction* succinctly, as well as glossing *autofiction*'s complex, 'undecidable' relationship to the truth/falsehood binary.

20. See Eakin, 'Foreword', p. ix.

21. While, in my fifth and final chapter, I offer a gloss on the conceptualizations of gender and engenderment elaborated in the post-Foucauldian writings of Judith Butler, and briefly invoke her particular perspective on the sex/gender relation, I do not intend here in my Introduction or elsewhere in my volume to resume or engage in detail with debates about what gender 'is', where it comes from and how the interrelated notions of gender and sexual difference 'interact'. The terms I use, and the issues and theoretical contexts associated with them, are sufficiently established in the late twentieth-century consciousness to render the need to do so redundant. A useful introductory summary of the debates around gender and of the history of the terminology used by different 'camps' within the gender studies field is offered in Elaine Showalter (1989), 'Introduction: The Rise of Gender', in E. Showalter (ed.), *Speaking of Gender*, London and New York, pp. 1–13. Showalter's essay (cf. p. 3) explains, *inter alia*, that 'sexual difference' and 'gender', as concepts, are often used interchangeably, but that the former can be taken to encapsulate difference in identity, subjectivity and language as it is theorized in psychoanalytic and poststructuralist discourse, while the latter is habitually used by materialist theorists to invoke the social and cultural production of masculinity/femininity, and the ideological processes that feed into it.

22. 'Autobiography and Questions of Gender', p. 10.

23. D. Stanton (ed.) (1984), *The Female Autograph: Theory and Practice of Autobiography from the 10th to the 20th Century*, Chicago and London.

24. S. Benstock (ed.) (1988), *The Private Self: Theory and Practice of Women's Autobiographical Writings*, London and New York.

25. B. Brodzski and C. Schenck (eds), (1988), *Life/Lines: Theorizing Women's Autobiography*, Ithaca.

26. L. Gilmore (1994), *Autobiographics: A Feminist Theory of Women's Self-Representation*, Ithaca and London.

27. See Stanley, *The Auto/biographical I*, p. 94.

28. See 'The Rise of Gender', especially p. 6, p. 8.

29. Showalter's own, edited anthology, *Speaking of Gender*, seeks precisely to 'speak of gender' *inclusively*, by engaging with a diversity of male- and female-authored, generically varied Anglophone texts. In her Introduction, 'The Rise of Gender', she makes it clear that a key inspiration for her collaborative project was work done in the 1980s on masculine modes of creativity and representation: work produced, notably, in the field of gay studies in the aftermath of the emergence/proliferation of feminist critical practices.

30. See 'Autobiography and Questions of Gender', p. 6. Neuman's point, here, meshes with Showalter's contention that if masculinity and male creativity have not been properly studied/dissected in gender-focused scholarship, this is because patriarchy constructs masculinity as 'natural', 'unproblematic' and somehow 'transparent'. See 'The Rise of Gender', p. 6. In his forthcoming essay 'Changing the Script: Women Writers and the Rise of Autobiography', Michael Sheringham argues that if women's autobiographies have been the particular target of gender-focused readings, this is because issues of gender are particularly prominently inscribed within them. His argument, while certainly valid, neglects adequately to acknowledge the connection between the 'gender markings' manifest in women's autobiographical discourses and the way in which, under patriarchy, women rather than men are engendered as the 'marked' – that is the different, 'other' – sex.

31. To be fair to Lejeune, he does direct his attention – somewhat voyeuristically – to women's life-writing in *Le Moi des demoiselles: Enquête sur le journal de jeune fille* (Paris, 1993).

32. A gender-conscious perspective is, however, prominent in M. Sheringham (1998), 'Invisible Presences: Fiction, Autobiography and Women's Lives – Virginia Woolf to Annie Ernaux', *Sites*, vol. 2, pp. 5–24, and in the forthcoming 'Changing the Script'.

33. See *L'Autobiographie*, pp. 95–124.

34. L. Hewitt (1990), *Autobiographical Tightropes*, Lincoln and London; R. L. Ramsay (1996), *The French New Autobiographies: Sarraute, Duras and Robbe-Grillet*, Gainesville.

35. See *Autobiographical Tightropes*, p. 8. Hewitt's study examines texts by Beauvoir, Duras, Sarraute, Monique Wittig and Maryse Condé.

36. D. Brahimi (1991), *Appareillages*, Paris.

37. Ibid., p. 8.

38. I address the phenomenon of 'heteropolarization' in Chapter 5, in my discussion of Butler's account of gender production.

1

Childhood Memories: Textual Burial and 'Obsessional' Narrative in Violette Leduc's *L'Asphyxie* and Jean-Paul Sartre's *Les Mots*

Obsessional discourse, its analysts concur, is characterized by encryptment.[1] In an essay published in 1965, 'Le Discours de l'obsessionnel dans les romans de Robbe-Grillet', Didier Anzieu suggests that inherent in such discourse, in its literary incarnation, is a process of defensive burial that manifests itself especially in aspects of style. This process, he argues, produces a narrative weave resembling an iron-barred structure – an *échafaudage grillagé* – behind which a neurosis is screened out, 'disarticulated' and interred.[2] Analogously, in the more recent 'L'Obsessionnel et sa mère' (1993), Julia Kristeva construes the language of the obsessional subject as an impenetrable armour (*armure impénétrable*) that covers a trauma up, denying the affect attendant on it access to symbolization, at least in direct, verbal form.[3] She signals, further, that obsessional signification turns on a 'double semiology' that brings 'blocking', 'disinvested' language and non-verbal, more communicative semiotic phenomena into conjunction.[4]

Having embarked on the autobiographical enterprise unexceptionally, by producing tales of childhood,[5] Violette Leduc and Jean-Paul Sartre offer as their autobiographical débuts exercises in self-inscription (*L'Asphyxie* (1946), *Les Mots* (1964)), neither of which lays claim to pure referentiality or objective, total 'truthfulness'. Unquestionably, in *Les Mots* and *L'Asphyxie*, Sartre and Leduc go about invoking youthful experience in highly dissimilar ways. The narratives in which they do so came into being, moreover, under very different conditions: *L'Asphyxie* was the work of an unknown, and inaugurated Leduc's trajectory as an *écrivaine mineure*, whereas *Les Mots* was the fruit and the logical extension of an engagement with 'secondary' modalities of life-writing – biography, diaristic record – that spanned decades of Sartre's intellectual career.[6] Yet their *récits d'enfance* are comparable inasmuch as both bear signs of the silencing, burying tendencies that Kristeva and Anzieu isolate as the hallmarks of obsessional language and discourse. In this first chapter of *Heterographies*, my project is to establish what it is that the autobiographical childhood histories of these authors occlude, and to speculate as to the causes of the discursive encryptments they effect. More specifically, I want to construct an account of the diverse ways in which, in each of the texts I shall scrutinize, (sexuality in) the maternal/feminine comes to be elided, and to offer a comparative reading of the elisions incorporated into them.

Playing with Mother in *L'Asphyxie*

In 'L'Obsessionnel et sa mère', in relation to the obsessional neuroses displayed by a number of her analysands, Kristeva comments as follows:

> I was able to observe, on the one hand, that these patients spoke rarely about their infantile relations with their mother. Always willing to evoke their conflictual dealings with their fathers or their brothers [. . .], *they buried their mothers deep within their psyche*. On the other, this 'buried mother' seemed to me to represent the focus of a violent libidinal attraction which had been satisfied in perpetuity and which, for that very reason, was cut off from all forms of symbolization other than visual, tactile or acoustic, and was torn from the realm of language.[7]

In the above remarks, Kristeva is addressing psychical and linguistic symptoms produced by male obsessionals: however, the maternal encryptment she views as intrinsic in their discourse is equally, I shall argue here, a feature of *L'Asphyxie* (LA), the first of a number of autobiographical novels published by Leduc in the 1940s and 1950s, and a work in which (unassuaged) filial desire is certainly identifiable. For readers familiar with Leduc's inceptive *opus*, this contention might seem surprising. *L'Asphyxie* constitutes, after all, like much of its author's creative corpus, the textual mirror of an intensely personal universe in which the figure of the mother and the mother–daughter relation occupy a primordial place. That said, it is possible nonetheless to locate, within what is incontestably an 'obsessional' narrative production, evidence of writing strategies that serve to block the mother out, and to abstract from the domain of open symbolization particular elements of the maternal. What is more, maternal occlusion likewise leaves its stamp on that segment of *La Bâtarde* (LB) (1964),[8] Leduc's first autobiography 'proper', in which Leduc addresses her reasons for writing *L'Asphyxie*: that is, for producing, long before *La Bâtarde* itself was published, a work of self-representation that fights shy of autobiographical orthodoxy and suppresses proper names, notably that of her mother Berthe.[9]

In creating *L'Asphyxie*, *La Bâtarde* informs us, Violette Leduc – or, rather, that manifestation of her profiled in her *récit autobiographique* – was driven by twin desires. The first was to comply with the dictates of the writer Maurice Sachs, with whom, in 1942, Leduc left war-torn Paris for Normandy and who, irked by her tales of childhood woe, exhorted her to turn them into literature (LB, p. 399/B [trans.], pp. 403–4). The second was to afford her beloved grandmother Fidéline a rebirth in writing, and to become in so doing the genetrix of a woman whose unconditional devotion she had all too briefly enjoyed (LB, p. 400/B, p. 404). In the roll-call of writerly motivations proffered by *La Bâtarde*'s autobiographical narrator, no explicit connection is established between Leduc's *venue à l'écriture* and her troubled relationship with her mother, even though that relationship is the fulcrum of *L'Asphyxie*. The presence, within the first of Leduc's 'classic' auto-biographies, of this instance of the unsaid indicates that critical approaches to *L'Asphyxie* grounded in an awareness of the phenomenon of maternal erasure are by no means misplaced. In the discussion that follows, I shall outline those areas of Leduc's text in which this phenomenon makes its mark, concentrating particularly on its elision of maternal sexuality. First, however, I want to address the ways in which, in the founding work of her narrative corpus, Violette Leduc 'writes the mother', signalling as I do so some of the thematic preoccupations and narrative characteristics peculiar to *L'Asphyxie*.

Critics concur that *L'Asphyxie* is a fragmentary, episodic text, focalized predomi-nantly through the consciousness of the child its nameless narrator once was, but narrated by an adult voice.[10] They have tended, further, to emphasize the accusatory dimension of Leduc's autobiographical novel, and to associate its fragmented, tableaux-based structure with the denunciatory impulses they detect within it.[11] René de Ceccatty notes, for example, that '*L'Asphyxie* presents itself as a trial, or, rather, as the reconstruction of a crime: its episodes follow each other like so many "exhibits".'[12] On one level, Leduc's narrative certainly represents a *roman-procès*, in which a narcissistic, denying mother who neglects to love her adoring daughter sufficiently is roundly condemned. Replicated in miniature in its nineteenth 'chapter' (LA, pp. 141–7), where a daughter-protagonist who is not the heroine of *L'Asphyxie* vilifies her own mother openly and violently on behalf of her dead younger sister, its denunciatory aspect derives from its narrator's cumulative display of a series of 'pieces of evidence' that are made all the more indictory by virtue of the fact that, in general, no explicit commentary accompanies them. Equally, however, *L'Asphyxie* constitutes a work endowed with a marked hermeneutic dimension: that is, with a textual stratum centred around a conundrum the reader must seek to unravel.[13] This dimension has its origin in the opening sentence of Leduc's text, 'my mother never gave me her hand . . .'[14] – a sentence that receives no elaboration and, left unexplained, implies the presence of a narrative mystery. Our awareness of its existence is reinforced by *L'Asphyxie*'s closing words ('as a mother, she was beyond reproach'),[15] which contradict Leduc's narrator's initiatory phrase in a highly puzzling manner. It is highlighted, further, by narrative elements that evoke the 'impossibility' the mother incarnates (LA, p. 182), illuminate the 'impenetra-bility' of her hard blue gaze, and thereby hint that *L'Asphyxie* incorporates some sort of maternally-related textual enigma. Its inclusion of a hermeneutic component allows us to read *L'Asphyxie* as a text that turns on an invitation to decode: an invitation whose focal point is a maternal protagonist transformed by Leduc's writing practice into a hermetic narrative riddle. If, though, *L'Asphyxie* can be said to 'enigmatize' its central mother-figure as much as it culpabilizes her, then how, precisely, does it do so?

Above all, maternal enigmatization proceeds from the fact that a number of interpretative possibilities emerge in relation to the anonymous maternal protagonist of *L'Asphyxie*, none of which satisfies definitively.[16] We may, for example, read her simply, and naively, as a cipher for sadism-in-the-feminine. Conversely, exploiting our extratextual knowledge of her creator's wretched familial history, and paying careful attention to 'clues' incorporated into Leduc's tale, we may view her, in materialist terms, as a product/construct/victim of a sociosexual situation generated by the humiliations meted out in turn-of-the-century France to women with illegitimate offspring. In this second perspective, the mother-figure of Leduc's *roman autobiographique*, for all the unkindnesses she manifests, becomes pitiable (*irréprochable*) rather than criminal. On the other hand, if we approach *L'Asphyxie* through a psychoanalytic, Kleinian optic, we can construe the key maternal player of Leduc's text as a narrative phantasm: a 'bad' part-object of the kind produced by the infantile ego when, exposed to the antithetical experiences of maternal deprivation and maternal nurturance, it splits the mother in two.[17] A Kleinian 'take' on Leduc's first novel establishes its 'bad' mother as an avatar of the archetypal Wicked Mother in whom, Roland Barthes claims, all forms of affective abandonment find their emblem.[18] Further, a Kleinian interpretation 'explains' the opposition of good and bad models of maternity that Leduc's text mobilizes, and calls its authenticity into question. This opposition is played out, in *L'Asphyxie*, by means of a constant counterpointing of its child-heroine's punitive, unloving, unavailable mother and her loving, beneficent grandmother. A Kleinian diagnosis of *L'Asphyxie*'s maternal dialectic consigns it to the domain of unconscious fantasy, and intimates the possible *in*divisibility, and unreality, of the apparently separate, twin mother-figures who provide the maternal 'poles' of Leduc's narrative.

If, in short, *L'Asphyxie* 'enigmatizes' its key maternal persona it does so, primarily, by representing her in a manner that deters us from establishing any single and definitive reading of what she 'means'. Her status as a narrative 'puzzle' issues, additionally, from *L'Asphyxie*'s narrator's reluctance to offer overt, explicit decodings of the phenomena her *récit* records – a reluctance that in turn relates to the fact that her account is focalized through a/her juvenile consciousness: a consciousness that *cannot* decode.[19] For all that enigmatization can in itself be construed as an occlusive procedure, my remarks so far might seem to make nonsense of the notion that *L'Asphyxie* is a text in which maternal elision plays a primordial role. Once, however, the reader turns his/her attention to the manner in which Leduc's narrative is organized, maternal effacement/burial starts to communicate its workings more forcefully.

Leduc's autobiographical fiction offers a darkly humorous chronicle of rural life in the France of the early years of the present century. This chronicle is arranged

A = 'bad' mother is present; B = 'good' grandmother is present; C = both maternal personae figure in the text; D = non-maternal focus.

in such a way as to generate a counterpointed, achronological, oneiric narrative in which vignettes focusing more or less exclusively on the twin, maternal mother-and-grandmother-figures of Leduc's text, themselves already counterpointed each against the other, are repeatedly played off against chapters in which the key focus is external and non-maternal, and which constitute so many 'scenes of provincial life'. Its structure is illuminated in the diagrammatic schema of *L'Asphyxie*'s narrative 'segments' provided above. In this schema, the 'A', 'B' and 'C' segments are those in which one or the other of Leduc's divided maternal figures, or both, represent the primary object of narrative scrutiny, while 'D' segments constitute those where the non-maternal is privileged, even if a mother-figure is interstitially present. The narrative interaction that prevails between, on the one hand, its 'A', 'B', and 'C' fragments and, on the other, its 'D' fragments suggests that *L'Asphyxie* is informed by a kind of alternating rhythm, generated by its contrapuntal play of maternalized and dematernalized narrative 'blocks'. Fundamental to this rhythm is a process of intermittent maternal erasure. How, though, should we understand the function that (interrupted) maternal occlusion performs within *L'Asphyxie*'s narrative evolution?

The alternating currents that govern *L'Asphyxie* engender a process of reiterated maternal fading, in which both the mother-figures of Leduc's text, its heroine's 'bad' mother and her 'good' grandmother, are implicated. Cognizant of Barthes's apprehension that the 'fade-out' of the loved object is occasioned by anxious affect,[20] we could opt simply to interpret the maternal intermittences of Leduc's *opus* as symptomatic of a hopeless, obsessive mother-love we can read as peculiar not only to its child-heroine, but to her adult, narrating avatar as well. We can also, however, decode the absence/presence paradigm subtending *L'Asphyxie*'s deployment of its twin maternal players (or 'composite' maternal entity) rather differently. In *Reading for the Plot*, Peter Brooks suggests that 'narrative always makes the implicit claim to be in a state of repetition, as a going over the ground already covered: a *szujet* repeating the fabula, as the detective retraces the tracks of the criminal'.[21] The rhythm of *L'Asphyxie*, grounded in a reiterated juxtaposition of the maternal and the non-maternal, precisely stages the repetitive movement that Brooks views as intrinsic in the narrative act. Equally, Leduc's repeated maternal fadings recall that reiterative game of *fort* and *da* that, Freud suggests in *Beyond the Pleasure Principle*, is played by children – and artists – bent on counterpointing presence and absence imitatively and vengefully, so that some control of the maternal might be realized. The *fort/da* repetition-game, Freud claims, allows the human subject to master a source of distress – namely, maternal absence – and to transform the unpleasurable into that which, in the end, yields its own kind of gratification.[22] Manifested and harnessed as formalized narrative repetition, argues Brooks, the *fort/da* model generates, eventually, a significant, because deferred, release of pleasure.[23]

The insights that Freud and Brooks provide usefully illuminate the ongoing, highly formalized reproduction, across *L'Asphyxie*, of maternally-focused and maternally-occlusive narrative tableaux. They enable us to view Leduc's text as the site of a process of repetition-induced narrative retardment, in/via which the phenomenon of maternal absence/lack – a key thematic focus of *L'Asphyxie* – is repeatedly dramatized on a structural level, the pain attendant on it is worked through, and a movement from passivity to pleasurable, maternally-oriented mastery is achieved. They encourage us, in other words, to construe *L'Asphyxie* as the locus of a narrative 'project' predicated at once on a domination of the maternal rendered possible by the *fort/da* games that Leduc's narrator plays, and on a libidinal satisfaction stimulated by her structurally-anchored actualization of maternal control.

If the maternal *per se* is (intermittently) blocked out in Leduc's text, then so too is sexuality-in-the-maternal. As I have suggested above, the maternal 'fade-outs' that *L'Asphyxie* stages can be read as an indication that its narrative development is imbued with, or founded in, a discharge of pleasure/gratification. However, its elision of maternal sexuality can be taken to signal its inflection by a quite different type of affective reaction. The nature and basis of this reaction will provide my focus in the concluding section of what follows. But, before I dissect it in detail, I want to unpick the workings of the erotically occlusive facet of Leduc's narrative artefact.

Sexual episodes proliferate in *L'Asphyxie*, introducing the reader to an aberrant erotic universe in which exhibitionism (LA, pp. 23–5), fetishism (LA, pp. 148–69), satyriasis (LA, pp. 103–9), child-abuse and incest (LA, pp. 32–6) apparently flourish unchecked. However, the majority of these episodes – marked with an 'X' on the schema provided above – do not coincide with those that are maternally-centred. What is more, the twin mother-figures of Leduc's text – the 'good' grandmother, who is likened to an 'ageless priest' (LA, p. 13), and, equally, the 'bad' mother, who is revealed as favouring monochrome, 'monastic' outfits (LA, p. 73) – are consistently cast as curiously sexless. In short, maternal sexuality is not (as it is, for instance, in *La Bâtarde* (LB, p. 38 /B, p. 38)) openly addressed in *L'Asphyxie*.[24] But this does not mean that it is entirely absent from, or unsymbolized within, Leduc's *récit d'enfance*. While their maternalized aspect is by no means immediately visible, a number of *L'Asphyxie*'s erotic episodes can be taken to inscribe sexuality-in-the-maternal in a dissimulatory, masking manner. Their encrypting dimension returns us to the Kristevan notion of the 'buried mother' invoked at the start of this discussion. Likewise, it reminds us of the Freudian credo that the elimination or negation of something stands as a cipher for its fundamental significance.

L'Asphyxie presents us with three female figures who *are* explicitly sexualized. The first is its heroine's schoolfriend Mandine, who vainly attempts in its eleventh tableau (LA, pp. 66–71) to seduce a flea-infested tramp. The second is Mme

Barbaroux, who is introduced in tableau 14 (LA, pp. 83–97) as a housework-obsessive driven to orgasm-inducing bouts of domestic activity by the sexual coldness of her consort. The third is Mme Panier, who tells in tableau 16 (LA, pp. 103–9) of the pleasure her husband's satyriasis afforded her before he took to wearing restraining gloves. Viewed/represented through the fascinated perspective of Leduc's self-projective child-heroine, two of these sexual subjects, Mme Barbaroux and Mme Panier, emerge as grotesque, while the third, Mandine, appears unsettlingly predatory.

At first glance, none of these seems especially 'maternal'. But a careful dissection of Leduc's text reveals that they are in fact endowed with a number of linguistic, vestimentary and gestural traits that bind all three of them to the twin mother-figures of *L'Asphyxie* and, especially, to its 'bad' mother (cf. LA, pp. 68, 71, 86, 91, 93, 96, 103, 105, 108, 120, 121, 150). This paralleling phenomenon implies two things.[25] The first is that La Barbaroux and co. can be construed as displaced maternal doubles: that is, as objects constructed as substitutes for Leduc's narrator-heroine's genetrix by and within a transformative, phantasmic process mobilized by *L'Asphyxie*'s narrative unconscious. The second is that we can read into the eroticism that Mandine, Mme Barbaroux and Mme Panier openly incarnate a projective, disguised and disguising vision of a maternal sexuality that Leduc's *récit*, it appears, will represent only obliquely, or metaphorically. The fact that, in *L'Asphyxie*, sexuality-in-the-maternal is given voice by means of a desymbolizing, metaphorical deployment of sexualized maternal substitutes reminds us of Anzieu's argument that in encrypting obsessional discourse, doubles are frequently used to masking effect.[26] Equally, it recalls Kristeva's contention that, in the language of the obsessional subject, direct and indirect semiotic modes are habitually conjoined. But what purpose does this effacing narrative practice serve? Aspects of *L'Asphyxie* highlight two possible responses to this question, the second of which would seem finally to be more satisfactory than the first.

In *Œdipe masqué*, her psychoanalytic study of Leduc's second novel *L'Affamée* (1948), Pièr Girard catalogues the narrative manifestations and consequences of an archaic, forbidden desire that, she argues, the text's narrator-heroine lastingly cherishes with regard to her distant, elusive mother.[27] Evidence of an analogous, denied desire is furnished by tableau 1 of *L'Asphyxie* – one of the few maternally-focused segments of Leduc's text in which maternal sensuality *is* alluded to. Here, in a scene where Leduc's heroine's mother parades seductively before a mirror, watching herself and herself alone as her daughter tracks a maternal gaze in which she has no place (LA, p. 8), we find signs not only of a desire-for-the-mother that Leduc's child-self cannot apparently cast aside, but also of the mother's interdictory refusal to acknowledge and thus to permit its expression and its very existence.

The mother's elected status as a taboo object (intimated by the fact that, in the episode evoked above, she features in veiled guise) allows us to elaborate a first way of understanding the presence, in *L'Asphyxie*, of a set of eroticized female figures who are/are not 'maternal' and of a number of narrative episodes in which maternal sexuality is inscribed phantasmically and deflectedly. It permits us to identify, within those sections of Leduc's *récit d'enfance* that introduce its secondary maternal doubles and articulate their sexualized aspect,[28] the lineaments of an enduring, maternally-oriented desiring impulse that remains largely non-verbalized; that is common, the reader senses, to Leduc's daughter-heroine and her older narrating persona alike; and that must, it appears, projectively generate a series of phantasmic, erotically active object-substitutes in order to achieve a licit conduit for expression/satisfaction. In his essay series 'Contributions to the Psychology of Love', Freud reads the tendency of certain male subjects to degrade the mother – by reducing her, in fantasy, to the level of a prostitute – as motivated by a wish to transform the maternal figure from an idealized, forbidden object into an accessible object of sensuality: an object that can be desired.[29] *L'Asphyxie*'s inclusion of its trio of mother-doubles, read in tandem with the sexual *bizarrerie* that each of them emblematizes, would seem to attest to the operation, in Leduc's female-authored/ narrated *opus*, of a similarly transformatory, debasing move – the aim of which, we may suppose, is to bring some measure of release for its narrator-heroine's ongoing, illicit, 'blocked' mother-love.

As the foregoing observations indicate, we can choose to read Leduc's self-referential narrator's recourse to a mode of imag(in)ing that produces *L'Asphyxie*'s eroticized, phantasmic mother-substitutes as symptomatic, simply, of a forbidden desire that has to be discharged deflectedly, if it is to be discharged at all. But to opt exclusively for an interpretation of this type is to fail to get to the bottom of the wierd dimension of the trio of erotic female object-doubles engendered by Leduc's dissimulatory representational strategy. *L'Asphyxie*'s mother-substitutes all incarnate a sexuality that not only serves to obscure, palimpsestically, the sexuality of its central, 'bad' mother, but is also imbued with an uncanny strangeness. They constitute the origin, and the target, of a narrative unease that is not articulated explicitly in Leduc's self-history, but nonetheless leaves its mark on its textual fabric, notably in tableaux 11, 14 and 16. This unease is imbricated in the troubling, aberrant aspect of *L'Asphyxie*'s ersatz erotic mother-figures. It provides a point of departure for the second reading of Leduc's occlusive treatment of sexuality-in-the-maternal performed here. My reading will work towards illuminating the causal role played within the sexual elisions effected in Leduc's autobiographical novel by a primitive anxiety whose foundation is the phenomenon of maternal Lack.

In an early section of *Pouvoirs de l'horreur* (1980),[30] her seminal treatise on abjection, Kristeva establishes a series of connections that bind the existence of a phobia both to the employment of metaphoric or substitutional language and to the literary act. These connections enable her to frame the creative writer as a phobic subject who 'metaphorizes' in order to overcome terror, and to thrive and survive through substitutive semiological activity.[31] If, as Kristeva suggests, the narrative practice of metaphorical substitution constitutes a protective, contraphobic procedure – a procedure that serves to mask and manage a source of fear – then we need to ask ourselves what fear, exactly, is it that inspires the metaphoric (because indirect), anxious articulations of maternal sexuality introduced into *L'Asphyxie* by virtue of its author/narrator's play with maternal substitutes, and with a mode of symbolization that inters the sexualized aspect of its primary mother-figure by displacing it in- and onto extrafamilial female textual personae?

In tableau 8 of *L'Asphyxie* (LA, pp. 39–53), a centrally significant fragment of Leduc's autobiographical fiction, her child-heroine witnesses a painful encounter between her mother and the wealthy young man who sired her, in the course of which the mother tries and fails to extract from her former lover a pension for their bastard child and some kind of recognition for herself. When the encounter is over, Leduc's child-self must confront the spectacle of the twisted mouth (*bouche déformée* LA, p. 50) and vulnerable flesh ('la chair même offerte à la douleur' LA, p. 50) of her weeping, impotent progenitrix. This spectacle, *L'Asphyxie*'s narrative voice informs us, fills her with horror: 'It was a forbidden sight. I was ashamed of my mother. I wanted her to be harsh, authoritarian. I should have preferred her to have beaten me. She paralyzed me.'[32]

The symbolically resonant episode staged in tableau 8 – an episode in the course of which Leduc's heroine's mother loses her umbrella (LA, p. 48) – patently dramatizes that archaic moment in the female psychosexual trajectory at which the 'fact' of maternal castration is finally acknowledged. There can be no doubt but that, in a concessional gesture towards Freudian orthodoxy reproduced elsewhere in Leduc's *oeuvre*, its allusions to the mother's deformed, martyred flesh and her grief-stricken powerlessness profile the spectre of maternal phallic denudation. On one level, this phenomenon is conveyed by Leduc's narrative in a blackly, bleakly comic manner. Concomitantly, however, it is tacitly presented as a source of shame and fearful anguish to Leduc's textual child-self – and, we sense, to her older narrating persona as well.

The anxiety that tableau 8 imputes to Leduc's child-heroine (an anxiety that is castration-related, and that we can ally with the fact that the 'discovery' of maternal *manque* puts the daughter's primordial mother-love – a key affective component of *L'Asphyxie* – at risk)[33] subsides in subsequent narrative fragments. We may, however, relate its narrative emergence to the existence of those other textual episodes of *L'Asphyxie* in which the sexual misfortunes and frustrations of Mandine, Mme Barbaroux and Mme Panier are variously depicted. In diverse ways, each of these episodes foregrounds female *sexual* lack. In all of them, the existence/evidence of that lack is evoked in words and images informed by the barely verbalized narrative discomfort I invoked above. Finally, each episode has a disguised, displaced maternal dimension, generated by its focus on a (sexually deviant) mother-substitute. This combination of factors must surely be significant. It suggests that, in certain segments of her story, Violette Leduc takes a phenomenon – maternal *phallic* Lack – that is phobia-inducing and induces disquiet both in the textual child-double her autobiographical fiction creates and in her older narratorial counterpart, and subjects it to a process of substitutional deflection, or displacement, that enables the anxiety it inspires to be expressed *indirectly*, and thereby mastered. I indicated above that *L'Asphyxie* offers us two interpretational purchases on the sexual occlusions that operate within it. The second reading I am proposing here is centred on the notion that if Leduc's *roman autobiographique* constitutes a text that works to veil sexuality-in-the-maternal metaphorically, by transferring it onto/ interring it within phantasmic, lacking substitute-characters, this is because her *récit d'enfance* turns on an anti-phobic effort to use substitution to 'manage' that sexuality, and to manage – that is, to defuse – the frightening 'deficiency' it emblematizes and vehicles. If, in other words, the sexual aspect of the maternal is desymbolized and buried in *L'Asphyxie*, its burial, achieved through substitutive narrative activity, is a function of the employment, in Leduc's *opus*, of a transforma- tive strategy designed to mutate a source of horror (maternal Lack/castration) into something that is 'defamilialized', defamiliarized, and therefore (relatively) anodyne.

Girard's *Œdipe masqué* pinpoints Violette Leduc's sense of the 'shameful' character of castrated femininity, and her lasting, anxious need to heal the wound constituted by the missing maternal phallus.[34] Its unimaginative deployment of Freudian doxas notwithstanding, Girard's study supports my feeling that, in *L'Asphyxie*, the occlusion of maternal sexuality/eroticism engendered by the sexual displacements that Leduc's text effects is fundamentally phobic in origin. In *Les Mots*, as I shall argue in the next section of this chapter, female eroticism is likewise masked. However, Sartre's lengthily-matured rendition of the youth of his child- self Poulou and his relations with a bourgeois clan comprising his mother Anne- Marie, his grandmother Louise and his grandfather Charles (Karl) Schweitzer encrypts feminine sexual phenomena by means of a manipulation of narrative 'layers' that accords sexuality-in-the-maternal even less (open) recognition than Leduc's deflectional strategy. Further, as I shall work to demonstrate here, *Les Mots*'s gynosexual elisions can be taken to derive from a narratively-grounded desire quite unlike the lack-oriented anxiety that haunts the female-authored pages of *L'Asphyxie*.

Reading, Writing and Erotic Erasure in *Les Mots*

A number of features of *Les Mots* (LM) – notably, its regular recourse to images of burial – hint that encryptment is a significant facet of Sartre's autobiographical *opus*. This, in turn, taken in tandem with Sartre's categorization of *Les Mots* as a narrative constellated with *sous-entendus*,[35] might lead us to suppose that he wanted his text to be read in the same manner as the detective stories of which he was fond: that is, as the site of an enigma destined for discovery. I am not persuaded, however, that *Les Mots* does in fact invite us to adopt as a lectorial model the friend whom, towards the end of his account, its narrator denounces as a fanatic bent on unearthing the dead (LM, p. 201/W [trans.], p. 149). On the one hand, as I shall argue here, Sartre's self-history does incorporate, beneath its surface fabric, a (superficially) buried narrative 'strand' that we are, it would seem, encouraged to disinter. Concomitantly, however, his *récit* contains at least one further, hidden narrative seam that is not elaborated in such a way as to incite the reader to uncover it. *Les Mots* is not only marked, in other words, by a tension between the overt and the covert, but can also be read as combining dissimilarly encrypted narrative elements.

Incontestably, the nexus of open and (differently) covered narrative facets that exists within Sartre's autobiography can be taken to evince *Les Mots*'s strongly obsessional aspect — itself masked by the almost clinically detached, self-parodic tenor of Sartre's tale. In the discussion that follows, the workings of this nexus will provide my object of scrutiny. Because, however, I am concerned here, primarily, with the profoundly buried narrative elements that lie at its heart, I shall dwell only briefly on *Les Mots*'s 'surface' and incompletely encrypted narrative levels, 'disinterring' them with a view to elucidating what it is that they combine to inter.

Amongst the numerous references to the hidden, the subterranean and the veiled that *Les Mots* contains, one appears especially significant. It features in a passage where Sartre's mature narrating persona recalls how his youthful readerly encounters with Corneille led him to ruminate on the significance of the word *amante* (mistress, female lover). 'Beneath the glossy surface of the idea', he affirms, 'I sensed a hairy body' (W, p. 36).[36] In many ways, this remark encapsulates the essence of the burying game elaborated in *Les Mots* — not least because the text's chief agent of occlusion, and the foundation of its 'dominant', overt narrative dimension, is the analytical, self-critical disquisition on childhood-as-ontological-apprenticeship that Sartre evolves within it.

As numerous critics have signalled, and in marked contrast to Violette Leduc, Sartre resorts to life/self-writing in *Les Mots* in order to produce, in autotheoretical mode, a philosophically-inflected, politically incisive reconstruction of data drawn from his formative years.[37] Refashioning *sur mesure philosophique*[38] elements of his childhood experience, he textually reinvents the child he used to be as the self-deceiving bourgeois boy-hero of a series of adventures in bad faith, *comédie* and existential anguish.[39] In so doing, he works up an autobiographical (more precisely, perhaps, an 'autofictional') story[40] that not only explodes mythic notions of auto-biography as transparent narrative recollection, but also provides a literary illustration of concepts and theories drawn from *L'Etre et le Néant* (1943) and from the 1957 essay *Questions de méthode*. Linguistically, this story is grounded in a discourse that plunders a lexis highly familiar to devotees of Sartrean thought, even as it deploys a variety of language-forms in a display of 'theoretico-stylistic' virtuousity.[41] Structurally, it relies not only on a bipartite surface organization generated by its account of Poulou's 'comedic' readerly and writerly activities, but also on a 'dialectical', achronological sub-patterning that, Philippe Lejeune contends, affirms its philosophical orientation by segmenting it into five dynamically-connected 'acts' predicated on phenomena such as inauthenticity and *nausée*.[42]

The central role accorded in *Les Mots* to Sartre's reconstructive tale of his youthful confrontations with contingency, choice and 'imposture', and the use that is made, in its elaboration, of an existentialist theoretical apparatus, ensure that Sartre's (arguably) 'autofictional' account comes to be encased within, and to bear the stamp of, a conceptual corset or *armature logique* afforded visual form in the semi-diagrammatic schema of its component parts included in Lejeune's seminal 'L'Ordre du récit dans *les Mots* de Sartre'.[43] This functions to deprioritize those elements of *Les Mots*'s narrative web that stand outside the philosophico-political, and to consign them to the realm of the 'decorative', the supernumerary.[44] Auto-biographical works that tend to the ideological, as *Les Mots* indubitably does, are prone, generically, to display an occlusive 'armature' of this type. But the repressive effect exerted by the pervasive, philosophically-inflected 'dialectical fable' Sartre weaves into *Les Mots* does suggest that narrative occlusion represents a procedure in which, as an autobiographical practitioner, he is personally (and obsessionally) invested.[45] In order to start to address the notion that narrative burial constitutes a phenomenon that Sartre, like Leduc before him, needs and wants to realize, we must first establish what gets buried – and how – under the *armature logique* he places over and around his *récit*.

An impressive cohort of Sartrean commentators[46] concurs that a key element obscured by the philosophizing spin Sartre puts on his boyhood years is constituted by the sexual. Philippe Lejeune, for instance, remarks on the radical, logical absence, in Sartre's *autobiographie à thèse*, of any sort of sexual recollection, arguing that since Sartre is keen to present the child he was as a youthful, anguished subject detached by familial and personal delusions from the real and cast into bad faith by activities pursued in the readerly and writerly realms, he must necessarily exclude all evidence that he also enjoyed, in the public sphere, an existence as an active desiring being.[47] Sexual issues do, incontestably, come to be buried in *Les Mots*, and to be buried by virtue of the narrative *échafaudage* engendered by its system-atically philosophical reconstruction of its author's past. That said, certain of the sexual phenomena that Sartre's *récit théorique* covers up are covered more comprehensively than others.

In general, if not exclusively, critics who have combed *Les Mots* for signs of the (buried) sexual have scrutinized its narrative substrata for manifestations of the oedipal/pre-oedipal, employing phallocentric psychoanalytic paradigms in support of their exegeses.[48] That they have done so is consistent with Anzieu's contention that, in male-authored, 'masking' literary discourse of an obsessional stripe, what is masked is the desire the writing subject primitively exchanged with his mother, as well as a paternal interdiction against it that is never entirely accepted.[49] But it is important to recognize that the oedipally-oriented aspect of Sartre's autobiography/*autofiction* – an aspect entrenched in the Poulou/Anne-Marie/Karl relational triangle – represents that sphere of his narrative construct I earlier qualified as its imperfectly occluded dimension.[50] On the one hand, this level of *Les Mots is* covered up, in a vertiginous range of ways. It is obscured by the 'theoretical' emphasis that Sartre's narrator places upon the 'comedic' (as opposed to the libidinal) slant of the family dynamics he chronicles. Likewise, it is elided by *Les Mots*'s insistent, negatory desexualization/de-oedipalization of the Schweitzer family drama and its key players. (Evidence of this is provided by *Les Mots*'s account of the 'platonic', brother–sister (LM, p. 48/W, p. 36) or female–female (LM, p. 41, p. 184/W, p. 31, p. 137) nature of the Poulou–Anne-Marie relation;[51] by its vision of Anne-Marie as an undesiring subject and an undesired object (LM, pp. 16–21/W, pp. 13–16); by its insistence on her need to subtitute a girl-child/mirror for her boy-child/phallus (LM, p. 88/W, p. 65);[52] by its fantasy of Poulou as a tranquilly sexless, unjealous being (LM, p. 25/W, p. 19); and by its reluctance (LM, p. 22, p. 25, p. 47/W, p. 17, p. 19, pp. 35–6) properly to acknowledge Karl's status as the third, paternal, authoritarian player in an oedipal triangle in which Poulou's childhood, however 'fatherless', is imbricated.)[53] Equally, the oedipalized character of the Poulou/Karl/Anne-Marie nexus, and, more generally, the oedipalized dimension of *Les Mots*, is masked by its inclusion of statements such as 'If he had lived, my father would have lain down on me and crushed me' (W, pp. 14–15)[54] and 'my father's hasty retreat had conferred on me a very incomplete Oedipus complex: no superego, I agree, but no aggression, either' (W, p. 19).[55] These remarks not only attest, by dint of their mechanistic recourse to analytic concepts, to Sartre's sceptical-but-concessional, complex relationship to Freudian psychoanalysis,[56] but also tell us that one of the stories that does *not* inhere in his self-history is a story of active, possessive, mother–son desire and its triangularized paternal truncation.[57] At the same time, however, the extensive use made in *Les Mots* of instances of oedipally-oriented negation (qualified by Pacaly as unconvincing),[58] as well as of 'signal' vocabulary drawn from the psychoanalytic lexicon, invites us to intuit that an oedipal narrative grounded in (thwarted) mother–son desire and (grand)paternal intervention may well exist below the surface of Sartre's *récit*, constituting a discursive strand that is buried only incompletely, and must be taken account of.

If the oedipal stratum of *Les Mots* is (un)symbolized by its author in a manner that encourages us to read it into his retrospective account, and to read it as a story that Sartre, his ambivalence towards (classic) psychoanalysis notwithstanding, teasingly encourages us to see, then what aspect of the sexual does his narrative production really encrypt? What element of *Les Mots* represents that which Sartre wants and needs to bury deeply and definitively? I want to propose that one, at least, of the sexual narrative facets his self-history suppresses genuinely and 'obsessionally' turns on a female erotic pleasure that does not take a (or Poulou as its) phallic object (Sartre 'outs' this latter pleasure occasionally, for example in his account of Anne-Marie's enjoyment of her 'portable' son/fetish (LM, p. 114/W, p. 85)), and that Poulou can access solely as a spectator. That this female pleasure represents a fundamental object of *Les Mots*'s encryptments *is* announced by the feminine connotations of the 'hairy body/*masse velue*' segment of the image cited above as a cipher for Sartre's burying narrative practice.[59] It is accorded, however, a quite different, far more occlusive mode of semiosis than the oedipal 'strand' of his tale. Many elements of Sartre's self-referential *histoire* work to elide it. For one thing, the pleasure in question – and the narrative seam it supports – is buried by virtue of the fact that a key overt message of *Les Mots*'s *incipit* is that non-pleasure is the proper of women (LM, pp. 12–16/W, pp. 10–13),[60] just as linguistic violence is that of the male (LM, pp. 12–17/W, pp. 10–14). More importantly, its manifestations are masked by their imbrication in the activity of reading: an activity whose evocations, in Part I ('Lire') of *Les Mots*, seem simply to belong to that (open) layer of Sartre's narrative in which he critically dissects the *comédies* played out in his childhood environment (cf. LM, p. 43/W, p. 32). How, then, does Sartre conjoin the (gyno)sexual and the lectorial?

Books are not simply established in *Les Mots* as emblems of the cultural capital that every member of the Schweitzer clan, albeit to varying degrees, possesses. They are also made into sexualized entities: objects that are introduced as phallic avatars (LM, p. 36/W, p. 28) but are subsequently imbued with feminine, vaginal characteristics: 'I sometimes got close enough to observe these boxes which opened like oysters and I discovered the nakedness of their internal organs' (W, p. 28).[61] Similarly, as it is in Gide's *Si le grain ne meurt* (discussed in Chapter 3), the act of reading is allied with sexual difference. Men are revealed as reading 'high' or educational literature in a penetrative mode illuminated by Sartre's accounts of Karl's defloratory encounters with printed material (LM, p. 39, p. 58/W, pp. 29– 30, p. 43), whereas women are shown to read more popular works (notably novels, construed as feminine in the French cultural imaginary)[62] less violently, for enjoyment's sake. Reading for pleasure might seem to represent an everyday, anodyne activity, that requires no critical attention. But the nature of the pleasure articulated in Sartre's descriptions of the readerly adventures of Poulou's female entourage merits careful scrutiny.

The extensively elaborated record of lectorial episodes that *Les Mots* contains incorporates four key scenes of female reading. None of them involves 'high', classical literature (the province of Karl-the-patriarch),[63] and all of them, if they are assimilable into that strand of his self-history where Sartre anatomizes the 'Comédie de la culture' enacted by Poulou and his tribe, seem also to be about something else. The first (LM, p. 13/W, p. 11) evokes the convulsions that rack Poulou's determinedly 'refined' grandmother Louise as she peruses the 'suggestive stories' of popular authors such as Adolphe Belot (a writer known, amongst other things, for his cautionary accounts of the moral perils of lesbianism). The second illuminates the complicitous pleasure Louise and Anne-Marie share as they finger the open pages ('internal organs') of the 'trashy' potboilers that Louise borrows from her local library (LM, pp. 37–8/W, pp. 28–9), and which are presented as the objects of a 'culte mineur, exclusivement féminin': '[My grandmother] used to [. . .] sigh with pleasure and weariness, and lower her eyelids with a delicately voluptuous smile which I have subsequently discovered on the lips of the Mona Lisa; my mother would fall silent, inviting me to keep quiet. [. . .] From time to time, Louise would give a chuckle; she would call to her daughter, point at a line and the two women would exchange a conspiratorial look' (W, p. 29).[64] The third reveals the mysterious, deathly languor that overwhelms Anne-Marie as she reads aloud fairy tales specially adapted for children: 'She leant over, lowered her eyelids and went to sleep. From this mask-like face issued a plaster voice. I grew bewildered [. . .] my mother had disappeared: not a smile or trace of complicity. I was an exile. And then I did not recognize the language' (W, p. 31).[65] The fourth chronicles the curiously caressive, 'malicious' looking she indulges in with a friend, Mme Picard, and the flushes that overcome her[66] as the two women, pursing their lips and leaning against each other, scrutinize Poulou's scribblings in the book of questionnaires Blanche Picard offers him (LM, pp. 92–3/W, p. 68).

In each of these scenes of ('low') reading, what appears to be intimated and imagined, even though it is in no way their surface or explicit focus, is a (maternal) *jouissance* that belongs squarely in the realm of the feminine and the *entre-femmes*, is somehow 'excessive' and 'masturbatory', is wholly self-sufficient and, in fact, invokes that phallically-disconnected pleasure that Luce Irigaray envisions in parts of *Ce Sexe qui n'en est pas un* (1977) that elaborate, in 'strategic' essentialist mode, alternatives to the figurations of female sexuality institutionalized under patriarchy.[67] This 'other', inter- and intrafeminine *jouissance* is the antithesis of the sensual Lack that Sartre's text, its insistence on the femininity/non-pleasure equation notwithstanding, intermittently isolates as the lot of its masculine protagonists (cf. LM, p. 33/W, p. 25). Its existence in, and status as a narrative component of, *Les Mots* is never overtly or properly acknowledged. It is not articulated de-elidingly, through the kind of 'signal', charged, recognizable terminology that Sartre employs in connection with the oedipal dimension of his narrative. It remains unequivocally in the sphere of the covertly intimated, the hidden – most notably because of its displaced, lectorial aspect. Yet it haunts Part I of Sartre's autobiography, constituting a tacit element in his philosophical disquisition on reading-as-(in)authentic-act, and generating beneath the surface of his *récit* an occluded narrative facet that is neither ontologically- nor oedipally-oriented and is masked in a way that no other stratum of *Les Mots* comes to be.

The covered narrative layer I am working to uncover here is predicated on more than female (reading) pleasure alone. It turns, additionally, on the male response provoked by the inter/intra-womanly, maternal *jouissance* that reading-in-the-feminine, as *Les Mots* inscribes it, incorporates and in/visibilizes. Inherent in this response are: a linguistic impotence that contrasts with the masculine linguistic mastery evoked in *Les Mots*'s opening section; sexual envy; and anguish. The first of these reactions is sited primarily in Charles Schweitzer (cast as easily unsettled by female pleasure in any form (LM, p. 18/W, p. 14)), and is addressed quite openly in Sartre's self-history (LM, p. 38/W, p. 29). The latter two are the province of Poulou, and are narratively communicated no less covertly than the erotic phenomenon that engenders them.

Sexual envy features in, even as it is obscured by, those segments of 'Lire' that chronicle Poulou's initial contacts with reading material and his clandestine encounters with popular literature. Sartre represents his child-self's entry into the lectorial domain (more particularly, into that of 'high', 'male' reading) as part and parcel of his comedic compulsion to ape grown-up practices; as inspired by a desire to assume the role of the Other/elder that has nothing sexual about it; and as a consequence of the 'imposture' he is forced into by the adults who govern his world (LM, pp. 60–3/W, pp. 45–7). Less self-laceratingly, he presents Poulou's fondness for reading, in secret, stories that were popular rather than classic works (fairy tales, adventure serials, the novels of Jules Verne) and were fitting for a boy of his age as evidence that he was not, entirely, consumed by the 'Comédie de la culture' in which his grandfather, in particular, overinvested (LM, pp. 63–6/W, 47–9). Nowhere does Sartre openly recognize that the readerly adventures he ascribes to his textual child-self incorporate an erotic dimension or motivation. Yet tiny aspects of his account imply nonetheless that Poulou's incursions into that popular, 'unworthy' form of reading that *Les Mots* construes as feminine ('l'objet d'un culte mineur') and as sexually charged, and that Louise and Anne-Marie encourage him secretly to enjoy (LM, pp. 63–6/W, pp. 47–9) rest on a jealous need to access a domain of female, exclusive, erotic pleasure whose privileged geography he intuits and envies as he observes women at their 'light' books.

Sartre's description, for instance, of the swooning ecstasy his child-self experiences whilst pursuing his *vraies lectures* amongst the 'magic boxes' his mother and grandmother buy for him hints that behind Poulou's desire to read 'genuinely' and popularly lies a desire to get at and into a feminine *jouissance* that is somehow coextensive with popular, 'low' reading (LM, pp. 63–4/W, pp. 47–8). So, too, does his representation of Poulou as a 'low' reader who is also, concomitantly, a holidaymaker in a bordello (LM, p. 66/W, p. 49). Superficially, this representation simply signals that the type of *mauvaise lecture* Poulou unalloyedly appreciates constitutes a counterpoint to the 'high', culturally consecrated reading to which Karl encourages him to apply himself, and is therefore, in his grandfather's eyes at least, debased. But, implicitly, the parallel it establishes between Poulou's engagement with the feminized activity of popular reading and a sojourn in a brothel – a site of heterosexual exchange but equally, and in the male pornographic optic especially, an interfemale erotic space – also suggests something else. Sartre's metaphor conveys that Poulou's clandestine perusals of comic books and adventure stories – that is, of 'low' fictions linked to the feminine – involve, on some level, an envious, identificatory effort to penetrate a locus (a harem-space) that is sexualized, gynocentric, at heart fundamentally alien to the male and implanted in the domain of the *entre-femmes*.[68] Simultaneously, Sartre's vision of his readerly boy-self as someone who can only vacation in the brothel-space of (inter)female popular reading/*jouissance* hints that Poulou's masculine gender-situation, however unformed and inflected by the feminine (LM, p. 41/W, p. 31), ultimately debars him from constituting anything more than a shadowy, voyeuristic, temporary presence in the erotic gynaeceum whose contours *Les Mots*'s scenes of womanly reading intermittently and covertly illuminate.

That anguish, no less than envy, forms part of the response provoked in Poulou by the (reading) pleasure he detects in the female members of his family circle is both inferred and interred in segments of *Les Mots* adjacent to those that transcribe the lectorial activities of his mother and grandmother. One of the features of the account of Karl's virile proof-reading practices that Part I of *Les Mots* presents – an account that follows hard upon Sartre's rendition of Louise's voluptuous, fingering encounters with her ('feminine') library books – is its allusion to the 'ecstasy' Poulou experiences as he watches his grandfather 'penetrate' and deflower his virgin pages (LM, p. 39/W, p. 30). Inspired as it is by the spectacle of phallicized reading, Poulou's ecstasy, we sense, rests less upon pleasure *per se*, here, than on a relief generated by Karl's manifest remasculinization of the lectorial act. This, in turn, suggests that reading-in-the-feminine, and the gynocentric erotic phenomenon it encrypts/evinces, represents a source of some disquiet for Sartre's autobiographical protagonist. But his textual child-self's sexual unease itself remains unsymbolized.

Sexual anxiety is similarly detectable – and buried – in the section of *Les Mots* that records the aftermath of the Anne-Marie/Blanche Picard/questionnaire episode (LM, pp. 93–4/W, pp. 68–9). Here, Sartre's narrative does focus openly on Poulou's descent into *angoisse*. However, the *angoisse* it overtly chronicles is that ontological anxiety inspired by the shame that overwhelms Sartre's child-self when his role-playing 'imposture' (evident in the spurious reponses he inscribes in his *cahier de questionnaires*) is brought to light. Nowhere, in this particular part of 'Lire', is the fact that the anguish Poulou experiences also possesses a sexual dimension connected to women's capacity to (co)read erotically made explicit. Yet, a single element within the narrative segment where his ontological panic is evoked does, tacitly, point its sexualized dimension up. In the fragment in question, Sartre's autobiographical narrator states that 'before my eyes, a jellyfish was striking against the glass of the aquarium [. . .] In the darkness, I sensed a vague hesitation, a rustling, a banging noise, a whole living creature' (W, p. 69).[69] By virtue of the imagery, notably the marine imagery, that it incorporates, this passage offers a clue that Poulou's anguish *is* (partly) sexual, and that female sexuality/*jouissance* – enduringly connoted in the Sartrean imaginary as viscous, fishy, palpitating and alive – constitutes its bedrock.[70]

The anguish that Poulou's boyhood confrontations with female (reading) pleasure inspire (more precisely, the anguish that Sartre's reconstructive *récit* ascribes to its narrator's child-self) coheres with the disquiet evinced in relation to female sexuality by Sartre's adult creative and philosophical writings alike. In turn, our awareness of this disquiet – dissected by commentators such as Doubrovsky, who talks of Sartre's 'uncontrolled ambivalence' towards female *jouissance* and his fear of self-loss within it[71] – provides us with a point of interpretational entry into the sexual encryptments that *Les Mots* effects. Our knowledge, in other words, of Sartre's visceral wariness of sexuality in the feminine, of the engulfing, (mal)odorous female sexed anatomy[72] and of the consciousness-contaminating impact of embodied, eroticized womanhood[73] offers us one way of understanding why, in a narrative artefact focused not on invented female protagonists but on the women of his family clan, he might have elected to inter (inter/intra)female *jouissance* so profoundly. But we are by no means obliged to regard the sexual/textual burials inherent in Sartre's self-history simply as the symptoms of a sentiment grounded in an admixture of phobia and *pudeur*. Equally, indeed instead, we can read Sartre's encrypting autobiographical discourse – more particularly, its habit of occluding a sexual pleasure it envisions as interfeminine – as the product of a voyeuristic preoccupation with gynocentric sexuality and with the female–female erotic relation that constituted an enduring feature of its creator's mental make-up.

In a number of the (para)autobiographical documents by Sartre and by Simone de Beauvoir published in the 1960s and after, this preoccupation is illuminated as no less significant a facet of Sartre's psychology than the sexual unease isolated by Doubrovsky *et al*.[74] It is signposted, for instance, by *Les Mots*'s repeated recourse to the phrase *deux femmes* (employed once at the end of that section of Sartre's text qualified by Lejeune as its second 'Act' (LM, p. 71/W, p. 53), and twice at the start of its second (open) part, 'Ecrire'). It is manifest in Sartre's negatory, unconvincing recollection, in a segment of his *Entretiens* with Beauvoir that echoes his vision of Poulou as a *vacancier au bordel*, of the 'boredom' he experienced when, on holiday in Naples, he witnessed in a brothel the spectacle of two prostitutes making lesbian love in poses borrowed from Pompeii's murals.[75] It is likewise hinted at in a fragment of the *Entretiens* where Sartre describes the male–female sexual connection as somehow 'primitive'.[76] Similarly, it is highlighted by those sections of Beauvoir's *Lettres à Sartre* in which, in a gesture of deeply unpalatable complicity, she proffers for her partner's delectation accounts of her own wartime erotic adventures with the women of her pseudo-familial group.[77] Once we take cognizance of Sartre's ongoing interest in the female intersexual bond and in gynocentric eroticism, we can comprehend more completely why he might have chosen to incorporate (fantasized) scenes of autonomous, intra- or interfeminine female pleasure into his generally desexualized *récit*. We can read their narrative *inclusion* as a function less of sexual anxiety than of a form of sexual prurience. In order, however, to understand the *occlusion* to which feminine inter- or intraerotic episodes are made subject in Sartre's autobiographical self-history, we need to unpick *Les Mots*'s account of what writing meant to Poulou, its author's textual child-double, and to take stock of what Sartre's text tells us about the motivations underpinning his narrative boy-self's engagement with the literary enterprise.

In *Les Mots*'s second part, which chronicles Poulou's *venue à l'écriture* in depth and extremely densely, three 'models' of writing are pointed up more or less openly. Since none of them exists independently of the others, organizing them into a discrete taxonomy is, arguably, artificial. I shall, nonetheless, 'classify' them separately here, in order to highlight a fourth type of writing that is not (fully) anatomized in Sartre's autobiography but *is* discernable within it. Needless to say, this fourth facet of Poulou's literary practice, as it is narratively reconstructed in *Les Mots*, constitutes my central object of scrutiny in the remaining sections of this discussion.

Amongst the models of writing that 'Ecrire' addresses, the first and most dominant associates the writerly act with the pursuit of a (predestined, 'sacred') mission, and contextualizes Poulou's youthful, 'clerical' adoption of a literary vocation in terms of issues of necessity, contingency and bad faith. As Edmund Smyth has suggested, the parts of *Les Mots*'s second section in which this first type of writing is foregrounded constitute those in which Sartre brings to a climax his elaborate, ironic dramatization of (his own) *mauvaise foi*, and indulges in a 'thoroughly Sartrean' – that is, philosophically-informed – reading of his childhood.[78] The second model, on the other hand, casts Poulou's literary activities in psychological, oedipal terms, revealing them to be predicated on a desire to constitute himself as the future creator of a corpus of book-phalluses/fetishes destined to bring satisfaction and 'completion' to new generations of reading female (m)Others: 'Cherished object of a desire still unaware of itself, I joyfully continued to remain incognito for a while. Sometimes my grandmother would take me along to her lending-library and it amused me to watch tall, thoughtful, unsatisfied women glide from one wall to another in search of the author who would satisfy them; he was not to be found because it was I, that child round their skirts, at whom they did not even glance' (W, p. 108).[79] In contrast, the third model posits Sartre's child-self's nascent creative endeavours – specifically, his comic, comedic incursions into the poetic realm – as inspired by a need to realize a male-to-male, filial/(grand)paternal communion. It identifies ('high') literary practice, in other words, as, in part, a homosocial affair: 'The habit was formed; the grandfather and his grandson were bound by a new link; they talked, like Indians or the pimps of Montmartre, in a language forbidden to women' (W, p. 89).[80]

'Ecrire' evokes the above modalities of writing so unambiguously as to enable the reader easily to detect their lineaments. Concomitantly, however, Part II of *Les Mots* incorporates a vision of another kind of writerly practice, whose nature and ambit we have to work to understand and unearth from within Sartre's deliberations on writing-as-existential-*comédie*. Its existence is intimated at the very start of 'Ecrire': that is, in a section of *Les Mots* where the *deux femmes* motif is strongly in evidence. Recalled with great affection by Sartre in his *Entretiens* with Beauvoir,[81] this particular writing mode is revealed in his autobiography to constitute a form of creative activity to which Poulou is powerfully drawn. Like the taboo *vraies lectures* he is cast as exploiting with a view to accessing *jouissance*-in-the-feminine, and like the (pleasuring) 'lectures' of his female kith and kin, it is popular as well as clandestine. It is shown to involve Poulou in secret, plagiaristic authorial sessions during which he copies plots and episodes from the 'low', 'feminine' (adventure) fictions he has enjoyed perusing in an unmanly manner (LM, pp. 121–5/W, pp. 90–3). It is presented, further, as generative of a considerable degree of gratification ('In short, I wrote for my own pleasure' W, p. 93).[82] Equally, it is presented as the source of a discourse capable of adumbrating the contours of an alien, disquieting world, in a language whose marine orientation recalls that used in 'Lire' to evoke the anguish female reading/pleasure arouses in Poulou and that used by Sartre to invoke female sexuality/desire:

> I would push my little desk over to the window, my anguish would return, and the docility of my heroes, unfailingly sublime, misunderstood and vindicated, would betray their lack of substance; then *it* would come: an invisible, bewildering creature would hypnotize me [. . .] I would [. . .] remove my characters to another region of the globe – usually under the sea or underground – and hastily expose them to fresh dangers: changed on the spur of the moment into divers or geologists, they would discover the Creature's tracks, follow them and, all of a sudden, meet it. What then issued from my pen – an octopus with fiery eyes, a twenty-ton crustacean or a giant talking spider – was myself, a childish monster' (W, pp. 96–7).[83]

It is construed, in short, as a conduit that provides Poulou with a means of entry into a 'monstrous universe' whose geography haunts his memory (LM, p. 126–7/ W, p. 94), and whose inscription, in his scribblings, casts his mother into a fever of embarrassment and delighted alarm.

Elements of Sartre's self-history invite us to interpret Poulou's production of this latter type of ('low') writing as further proof of his resistance to Karl Schweitzer's class-based cultural dictates, and to the 'inauthenticity' in which they implicate him (LM, p. 124/W, pp. 92–3).[84] Equally, *Les Mots* encourages us to contextualize it metaphysically, *vis-à-vis* Poulou's *prise de conscience* of (his own) contingency, and his (frustrated) efforts to overcome it. But the terms and manner in which his engagement with popular writing is described permit us also to read that engagement rather differently. Poulou's 'writing-for-pleasure' may involve the creation of a model of literary discourse that, crammed with episodes of heroic derring-do, is superficially highly phallicized.[85] At the same time, however, its popular (hence 'female') foundation, and its imbrication in pleasure, anguish and a lexis consonant with that mined by Sartre in his articulations of the sexualized feminine, strongly imply that it can be construed as a creative mode that is manipulated by its child-author as a means to gain a definitive purchase on a delightful, if frightening, realm of *jouissance* (an *univers monstrueux*) that is sited in the inter/intra-feminine; that, for Poulou, is allied with the activity of womanly popular reading; that he is hindered from penetrating by his gender-status; and that is not rendered wholly accessible by his own, populist, 'feminine' *mauvaises lectures*.

Les Mots's second section in no way flags itself up as a narrative entity in which the phenomenon of writing-as-route-into-female-pleasure is a constitutive focus. But 'Ecrire' can, nonetheless, be interpreted as such. That this is the case is suggested by Sartre's depiction of his writerly boy-self as a 'Montmartre pimp'. Introduced in 'Ecrire's' second paragraph, this supports our intuition that one of the dramas staged in *Les Mots*'s account of Sartre's child-self's *venue à l'écriture* turns on Poulou's attempt to use the literary act in order to afford himself a sanctioned place inside that erotic gynaeceum intimated by and encrypted in feminine lectorial excitement, and imagined, in 'Lire', as a brothel-space.

If, though, 'Ecrire' dramatizes Poulou's efforts to use 'low' writing in order to pursue an erotically-oriented endeavour, it also illuminates them as doomed. Various elements within *Les Mots*'s second part associate popular writing – and writing in general – with failure. Sartre's self-projective narrator informs us, for instance, that his youthful incursions into populist literary practice proved 'too good to last' (LM, p. 131/W, p. 97). He states, later, that his writerly difficulties resembled those of a frigid woman bent on faking her elusive orgasms (LM, p. 174/W, p. 130). Later still, addressing his current, mature vision of the literary endeavour, he talks of the 'impotence' he senses it to incorporate (LM, p. 212/W, p. 157). These observations are open to a variety of interpretations. On one level, however, all of them can be taken to signal the ultimately unsuccessful nature of the intrusive, pleasure-centred writerly project that *Les Mots* tacitly presents Poulou as pursuing. Its failure is by no means left unexplained. Sartre's narrator strongly implies that, if his boy-self's attempts to employ a *mauvaise écriture* to get at and into gynocentric *jouissance* founder, this is because his grandfather intervenes, patriarchally, to pull him out of the popular, 'feminine' creative space he longs to inhabit and exploit, and into a literary vocation that is not only that of the minor writer but is also grounded in a thoroughly masculine, 'high', bourgeois, broadly realist literary practice wherein (female) pleasure has no place or articulation, and that cannot lead towards it:

> You may well believe that I appreciated my good fortune. The trouble was that I did not enjoy it [*je n'en jouissais pas*]. [. . .] Thus was my fate determined at Number One rue le Goff, in a fifth-floor flat, below Goethe and Schiller, above Molière, Racine, and La Fontaine, and facing Heinrich Heine, amidst continually interrupted conversations. Karl and I chased the women out, embraced closely, and whispered our muted dialogues to each other, every word of which left its mark on me (W, pp. 101–3).[86]

If *Les Mots* casts Poulou as a junior scribe who is thwarted in his desire to manipulate writing and discourse in order to penetrate a desiring domain from which his sex debars him, it also presents its mature, narrating persona – and, concomitantly, his 'real-life' author-counterpart, Sartre – as a being who shares its boy-protagonist's narratively elaborated desiring habits, but is far less naive about what writing and discourse can and cannot achieve. Sartre's *récit* does so by combining, in its concluding section, apparently contradictory affirmations, such as 'All the characteristics of the child [. . .] have survived in the fifty-year-old man' (W, p. 157),[87] 'I see clearly, I am free from illusions, I know my real tasks' (W, p. 157), and 'For a long time I treated my pen as a sword: now I realize how helpless we are' (W, p. 157).[88] Counterposed with its account of the frustrated nature of Poulou's erotically-directed, populist writerly endeavours, *Les Mots*'s articulation of the Poulou/Sartre 'gap' helps us to see why Sartre, as an adult, 'disabused' autobiographer, might have elected to employ an erasive, encrypting discursive mode to give (what is no more than a muffled) voice to a gynocentric pleasure he is no less fascinated by than his textual child-avatar. It allows us to understand that if Sartre opts, in his middle-aged incarnation, to bury that pleasure deep within a discourse rendered occlusive/desexualized not only by its 'disincarnated' philo-sophical inflection but also by its extreme literariness,[89] this is because he is aware, as Poulou is not, that the writer bent on accessing desiring phenomena that are both alien and seductive is better off introducing them into, and masking them beneath, the fabric of his own, multilayered writing, converting them thus into a private object of delectation, than seeking to use ('low') writing intrusively, to breach the libidinal space such phenomena represent.

Les Mots is a narrative construct in which a vertiginous gamut of meanings, messages, issues and textual strata are brought into contact. Informed by a range of conceptual perspectives – philosophical, political, psychoanalytic – it offers itself up to a diversity of interpretations. Amongst other things, we can read it as the site of a burying discursive practice that is employed by its author as a means to afford himself a privileged, voyeuristic purchase on a realm of *jouissance* located so deep within the weave of his narrative that it becomes a kind of personal, exclusive peep-show for one. In order, however, to construe Sartre's text as such, we must first unpack the writerly impulses to which it presents Poulou as succumbing, understand their (gyno)sexually-directed (and doomed) dimension, and contextualize Sartre's adult, autobiographical, sexually occlusive writing tendencies in counterpoint to them. In *Le Livre brisé*, Doubrovsky argues that, in spite of Sartre's manifest hostility towards his autobiographical child-self, it is Poulou who is the true author of *Les Mots*.[90] I would wish here, with regard to the erotically encrypting facet of Sartre's *opus*, both to endorse and depart from Doubrovsky's reading. The existence, in *Les Mots*, of a narrative stratum centred in/on female–female pleasure suggests that Sartre's *récit* is inflected by writerly desires that were Poulou's (as, at least, *Les Mots* reinvents him) long before they became his adult, authorial creator's. However, the (masking) manner in which this stratum is inscribed and elided reveals beyond all doubt that, as a writer in pursuit less of his own pleasure than of that of the female (m)Other, Sartre has indeed, as the conclusion of *Les Mots* affirms (LM, p. 199, p. 200/W, p. 148), put his past and his boy-self's writerly project behind him.

If, then, Violette Leduc and Jean-Paul Sartre elaborate childhood self-histories characterized by a common, not to say 'obsessional' effort to obscure or encrypt sexuality-in-the-feminine/maternal, they do so, it would appear, for very different reasons. While Leduc's narrative play with maternal fading can be viewed as imbricated in her pursuit of a pleasure grounded in the practice of maternal control, the sexual elisions that her *récit d'enfance* mobilizes may be taken to signal that a driving force behind *L'Asphyxie* is a/her dread of maternal phallic 'deficiency' and its anxiety-inducing potential – a dread reflected in the metaphorical, masking articulations of sexualized maternity that *L'Asphyxie* contains. We might have expected to locate castration anxiety-induced elision in *Les Mots* rather than in *L'Asphyxie*, given that anxiety of this ilk is habitually associated with the masculine subject. But, as the second section of this chapter affirms, Sartre's gynosexual occlusions can be construed as attesting not to a fear of the castrated feminine but to his fixation with, and his desire to achieve a private textual grip upon, a *jouissance* envisioned in the male-authored, prurient *Les Mots* as peculiar to women/ mothers.

In the fifth and final chapter of this study, I shall refocus on the phenomenon of narrative occlusion, dissecting its dynamics in Serge Doubrovsky's autofictional, hermeneutic *Un amour de soi*. For now, though, I want to turn my attention elsewhere. In Chapter 2, I shall address a second duo of narratives in which, as in *L'Asphyxie* and *Les Mots*, issues of maternally-oriented desire and maternal lack are thematized. My analysis of the texts in question – Hervé Guibert's *L'Image fantôme* (1981); Marguerite Duras's *L'Amant* (1984) – will not, however, concern itself exclusively with the treatment they accord the maternal/feminine. Rather, it will scrutinize the workings, in each of the narratives I have chosen to read, of a nexus of connections between autobiographical and visual (self-)representation, desire, and fetishism in the photographic sphere.

Notes

1. See for example D. Anzieu (1965), 'Le Discours de l'obsessionnel dans les romans de Robbe-Grillet', *Les Temps Modernes*, vol. 21, pp. 608–37; J. Kristeva (1993), 'L'Obsessionnel et sa mère', in *Les Nouvelles Maladies de l'âme*, Paris, pp. 75–99.
2. See 'Le Discours de l'obsessionnel', p. 625.
3. See *Nouvelles Maladies*, pp. 75–80.
4. Ibid., p. 80.
5. J.-P. Sartre (1964), *Les Mots*, Paris, translated as *Words*, trans. I. Clephane, Harmondsworth, 1967. No translation of *L'Asphyxie* (Paris, 1946) exists; translations are my own.
6. Manifestations of Sartre's protracted flirtation with life-writing include his autobiographical novel *La Nausée* (1938), his existential biographies of Genet and Baudelaire and the diaries and letters he wrote during the phoney war.
7. 'J'ai pu constater, d'une part, que ces patients parlaient rarement de leur relation infantile à la mère. Toujours prompts à évoquer leurs conflits avec leurs pères ou frères [. . .], *une véritable "mère enterrée" gisait au coeur de leur psychisme*. D'autre part, cette "mère enterrée" me semblait être le pôle d'attraction d'une libido violente, à tout jamais satisfaite et pour cela même indisponible pour une symbolisation autre que visuelle, tactile ou sonore, farouchement retranchée de la parole'. See *Nouvelles Maladies*, pp. 85–6 (my trans.).
8. V. Leduc (1964), *La Bâtarde*, Paris, translated as *La Bâtarde*, trans. D. Coltman, London, 1965. In this and my fifth chapter, page references to the French *édition blanche* will be signalled LB, while those from the English translation will be marked B.
9. See S. Marson (1995), 'Au bord de *L'Asphyxie*, *Littérature*, no. 98, pp. 45–58, pp. 47–8 and (1998), *Le Temps de l'autobiographie: Violette Leduc*, Saint-Denis, pp. 183–4. Marson's work usefully illuminates the autobiographical ambiguities of *L'Asphyxie* – which, in its most recent edition, is generically/paratextually designated neither as a *roman* nor as a *récit* (that is, as a referential narrative).

10. See, *inter alia*, I. de Courtivron (1985), *Violette Leduc*, Boston, p. 18.

11. See for example Colette Hall (1988), '*L'Ecriture féminine* and the Search for the Mother in the Works of Violette Leduc and Marie Cardinal', in M. Guggenheim (ed.), *Women in French Literature*, Saratoga, pp. 231–8.

12. '*L'Asphyxie* se présente comme un procès ou plutôt la reconstitution d'un crime: les scènes se succèdent comme autant de pièces à conviction.' See R. de Ceccatty (1994), *Eloge de la Bâtarde*, Paris, p. 222 (my trans.).

13. On the hermeneutic 'code' and its workings, and on the establishment, in narrative, of questions and enigmas, see R. Barthes (1970), *S/Z*, Paris. I shall return to the issue of narrative 'mystery' in Chapter 5.

14. 'Ma mère ne m'a jamais donné la main . . .' (LA, p. 7).

15. 'C'était une mère irréprochable' (LA, p. 188).

16. For a detailed discussion of these, see A. Hughes (1994), '*L'Asphyxie*: The Double Face of Maternity', in *Violette Leduc: Mothers, Lovers and Language*, London, pp. 15–39.

17. For a summary of Kleinian psychoanalytic theory that glosses the unconscious mechanisms on which it focuses (including maternal splitting, projection and introjection), see Juliet Mitchell (1986), 'Introduction', in J. Mitchell (ed.), *The Selected Melanie Klein*, Harmondsworth, pp. 9–32.

18. On the connection between the experience of loss/lack of love and the emergence, in the unconscious, of the archetype of the Wicked Mother, see R. Barthes (1977), *Fragments d'un discours amoureux*, Paris, pp. 129–33.

19. See Marson, 'Au bord de *L'Asphyxie*', p. 52; *Le Temps de l'autobiographie: Violette Leduc*, pp. 187–8.

20. See *Fragments*, pp. 129–30.

21. P. Brooks (1984), *Reading for the Plot*, New York, p. 97.

22. See S. Freud (1920/1922), *Beyond the Pleasure Principle*, London, especially pp. 12–16.

23. See *Reading for the Plot*, pp. 101–2.

24. This is not to say that the 'bad' mother of the text is cast as uninterested in sexually-oriented behaviour. Her narcissistic *coquetterie* is revealed in tableau 3, for example, and her efforts to find a husband are recorded in tableau 18.

25. For a detailed discussion of it, and of the role played by 'doubling' in *L'Asphyxie*, see my *Violette Leduc*, pp. 24–39.

26. See 'Le Discours de l'obsessionnel', p. 627.

27. See P. Girard (1986), *Œdipe masqué*, Paris. See also V. Leduc (1948), *L'Affamée*, Paris. No English translation of the latter exists.

28. I refer here to La Barbaroux and co. as 'secondary' doubles because the 'primary' double of *L'Asphyxie*'s dominant, 'bad' mother-figure is its heroine's 'good' grandmother. On the parallels that bind the 'good' mother to her 'bad' counterpart, see my *Violette Leduc*, pp. 27–9, 38–9.

29. See S. Freud (1912/1977), 'On the Universal Tendency to Debasement in the Sphere of Love', in *On Sexuality*, *Penguin Freud Library*, vol. 7, Harmondsworth, pp. 243–60, pp. 251–2.

30. J. Kristeva (1980), *Pouvoirs de l'horreur: essai sur l'abjection*, Paris, pp. 43–67.

31. Ibid., p. 49.

32. 'C'était un spectacle défendu. J'avais honte de ma mère. Je la voulais dure, autoritaire. J'eusse préférée qu'elle me battît. Elle me paralysait' (LA, p. 50).

33. In 'Femininity', Freud affirms that the daughter's preoedipal recognition of maternal castration encourages, not to say compels, her to drop her mother as a libidinal object. See S. Freud (1933/1973), 'Femininity', in *New Introductory Lectures On Psychoanalysis*, *Penguin Freud Library*, vol. 2, pp. 145–69, p. 160.

34. See, for example, *Œdipe masqué*, p. 205. The need to heal maternal Lack that Girard attributes to Leduc can be associated, as I intimated above, with the/ her daughterly fear of the threat posed to filial mother-love by the phenomenon of maternal phallic denudation.

35. See S. de Beauvoir (1981), *La Cérémonie des adieux, suivi de Entretiens avec Jean-Paul Sartre août–septembre 1974*, Paris, p. 306.

36. 'sous la surface lumineuse de l'idée, je pressentais une masse velue' (LM, p. 48).

37. See, for example, Beauvoir, *Entretiens*, p. 200. See also P. Lejeune (1975), 'L'Ordre du récit dans *les Mots* de Sartre', in *Le Pacte autobiographique*, pp. 197–243; S. Doubrovsky (1986), 'Sartre: retouches à un autoportrait', in C. Burgelin (ed.), *Lectures de Sartre*, Lyons, pp. 99–134.

38. Doubrovsky, 'Sartre: retouches à un autoportrait', p. 102.

39. There is no space to address, here, the details of the 'philosophification' of his youthful *vécu* that Sartre develops in *Les Mots*. On this subject, see Edmund Smyth (1995), 'Autobiography, Contingency, Selfhood: A Reading of *Les Mots*', in T. Keefe and E. Smyth (eds), *Autobiography and the Existential Self*, Liverpool, pp. 25–37; J.-P. Laffitte *et al.* (1996), *L'Ecriture de soi*, Paris, pp. 69–96; J. Walling (1996), 'Repression and Denial: The Absent Childhood Self in Sartre's *Les Mots*', *Romance Studies*, no. 27, pp. 49–61.

40. Unlike *L'Asphyxie*, *Les Mots* does flag its autobiographical status up, through the initiation of a distinctly 'loose' autobiographical 'pact': however, it has also been categorized as a self-inventive *autofiction*. On the connection between *Les Mots*'s autofictional aspect and its 'philosophication' of its author's childhood, see S. Doubrovsky (1991), 'Sartre: autobiographie/autofiction', *Revue des sciences humaines*, vol. 98, pp. 17–26. I shall discuss the generic hallmarks of *autofiction* in some detail, in Chapters 4 and 5.

41. See S. Doubrovsky (1989), *Le Livre brisé*, Paris, p. 107. This *autofiction* chronicles Doubrovsky's critical encounters with *Les Mots* and its author.

42. See 'L'Ordre du récit', pp. 209–24.
43. Ibid., p. 211. *Armature logique* is Doubrovsky's term. See *Le Livre brisé*, p. 263.
44. See *Le Livre brisé*, p. 263.
45. The term *fable dialectique* is Lejeune's. Walling (cf. 'Repression and Denial', p. 58) endorses the reading of the repressive nature of Sartre's 'intellectualized', existentialist self-history offered here. Sheringham (cf. *French Autobiography*, p. 245) discusses, more generally and more charitably, the narrative restraints/ constraints imposed by the ideological character of existentialist autobiography.
46. This includes Serge Doubrovsky; Geneviève Idt; Josette Pacaly; Jeffrey Mehlman; and Jean-François Chiantaretto.
47. See Philippe Lejeune (1996), 'L'Ordre d'une vie', in M. Contat (ed.), *Pourquoi et comment Sartre a écrit "Les Mots"*, Paris, pp. 49–119, p. 79.
48. See J. Mehlman (1974), 'Sartre and His Other', in *A Structural Study of Autobiography: Proust, Leiris, Sartre, Lévi-Strauss*, Ithaca and London, pp. 151–67; J. Pacaly (1980), *Sartre au miroir*, Paris, pp. 66–122; Geneviève Idt (1982), 'Des *Mots* à *L'Enfance d'un chef*: autobiographie et psychanalyse', in M. Issacharoff and J.-C. Vilquin (eds), *Sartre et la mise en signe*, Paris, pp. 11–30; M. Murat (1988), 'Jean-Paul Sartre, un enfant séquestré', *Les Temps modernes*, vol. 498, pp. 128–49; A. Leak (1989), 'The Staging of Desire', in *The Perverted Consciousness*, Basingstoke and London, pp. 79–102; A. Green (1992), 'Des *Mouches* aux *Mots*', in *La Déliaison*, Paris, pp. 340–70.
49. See 'Le Discours de l'obsessionnel', pp. 634–7.
50. Idt acknowledges this (cf. 'Des *Mots* à *L'Enfance d'un chef*', p. 28) by observing that the silence surrounding oedipal sexuality in Sartre's autobiography does not signify its negation. In 'Travail de la censure de "Jean sans terre" aux *Mots*' (in Contat, *Pourquoi et comment Sartre a écrit "Les Mots"*, pp. 359– 72, p. 359), in similar vein, Pacaly suggests that Sartre does confirm that the oedipal plays a role in *Les Mots*, even as he masks its sexual aspect, by allowing 'la problématique oedipienne' to prevail over 'la problématique narcissique'.
51. See Mehlman, *A Structural Study*, p. 154; Pacaly, *Sartre au miroir*, pp. 78–9; Leak, *The Perverted Consciousness*, p. 93, p. 97. We should note that while Sartre readily recognizes the sexual potential of the brother–sister relation *per se*, he desexualizes the 'fraternal–sororal' bond between Poulou and Anne-Marie.
52. See Mehlman, *A Structural Study*, p. 151; Leak, *The Perverted Consciousness*, p. 9.
53. See Pacaly, *Sartre au miroir*, pp. 69–70; Leak, *The Perverted Consciousness*, p. 93; J.-F. Chiantaretto (1995) '*Les Mots*, une lecture psychanalytique', in *De l'acte autobiographique: Le Psychanalyste et l'écriture autobiographique*, Seyssel, pp. 181–236, p. 215. Useful, also, are Marie Miguet-Ollagnier's

remarks on the vision of the 'anti-oedipal' father offered in *Les Mots*. See Marie Miguet-Ollagnier (1992), '"La saveur Sartre" du *Livre brisé*', in A. Hornung and E. Ruhe (eds), *Autobiographie et Avant-garde*, Tübingen, pp. 141–57, pp. 147–8.

54. 'Eût-il vécu, mon père se fût couché sur moi de tout son long et m'eût écrasé' (LM, p. 19).

55. 'la prompte retraite de mon père m'avait gratifié d'un "Œdipe" fort incomplet: pas de Sur-moi, d'accord, mais point d'agressivité non plus' (LM, pp. 24–5).

56. See Pacaly, *Sartre au miroir*, pp. 54–5. Pacaly's first chapter offers essential insights into Sartre's evolving relationship with Freudian, or 'empirical', psycho-analysis, which space-related considerations prevent me from glossing here.

57. In 'L'Ordre du récit' (cf. p. 204, p. 210), Lejeune suggests that what Sartre does in *Les Mots* is cast the death of Poulou's father as an event that regulates all forms of oedipal conflict before they arise.

58. See *Sartre au miroir*, p. 70.

59. Hairiness is associated with sexualized women figures in *Les Mots* (cf. LM, p. 15, p. 34/W, p. 12, p. 26).

60. Doubrovsky offers a commentary on this phenomenon. See *Le Livre brisé*, p. 113.

61. 'Quelquefois, je m'approchais pour observer ces boîtes qui se fendaient comme des huîtres et je découvrais la nudité de leurs organes intérieurs' (LM, p. 37). On the (bi)sexual character of books in *Les Mots*, see Pacaly, *Sartre au miroir*, pp. 83–4; Leak, *The Perverted Consciousness*, p. 101.

62. See M. Danahy (1991), *The Feminization of the Novel*, Gainesville.

63. In 'Les Souvenirs de lectures d'enfance de Sartre (in Burgelin, *Lectures de Sartre*, pp. 51–87, p. 52), Lejeune notes that three central types of literature are evoked in *Les Mots*: (i) texts belonging to the domain of the Classics, and housed in Karl Schweitzer's library; (ii) children's literature (including comic-type serial literature) and (iii) contemporary writings for adults (novels, etc.).

64. '[Ma grand-mère] soupirait de bonheur et de lassitude, baissait les paupières avec un fin sourire que j'ai retrouvé depuis sur les lèvres de la Joconde; ma mère se taisait, m'invitait à me taire [. . .]. De temps en temps, Louise avait un petit rire; elle appelait sa fille, pointait du doigt sur une ligne et les deux femmes échangeaient un regard complice' (LM, p. 38).

65. 'elle se pencha, baissa les paupières, s'endormit. De ce visage de statue sortit une voix de plâtre. Je perdis la tête [. . .] ma mère s'était absentée: pas un sourire, pas un signe de connivence, j'étais en exil. Et puis je ne reconnaissais pas son langage' (LM, p. 41). In 'Jean-Paul Sartre, un enfant séquestré' (cf. pp. 143–4) Murat remarks on the fact that this particular lectorial episode constitutes a scene of desire, but uses Lacanian paradigms to insert it into the oedipal stratum of *Les Mots*.

66. Like hairiness, redness is associated in *Les Mots* with sexualized femininity. There is an interesting play with whiteness and redness in this fourth scene of female reading that suggests that, in writing it, Sartre struggled both to suppress and to illuminate eroticism-in-the-feminine.

67. For a discussion of Irigaray's efforts to envisage female pleasure in a manner that makes no claim to empirical veracity but rests on an attempt to develop a different way of thinking the feminine from that permitted under phallocentric patriarchy and its representational system, see E. Grosz (1989), *Sexual Subversions*, St Leonards, pp. 115–17. In *De l'acte autobiographique* (cf. pp. 214–15) Chiantaretto offers a commentary on the role, in *Les Mots* and *L'Etre et le néant*, of the 'feminine-in-itself' that is also potentially relevant to the phenomenon discussed here.

68. In his interviews with Beauvoir (cf. *Entretiens*, p. 272), Sartre acknowledges that his popular *lectures* – disingenuously described as 'disinterested' – involved a feminine (grand)maternal identification. Chiantaretto (cf. *De l'acte autobiographique*, pp. 215–17) comments on Poulou's identification with the-mother-as-reader, without however relating this to his envy of feminine/maternal pleasure.

69. 'Sous mes yeux, une méduse heurtait la vitre de l'aquarium [. . .]. Dans le noir, je devinais une hésitation infinie, un frôlement, des battements, toute une bête vivante' (LM, pp. 93–4).

70. Numerous critics address this phenomenon. See, *inter alia*, Doubrovsky, 'Sartre: retouches à un autoportrait', in Burgelin, *Lectures de Sartre*, pp. 126–7; Leak, *The Perverted Consciousness*, pp. 12–31. The latter study helpfully illuminates the role played by images pertaining to swampiness and marine-/pond-life in Sartre's representations of the sexualized feminine. Equally, however, Leak's monograph enables us to see why the account of Poulou's existential panic provided by the section of 'Lire' under scrutiny here would almost inevitably have contained instances of language relating to feminine sexuality. In Existentialist terms, what happens, broadly, to Poulou when he is unmasked as a role-playing fraud is that his subjectivity collapses into objectness, becoming 'bogged down' in that state known as the 'Viscous', in which consciousness becomes muddied, corrupted and frozen in its flight. Since viscosity, as Leak explains, is explicitly associated with sexualized femininity in the Sartrean imaginary, it should come as no surprise that narrative episodes in which it is tacitly alluded to should evoke feminine sexuality somehow or other. This is not to say that the reading I am offering here, which construes Poulou's anguish as sexually *motivated*, is invalid.

71. See 'Sartre: retouches à un autoportrait', especially pp. 116–17, 124–6, p. 134; and 'Sartre: autobiographie/autofiction', especially pp. 25–6.

72. See Doubrovsky, 'Sartre: retouches à un autoportrait', p. 114; Leak, *The Perverted Consciousness*, p. 15, p. 27.
73. See Doubrovsky, 'Sartre: retouches à un autoportrait', p. 127.
74. Doubrovsky himself recognizes the fact/existence of this fascination, for example in the concluding section of 'Sartre: retouches à un autoportrait'.
75. See *Entretiens*, pp. 258–9.
76. Ibid., p. 406.
77. See for example S. de Beauvoir (1990), *Lettres à Sartre 1940–1963*, Paris, p. 23, p. 36, pp. 41–2, pp. 70–1, p. 127.
78. See Smyth, 'Autobiography, Contingency, Selfhood', p. 28.
79. 'Bel objet d'un désir qui s'ignorait encore, j'acceptais joyeusement de garder pour quelque temps l'*incognito*. Quelquefois ma grand-mère m'emmenait à son cabinet de lecture et je voyais avec amusement de longues dames pensives, insatisfaites, glisser d'un mur à l'autre en quête de l'auteur qui les rassasierait: il restait introuvable puisque c'était moi, ce môme dans leurs jupes, qu'elles ne regardaient même pas' (LM, p. 145).
80. 'L'habitude était prise, le grand-père et son petit-fils s'étaient unis par un lien nouveau; ils se parlaient, comme les Indiens, comme les maquereaux de Montmartre, dans une langue interdite aux femmes' (LM, p. 120).
81. See *Entretiens*, pp. 182–3, p. 188.
82. 'Bref, j'écrivis pour mon plaisir' (LM, p. 125).
83. 'je poussais mon petit bureau contre la fenêtre, l'angoisse renaissait, la docilité de mes héros, immanquablement sublimes, méconnus et réhabilités, révélait leur inconsistance; alors *ça* venait: un être vertigineux me fascinait, invisible [. . .] j'emmenai mes personnages en une toute autre région du globe, en général sous-marine ou souterraine, je me hâtai de les exposer à de nouveaux dangers: scaphandriers ou géologues improvisés, ils trouvaient la trace de l'Etre, la suivaient et, tout à coup, le rencontraient. Ce qui venait alors sous ma plume – pieuvre aux yeux de feu, crustacé de vingt tonnes, araignée géante et qui parlait – c'était moi-même, monstre enfantin' (LM, pp. 129–30). In the above passage, the octopus reference recalls that used by Garcin, the 'hero' of Sartre's *Huis Clos* to dismiss Estelle and the sexual advances she has made, while its evocations of crustaceans and spiders echo the imagery used by Roquentin in *La Nausée* to describe the genitals of a woman with whom he has casual sex.
84. For a useful analysis of Poulou's popular writing (and reading) as the site of a resistance to the ideological forms of bourgeois society, see Smyth, 'Autobiography, Contingency, Selfhood', p. 30.
85. On the role played in Poulou's boyhood scribblings by episodes drawn from the 'roman de cape et d'épée', see LM, p. 126/W, p. 94, and *Entretiens*, pp. 182–3, p. 188.

86. 'On pense bien que j'appréciais mon bonheur! L'ennui, c'est que je n'en jouissais pas. [. . .] Ainsi s'est forgé mon destin, au numéro un de la rue Le Goff, dans un appartement du cinquième étage, au-dessous de Goethe et Schiller, au-dessus de Molière, de Racine, de La Fontaine, face à Henri Heine, à Victor Hugo, au cours d'entretiens cent fois recommencés: Karl et moi nous chassions les femmes, nous nous embrassions étroitement, nous poursuivions de bouche à oreille ces dialogues de sourds dont chaque mot me marquait' (LM, pp. 136–8).

87. 'tous les traits de l'enfant sont restés chez le quinquagénaire' (LM, p. 212).

88. 'Je vois clair, je suis désabusé, je connais mes vraies tâches' (LM, p. 211); 'Longtemps j'ai pris ma plume pour une épée: à présent je connais notre impuissance' (LM, p. 212). In *Le Livre brisé* (cf. pp. 157–60), Doubrovsky offers an interesting commentary on such statements and on the conclusion of *Les Mots*.

89. As Smyth demonstrates (cf. 'Autobiography, Contingency, Selfhood', p. 25, p. 29), *Les Mots*'s literariness can be (paradoxically) associated both with the renunciation of the value of the literary vocation that Sartre stages in its conclusion and with the demystification of bourgeois literature that is one of its key elements. However, a further effect of the 'sparkling and controlled' (Mehlman, *A Structural Study*, p. 159), high-literary tone of Sartre's *autofiction* and its 'maestria du verbe' (Doubrovsky, *Le Livre brisé*, p. 107) is the creation of a material narrative surface that is so dense, prickly and dazzling that the reader is deterred from looking beneath/behind it.

90. *Le Livre brisé*, p. 160.

2

Photography, Desire, and Fetishism: Reading (and) the Autobio/photographical Writings of Hervé Guibert and Marguerite Duras

In the discussion that follows, my primary focus will be a pair of photographically-oriented narratives that were published in the 1980s by Guibert and Duras and that, while clearly concerned with the 'bio' of their authors, eschew conventions of life-writing and embrace generic slipperiness, or indeterminacy, in ways that the works dissected in my last chapter do not. I want to begin however by invoking *La Chambre claire* (CC)(1980),[1] the seminal, intensely personal essay born out of Roland Barthes's decision to abandon the mantle of the high-semiotician, and to abandon himself to the magical *experience* of photography.[2] Inspired by its author's 'ontological' desire for photographic understanding (CC, p. 13/CL [trans.], p. 3), *La Chambre claire* pinpoints issues that likewise inflect the Guibertian and Durassian texts I shall scrutinize here. Before, therefore, I embark on a readerly engagement with them, and by way of an introduction to the readings I shall presently perform, I want briefly to highlight some facets of Barthes's *Reflections on Photography*.

Famously, *La Chambre claire* addresses the phenomenon of photographic veracity, contending that photography (by virtue, in part, of its capacity to affirm '"That-has-been" (CC, p. 120/CL, pp. 76–7)) is a uniquely referential – and uniquely truthful – representational practice. Nowhere is this notion articulated more clearly than in Barthes's account of the 'Winter Garden' image of his recently deceased mother (CC, pp. 105–9/CL, pp. 67–70). On the one hand, Barthes's 'Photographie du Jardin d'Hiver' is established as incarnating the essence of photography itself (CC, p. 114/CL, p. 71). Concomitantly, in what Victor Burgin construes as a leave-taking of semiological science,[3] it is framed by Barthes not as a sign dispossessed of any ontological connection to the real, but rather as an artefact that delivers up the 'essential' truth of its subject (Barthes's parent), achieving the 'impossible science of the unique being' (CL, p. 71).[4]

If, by dwelling on the 'co-naturalness' of the photograph and its referent and on the seduction this exerts on the photographic reader, Barthes's *Note sur la photographie* foregrounds the question of photographic truthfulness, it also explores photography's relationship to desire. More precisely, it intimates the intensely fetishistic, fetishizable nature of the photographic artefact. A fetish may be understood, broadly, as an entity whose 'nearness' – whose contiguous, metaphorical or metonymic closeness – to an original, lost object of desire allows it to allay anxieties stimulated by the originary 'gap' that generates its own fetish-status.[5] In the Freudian schema, specifically, a fetish is something that stands substitutionally for the missing maternal penis, disavowing yet confirming its absence. Its existence affirms the fetishist's knowledge of maternal Lack, but signals, simultaneously, his will to keep his belief in maternal phallicity alive.[6] Provoked by a 'glance in childhood, unchanged and always active', the fetish's formation in the unconscious, Christian Metz suggests, is brought about by an immobilizing process not unlike that involved in photography.[7] And, in parallel, Metz likewise affirms, the visual products that the photo-take creates – because they not only represent but also preserve against erasure fragments of the real, affording a mirage of 'presence' even as they intimate their referents' evancescence – may be taken to possess the talismanic qualities of the fetish object proper and to constitute, like the fetish itself, inexhaustible reserves of (ambiguous) consolation.[8]

In Barthes's discussions of the Winter Garden photograph around which his *Chambre claire* is constructed, Metz's sense of the photo-image's fetishistic nature finds ample confirmation. The bittersweet, nostalgia-imbued pleasure that its discovery is cast as producing ('this Winter Garden Photograph was for me like the last music Schumann wrote before collapsing, that first *Gesang der Frühe* which accords both with my mother's being and my grief at her death' CL, p. 70)[9] powerfully implies that the Winter Garden image functions as a Barthesian totem of a fetishistic stripe. So, too, does the fact that Barthes's narrative sets it up, simultaneously, as the substitutive symbol of a lost, primordial object of desire – Barthes's dead mother – and as a 'consolatory', surrogate entity that fleetingly occludes the scandal of maternal absence. Like all fetish objects, in other words, Barthes's Winter Garden photo emerges as the target of an 'I know very well, but nonetheless'-type sentiment that combines the recognition of (maternal) lack and its temporary repudiation.[10] If, however, Barthes's 'essential' image can be read as a fetish-like 'presence' that permits its owner to 'forget' a traumatic absence, it is itself permitted to be no more present in *La Chambre claire* than the missing maternal Other it commemorates. Barthes abstracts the Winter Garden photograph from his text, explaining his reluctance to include it amongst the illustrations accompanying his photo-essay by arguing that it would mean nothing to anyone except himself (CC, p. 115/CL, p. 73). And in so doing, he secures his photo-image's status as a fetish object.[11]

Hervé Guibert's *L'Image fantôme*: Desire in/and the Autobiographical Photo-Essay[12]

The Image is the essence of desire, and to desexualize the image would be to reduce it to a theoretical abstraction . . .

This text exists because the image has failed to exist, and, worse than a blurred or fogged image, it is a phantom image . . .[13]

Published a year after *La Chambre claire,* Hervé Guibert's *L'Image fantôme* (IF) is a markedly Barthesian production, as well as a work that includes Barthes amongst its *dramatis personae.*[14] In it, the relationships between photography and truth, and between the (invisible) photographic artefact, fetishism and desire, are once again key focuses. So, too, is the bond between visual representation, writing, reading and what, for the moment, I shall term readability. In Part I of this chapter (Part II refocuses on the photography/fetishism/desire dynamic, exploring the ways in which Duras's *L'Amant* works it through), I wish, first, to tease out the detail of these Guibertian connections. Next, I shall move to examine the sexual politics – these centre on the issue of gay 'legibility' – that inhere in what might seem simply to be an individualistic account of the possibilities and limitations of photographic practice. But before I turn either to the convergences and divergences between visual and textual representation, reading and desire delineated in *L'Image fantôme* or to Guibert's politics of homosexual (un)readability, I want to outline some general features of his 'photo-text'.

While Guibert is popularly perceived as 'France's premier *sida* novelist',[15] his literary corpus includes some fifteen works in which AIDS is not (explicitly) an issue. Novels and *autofictions* apart, he also has two collections of photographs to his name (*Le Seul Visage* (1984) and *Photographies* (1993)), and wrote for *Le Monde*'s photography column for almost a decade. As the citations prefacing this section of my discussion indicate, his *L'Image fantôme* is a text in which photography is a central preoccupation. Guibert's *récit* offers, however, a by no means conventional exploration of the photographic.

Cohering as it (partially) does with the 'photo-essay' format, *L'Image fantôme* should, in principle, proffer for the reader's scrutiny a collage of photographs and words, pinpointing thereby the semiotic differences and mutual 'resistances' that obtain between verbal and visual representation. In fact, Guibert's text does no such thing. Devoid of any actual photographic images – described as 'alien' to *L'Image fantôme* (IF, p. 123) – it is composed simply of a series of reflections on photography and photographs. These are offered by a narrator who, if nameless, is patently identifiable as a projection of Guibert himself, and, as 'photobiographies', heterogeneously interweave photo-analysis and personal recollection, drawn in part from Guibert's diary.[16] Founded as they are upon photographic absence, the Guibertian autobio/photographical reflections incorporated into what is introduced as an *autoportrait* have been categorized as 'virtual photography'.[17] The textual fragments containing them – many of which address 'phantom' images that are never realized (IF, p. 124) – are interrupted by dialogic passages, in which Guibert's narrating *je* 'converses' with an anonymous other voice, identified sometimes as *tu*, sometimes as *vous*. The focus of these conversations is Guibert's self-referential narrator's status as the subject and object of photographic representation, as well as the content and evolution of his narrative.

Amongst the various things that it conveys about Guibert's relation to the photographic, *L'Image fantôme* reveals that even if he was especially fascinated by photo-images that barely existed as such – 'phantom images, images that didn't come out, latent images'[18] – he nonetheless shared Barthes's concern with the question of photographic *truth*. Commentators on his volume of fragments have generally isolated those features of it that suggest that Guibert took photography to be a representational form lacking in the capacity to conserve and capture *le vrai*. Alain Buisine, for instance, addresses Guibert's vision of photography as a 'forgetful practice' (*pratique oublieuse*, IF, p. 24), in order to argue that he not only viewed the photographic act as obliterative of the reality/essence of the referent, but also appreciated the 'deadly erasures' (*effacements mortifères*) that photography effects.[19] Elements of *L'Image fantôme* certainly imply a belief on Guibert's part that photography, if it offers the illusion of truthful transparency, is prone to reify and embalm its objects.[20] Other sections of the text, however, notably its *incipit*, qualify this belief, indicating that Guibert was ready, intermittently, to entertain a rather different, more 'primitive' vision of photographic practice. This fragment runs as follows:

> In one of my Bibi Fricotins [a child's comic], I came upon a fabulous invention that made me dream [. . .]: glasses that let you read other people's thoughts. Since then, I've discovered, from more or less dirty ads, that there are spectacles which see through [*transpercent*] clothes, undressing the person wearing them. And I imagined that photography could bring both of these powers into play, I was tempted to make a self-portrait . . .[21]

This section of Guibert's text, focused as it is on the optical/ocular, suggests that photography potentially constitutes a hyperpowerful mode of reading the real. It does so, in part, by engaging with the quasi-Barthesian notion of a 'reverse *punktum*' effect. In the Barthesian optic, the *punktum* elements (the stray, accidental, uncoded details) of the photographic image possess the power to 'pierce' the photographic reader erotically, so that s/he is left pleasurably wounded by his/her encounter with photography (CC, pp. 47–9 and *passim*/CL, pp. 25–7). Conversely, for Guibert, to judge at least by the *incipit* of *L'Image fantôme*, it is the photographic *object* that comes to be 'pricked' through the photographic act, and pricked in such a way that its 'truth' is revealed. For Guibert (specifically, the Guibert of the early 1980s), then, photography seems at least some of the time to function as a 'magical', caressive, kiss-and-tell medium that, by virtue of its preternaturally penetrative powers, can both read *and* render readable the 'essence' of that which it seeks to replicate.

If Guibert plays with the notion that the photographic gesture turns on an erotically penetrative act – an act by means of which the photographic *object* is stripped readably bare, in X-ray mode – he also suggests that photography possesses the capacity to 'legibilize' the erotic impulses and instincts of the photographic *subject*. By having *L'Image fantôme*'s narrator insist that the photographic image is *l'essence du désir* (IF, p. 89), and by making him assert that photography is an 'amorous practice' (IF, p. 11), and by suggesting, in *Le Seul Visage*, that his own photographic images bear witness to the love he feels for those close to him,[22] Guibert frames the photographic artefact as the product of a desiring movement that, once the photograph has been taken, can come potentially, and despite photography's 'forgetful' tendencies, to be visible within it. Guibert does then, as Buisine suggests, cherish the curiously naive notion that desire, for all its slipperiness, can be ontologically – and readably – present within the photographic image: 'That Hervé Guibert intensely desired the photographic image, in that it constitutes in his eyes the essence, indeed the very ontology of desire and in that it incarnates, stiffens and erects [*érige*] the body of the Other, irresistibly arousing those beings who seek to take pleasure from its intensely, desperately mimetic sex appeal, is beyond all doubt.'[23] If Guibert views the photo-image as constituting *l'ontologie du désir*, this is not, however, (or at least not simply, as Buisine implies) because the reification of the Other's body that the photographic act effects transforms it into a substitute phallus – a fetish object[24] – that cannot help but stimulate desire in the photographic *reader*. It is rather because, in the Guibertian optic, the photographic artefact represents a container for, and a precipitate of, the desire of its photographing *author* – a desire that has as its concomitant the metonymic replacement of human objects of desire with two-dimensional, filmic equivalents, and that we can construe as deeply fetishizing.[25]

The first titled fragment of *L'Image fantôme*, also entitled 'L'image fantôme' (IF, pp. 11–18), introduces Guibert's reader to the type of (truthful) photograph that, in Guibert's scheme of things, potentially 'ontologizes' and legibilizes its creator's desire. Perhaps unsurprisingly, two aspects of this narratively inscribed photograph, also invoked in Guibert's *Mes Parents* (1986),[26] recall Barthes's Winter Garden *ur-photo*. First, the image it proffers is an image of Guibert's narrator's mother. Second, the reader senses, it constitutes a talismanic, fetish-like object whose creation the Guibert persona of *L'Image fantôme* pursues self-protectively, in order to ward off and to disavow, even as he acknowledges its inevitability, the phenomenon of maternal mortality and the related, threatening spectre of Lack: 'I captured my mother on film: she was at that point at the height of her beauty [. . .]. [Once the session was over] she became once more her husband's wife, a forty-five-year-old woman, even though, as if by magic, the photo had momentarily halted the ageing process [. . .]. I wanted to forget her, to see her no longer, to focus for ever on the image we were about to extract from the fixing bath.'[27] In order to bring his filmic fetish-image into being – in order, in other words, to generate an object whose freeze-framed relation to the maternal real imbues it with maternal presence, diminishing the menace of maternal decay – Guibert's narrator senses that he must transform his model into a 'decensored' entity that corresponds to 'l'image de [son] désir' (IF, p. 15). For all photography's openness to fetishism, however, and for all his maternal manipulations – these take the form of efforts to alter his mother's physical appearance, so that it escapes her husband's control – visual gratification eludes Guibert's narrating counterpart. When he tries to develop the photographic image he has striven to produce, it emerges that he has failed properly to load his film into the camera that his father, excluded from what is an intensely oedipal photographic scene (IF, p. 12), has provided for the occasion. All Guibert's narrator is left with, at the end of his abortive photo-take, is the unsatisfactory spectacle of a virgin piece of film (*pellicule vierge*, IF, p. 17), resonant with the maternal absence he has endeavoured to exorcize.

Guibert's discussion, in the first essay of *L'Image fantôme*, of this doubly 'absent' photograph makes three things clear. The first is that, for Guibert himself, the desire that impels photography into existence is, above all, a desire to transgress an interdiction (here paternal), by transforming the photographic object into a 'forbidden image' (*image interdite*, IF, p. 14) that is desirable uniquely on his own (incestuous) terms. The second is that the kind of desiring photograph Guibert envisages – i.e., the kind of photograph that might allow its reader to read the truth of its *author*'s desire – proves, for Guibert, to be as slippery as desire itself. The third is that when photographic reproduction fails the Guibertian subject of desire, the only – and unsatisfactory – recourse that is left is literature. This is the sense of the second of the extracts cited at the start of this section of the present chapter. What this statement signals is that Guibert's narrative creation, *L'Image fantôme*, owes its existence to the photographic failure invoked in its opening fragment, and to the existence of a *photo manquée*. As Alain Buisine explains,[28] if Barthes's *La Chambre claire* exists around and because of a maternal photograph that exists but is never shown – and that, we sense, can *only* exist as a fetish object and a 'truthful' sign as long as it remains unavailable to the public gaze – Guibert's *L'Image fantôme* comes into being, as text, as textual self-portrait and as 'virtual photography', by virtue of the (in)existence of an 'image effacée, fantomatique'.

The fact that *L'Image fantôme* exists as a textual artefact because visual representation eludes him inflects the form as well as the content of Guibert's narrative. His text not only dissects real and imaginary photographs, but also constitutes an example of what Guibert himself terms *écriture photographique*. This is defined in *L'Image fantôme* (IF, pp. 73–7) as a mode of writing that possesses a 'visual' immediacy analogous to that of the photograph (IF, p. 75), and operates in the same 'penetrative' fashion as the photographic act itself.[29] Guibert's own text may be taken to deploy an *écriture photographique* for three reasons. The first is that the organization of *L'Image fantôme* – involving a series of short, highly-focused texts, arranged associatively and interspersed with sections of commentary – signally mirrors the layout of a photo album. The second is that *L'Image fantôme* fetishistically substitutes sections of narrative for absent photographic objects much in the same way that photography substitutes pieces of film for absent elements of the real. The third is that *L'Image fantôme is* a 'penetrative' text. It 'penetrates' in so far as its sequence of essays pierces and elucidates the essence of Guibert's relation to photography much as the X-ray photograph of his adolescent body – set up as a kind of photographic *mise-en-abyme* in the essay 'la radiographie' (IF, p. 68) and used elsewhere in Guibert's *oeuvre* as a metaphor for writing practice – penetrated and revealed his own corporeal essence, engendering, Guibert claims, 'the most intimate image of myself'.[30]

Its status as a 'photographic' production (albeit as a 'negative', generated by a photographic failure) poses the question of how, as a whole, *L'Image fantôme* relates to *desire*. His/her encounter with Guibert's *photo-écriture* necessarily provokes the reader into wondering whether the gamut of tableaux constituting his textual *autoportrait* combine to 'legibilize' the (sexual) desire(s) of their creator in the same way that a photograph might, and what the desiring truths might be that *L'Image fantôme* permits us to intuit.

In a central segment of *L'Image fantôme*, in one of its dialogic passages, the 'other voice' of Guibert's narrative tartly informs its Guibert persona that most of his fragments ooze (with) homosexuality.[31] Guibert's narrator readily accepts that the essays of *L'Image fantôme* exude the homoerotic. He argues that, since his subject is the photographic image, about which it is impossible to talk without talking also of desire, it is unsurprising that his text should bespeak the specificity of his own erotic proclivities. Indeed, he states, it is desirable that this should be so, since, were he to mask or despecify his desire, the 'truth' of the reflections contained in *L'Image fantôme* would be adulterated (IF, p. 89).

The inclusion of this dialogue might encourage Guibert's reader to surmise that the sole desire rendered readable in *L'Image fantôme* is homoerotic desire (that is, a desire whose objects are marked and made desirable by the fact of sexual sameness). The contents of certain of the *récits* making up Guibert's text suggest that we would not be wrong to do so.[32] But there is another, 'secret' desire at play in *L'Image fantôme*, which is immisced with homosexual desire and which we cannot help but read, eventually, within Guibert's textual self-portrait, even though we are not bidden explicitly so to do. This is a desire, I want to propose, whose focus/object is the erotically unreadable, the sexually unmarked. That this latter desire not only obtains in Guibert's photo-text but also stands in a complex relation to homosexual desire is signalled in the final narrative 'snapshot' of *L'Image fantôme*: 'L'Image cancéreuse' (IF, pp. 165–9). Consequently, in the next section of this discussion, the patterns of desire that this essay legibilizes will be scrutinized in detail.

The photograph that 'L'Image cancéreuse' takes as its focus proffers an image to which the narrator of *L'Image fantôme* – Guibert's self-projective double – is so fetishistically attracted that he coddles it, sleeps with it and, eventually, sellotapes it to his body, so that, mingled finally into the pores of his flesh, it becomes his *own* double, or 'second brother'.[33] Constituting as it does no less talismanic an entity than the unrealized *image fantôme* that Guibert's photo-text begins by invoking, it seems likely that this actualized photo-image – or, rather, the essay that Guibert's unillustrated narrative offers us in its stead – holds clues to the nature of Guibert's most intimate desires. That said, some of the desiring impulses that 'L'Image cancéreuse' incites us to read are less than immediately foreseeable.

The photograph that 'L'Image cancéreuse' addresses is imprinted with the image of a blond, anonymous teenage boy. Elements of this image, as it is 'verbalized' in the opening section of Guibert's *récit*, recall the timeless grace of the ephebe featured in Visconti's *Death in Venice* and evoked as iconically desirable in the first essay of *L'Image fantôme* (IF, p. 15). The boy's 'uniform', however – black leather jacket, white shirt, studded leather bracelet – has more contemporary, s/m resonances, and his displayed body, aloof and yet available, seems overtly to signal itself as different from the male heterosexual body.[34] The photographic image, then, that 'L'Image cancéreuse' reconstitutes emits messages that are mixed, but that combine to transform it into a markedly coded visual sign, wherein homosexuality is connoted, and connoted in a highly readable fashion. Given the homoerotic quality this sign possesses, and given the central presence it is accorded in Guibert's narrative, Guibert's reader might opt to conclude that the only desire evinced in his *récit* is a desire that is exclusively homosexual. To do so would, however, be unwise. As Guibert's essay progresses, and as its focus becomes the progressive deterioration to which the photographic image reconstructed within it falls victim, another desire comes to be readable in 'L'Image cancéreuse', and to dominate its second section (IF, pp. 167–9).

The latter part of Guibert's *nouvelle* charts the delegibilization that gradually befalls the desired image of the unknown boy. The image's growing unreadability – caused by damage inflicted on the snapshot it is etched on by the glue attaching the photo to its mount, and likened by Guibert's narrator to a disease – ensures that it comes in the end to be as empty of content as the 'absent', eroticized maternal fetish-image invoked in *L'Image fantôme*'s opening *récit*. Predictably, the invisibility that encroaches on Guibert's photo-image erases the homoerotic quality it initially manifests. Unpredictably, the 'cancerous' process of (homo)sexual delegibilization to which his cherished image succumbs – a process lovingly detailed in the closing sections of his *récit* – appears to appeal to Guibert's narrating double; so much so, in fact, that he chooses not to retouch the damaged photo in order to return it to its original, easily readable state.

That (homo)sexual unreadability is somehow attractive to the Guibert persona of *L'Image fantôme* is implied both in earlier essays of the volume[35] and in a central section of 'L'Image cancéreuse' (IF, p. 166), where Guibert's narrator reveals that he was first drawn to the photograph of the boy because, even intact, it showed only the upper, unsexed, androgynous torso of its object. The fact of its attractiveness elucidates the pleasure permeating the closing part of Guibert's narrator's *récit* – a pleasure stimulated by the detioration of what was once a legibly (homo)sexualized photographic artefact. What, though, does this pleasure tell us about the desires that inhere in 'L'Image cancéreuse'?

Its textual articulation attests, we sense, to the fact that the desire that 'founds' 'L'Image cancéreuse' and is gradually legibilized within it is less homosexual desire *per se* than a desire for that which, in erotic terms, is readable only as sexually non-specific, as homosexually *un*readable. What is more, the expression/manifestation, in 'L'Image cancéreuse', of this latter, 'founding' desire would seem to signal the narrated existence, in *L'Image fantôme*, of a yet other, and associated, Guibertian desire. Sexual illegibility (the fundamental focus of desire in 'L'Image cancéreuse') is incarnated in an erotic object (the boy of the narratively reconstituted photo-image) who is cast in Guibert's essay as the symbiotic double (*second frère*) of Guibert's narrator – who is, in turn, a self-projective avatar of Guibert-as-author. In other words, 'L'Image cancéreuse' not only pinpoints (homo)sexual unreadability as intrinsically desirable, but also pinpoints parallels that trouble the boundaries between the Guibertian authorial/narrating self profiled in *L'Image fantôme* and the textually inscribed, desired, sexually unreadable Other. This implies that the desire for homosexually non-legible *objects* of desire adumbrated in the concluding *récit* of *L'Image fantôme* incorporates a desire on Guibert's (authorial) part to embrace, and to *identify* himself with, the homoerotically unreadable. In short, Guibert's five-page disquisition on photographical 'cancer' may be taken to establish homosexual illegibility as something that is not only desired (by its author/narrator), but is desired both *in* the erotic object and *as* a subjective state.

The question of gay 'readability' is treated at length in Lee Edelman's 1994 essay 'Homographesis'. I want therefore to pause, briefly, even though its complexities do not lend themselves lightly to recapitulation, to delineate some of the central contentions mooted in Edelman's polemical piece. Edelman opens 'Homographesis' by establishing homosexual 'legibility' as something that, paradoxically, both the gay advocate *and* the homophobe invest with a sense of urgency.[36] He goes on to argue that while the imperative to make 'homosexual difference' visible/readable and to subject it to investigative scrutiny is an integral part of a gay liberationist politics 'committed to the social necessity of opening, or even removing, the closet door',[37] we must never forget that the conceptualization of the gay subject, and more particularly the gay *body*, as entities stamped with the hallmark of a homosexual specificity that can and must be read is not unproblematic. Edelman's point, put simply, is that the political promotion of gay legibility/legibilization carries with it certain risks, in view of the fact that homosexual 'readability' is something that heterosexual culture requires and desires. That this is the case, argues Edelman, reflects the fact that the heterosexual order needs a markedly identifiable sexual Other in order to reinforce its own authority/naturalness, and deploys a series of disciplinary knowledges in order to bring that Other into (legible) being.[38]

Having glossed the problems inherent in the categorization of homosexuality as a reified, readable modality of difference that is inscribed, legibly, on the gay body, and with reference to literary and sexological writings of the present and past, Edelman turns his attention to the phenomenon of 'homographesis' itself. This term relates to the inscription and production of homosexuality within writing and textuality.[39] Edelman defines it in two, antithetical, ways, contending that 'like writing, [. . .] homographesis would name a double operation: one serving the ideological purposes of a conservative social order intent on codifying identities in its labor of disciplinary inscription, and the other resistant to that categorization, intent on *de*-scribing the identities that order has so oppressively *in*scribed'.[40] First, he casts 'homographesis' as a regulatory 'putting into writing of homosexuality' that institutionalizes homosexual difference, by marking it out as a discrete and legible identity-mode, and does so in the service of heterosexual power relations.[41] Second, however, he suggests that 'homographesis' is also a *deconstructive* writing practice that works *against* homographesis in its first sense, by inscribing homosexual possibilities in such a way as to operate a *refusal* of the specifications of sexual identity/difference on which heterosexuality, and the cultural practice of regulatory homographesis, rely.[42] Homographesis, then, for Edelman, in its 'alternative' guise, appears to constitute a writing mode that works towards a form of homotextual *de*categorization. It functions to undermine that binary logic of homo/heterosexual difference on which, within the heterosexual order, notions of symbolic identity are grounded. Consequently – and for all that it refuses to commit itself to the valorization of homosexual visibility – the 'homographic' text, according to Edelman's deliberations, is one in which a subtle form of politico-textual resistance comes into operation.

If, in parenthesis, space has been devoted here to a reiteration of some of the theses of 'Homographesis', this is because it is not only possible but also productive to read 'L'Image cancéreuse' – and *L'Image fantôme* as a whole – in tandem with

Edelman's analysis of gay legibility, and the uses heterosexism makes of it. As I have already established, 'L'Image cancéreuse' chronicles a process of (homo)sexual delegibilization. In so doing, Guibert's *récit* – with its loving attention to the erasures that befall the marks of sexuality inscribed on the boyish photo-body whose fate is its focus – invites its reader to envision the gay male body not as a body on which homosexual difference is necessarily and indelibly stamped, but rather as a markedly less 'coded' body whose sexual orientation potentially eludes readability and legibilization. Within the terms of Edelman's argument, these features of 'L'Image cancéreuse' signal a contestation of the (heterosexist) notion that the 'indiscreet anatomy' of the gay male subject must ineluctably bear witness to a 'deviant' sexual identity that is 'written immodestly' upon it.[43] They suggest, moreover, that Guibert (consciously? unconsciously?) wrote at least one of the *nouvelles* of his photo-text in order to expose, and undercut, the compulsory fabrications imposed on the homosexual subject/body by the disciplinary order of heterosexual normality and by its need for a visibly identifiable homosexual other. The apparently apolitical disquisition on photography that Guibert offers us in *L'Image fantôme* can, consequently, be viewed as a 'homographic' production, if only by virtue of the contents of 'L'Image cancéreuse'. Guibert's collection of photo-essays can, therefore, up to a point at least, be aligned with some of his later, more 'militant' writings in which, as Murray Pratt explains, he pursues a series of textual self-reinventions, in order to shrug off a 'homosexual identity' constructed, ultimately, by and within the determinations of regulatory heterosexuality.[44]

I signalled above that my intention, here, was to examine the sexual/political impact of *L'Image fantôme*. My analysis of the 'delegibilizing' dimension of Guibert's text – a dimension that emerges most powerfully in 'L'Image cancéreuse', but is implicit elsewhere in Guibert's volume – has sought to illuminate its contestatory potential. I want, however, to conclude my investigation of Guibert's *photo-écriture* by dwelling further on the sexual/textual politics of *L'Image fantôme*.

In view of the fact that 'L'Image cancéreuse', the concluding essay of Guibert's photo-text, profiles a desire that is 'resistant' in so far as its object – gay illegibility – runs counter to the identitarian requirements of the heterosexual order, Guibert's readers might choose to classify *L'Image fantôme* as a work in which sexual/political contestation wins the day. But I am not convinced that to do so is wholly justifiable. In order to establish why not, I want to turn to the *coda* of Guibert's narrative, an untitled dialogic fragment:

'Telling you this story ['L'Image cancéreuse'] has left me feeling quite empty. The story's my secret, you know?'
'And?'
'I don't want to say, to you of all people, "please don't tell it to anyone else".'
'OK. But your secret has also become my secret now. It is part of me and I will treat it

as I treat all my secrets; disposing of it when the moment comes. And it will become someone else's secret.'

'You're right. Secrets need to circulate.'[45]

Amongst other things, this fragment suggests that the 'political' desire subtending 'L'Image cancéreuse' has been, hitherto, a hidden desire, a secret. In addition, it reveals that this desire, once unmasked and legibilized within 'L'Image cancéreuse', comes to constitute an *open* secret that – like the majority of the secrets Guibert's writings evoke – gets transformed into an object of exchange.[46] In *The Novel and the Police*, D. A. Miller has pertinent things to say about secrecy and secrets. On the one hand, he suggests, the hidden secret is a force for subversion. He explains that 'in a world where the explicit exposure of the subject would manifest how thoroughly he has been inscribed within a socially given totality, secrecy would be the spiritual exercise by which the subject is allowed to conceive of himself as a resistance: a friction in the smooth functioning of the social order'.[47] Conversely, however, the open secret, for Miller, is not subversive at all, in that it merely 'registers the subject's accommodation to a totalizing system that has obliterated the difference he would make'.[48] Miller's highly Foucauldian association of avowal and accommodation helps us to assess the political punch – or lack of it – packed, ultimately, by Guibert's *L'Image fantôme*.[49] In this text, a desire that countermands compulsory homosexual legibility is mutated, by virtue of the narrative act that is 'L'Image cancéreuse', into an avowed, readable secret – a secret shared with the dialogue-partner of Guibert's *L'Image fantôme* and with Guibert's reader. In itself, this desire is distinctly subversive. Once, however, it is acknowledged and 'outed' – and the *coda* of Guibert's narrative confirms that this is what happens in 'L'Image cancéreuse' – then it is arguably the case (at least within the terms of Miller's analysis) that its legible presence in Guibert's *opus* robs *L'Image fantôme* of the contestatory force that the Guibertian reader might have been moved to detect within it.

Marguerite Duras's Photo-Fetishism: Photography, Autobiography, Lack

That image, that unphotographed absolute image, entered into the book [. . .] it will have been and will remain indicated; its existence, its *"retinian"* permanence will have been placed there.[50]

Proximate publication dates aside, it might appear that Guibert's *L'Image fantôme* and Duras's *L'Amant* (LA)[51] have little in common. In fact, differences of genre notwithstanding, Duras's *récit* connects with Guibert's photo-text in a variety of ways. Firstly, because it incorporates (what is generally assumed to be) personal history into a narrative that dramatically destabilizes the chronological organization and identitarian certainties of 'classic' autobiography, Duras's *opus* is no less generically elusive than Guibert's autobio/photoessay.[52] Secondly, in 'Guibertian' mode, Duras's temporally and pronominally fluid rendition of her colonial Indochinese childhood is inaugurated yet unillustrated by a 'latent' (in the case of *L'Amant*, imaginary) photo-image that is never actually realized, but is proffered nonetheless as an object of spectatorship for the reader's gaze. Thirdly, and in consequence, like Guibert's *récit photographique* before it, *L'Amant* echoes Alain Buisine's assertion that 'if a text turns upon an image [. . .], it cannot fail to be the case that text and image will immediately miss each other, that each will be absent to the other'.[53] Fourthly, the space of writing constructed in *L'Amant* is characterized by 'photographic' formal features (these include a bric-à-brac organization of snapshot-like textual segments) that are equally apparent in *L'Image fantôme*.[54] Finally, and most importantly, *L'Amant*'s 'photographic' narrative opens by presenting for our inspection an 'unphotographed absolute photograph' that is as much a target of the fetishizing impulse as Guibert's 'phantom' maternal image and, indeed, Barthes's seminal 'Photographie du Jardin d'Hiver'. The 'presence', within *L'Amant*, of this absent fetish-photo legibilizes, moreover, a key element in the matrix of desires mapped in Duras's autobiographically-inflected tale. In view of this, the detail of the role played by fetishism in Duras's photographically-stimulated *écriture* will constitute, in this final section of Chapter 3, my (not unfetishistic) object of investigation. In particular, I shall address the 'aberrant' nature of Duras's female photo-fetishism, exploiting psychoanalytic theory in order to do so, and working, amongst other things, to present it as a less self-oriented phenomenon than the photo-fetishism of Hervé Guibert.

The 'image' from which the *récit* contained in *L'Amant* derives its impetus is a verbalized, fantasized image; a 'fantasme de photographie'[55] that Duras's nameless adult narrator progressively 'develops' before our eyes, in the *incipit* of her story (LA, pp. 9–21/TL [trans.], pp. 7–17). It exists because of, and as an *après-coup* substitute for, a photo-image that has previously *failed* to materialize at the point in time at which its realization became a possibility. The product of a 'photo-take' that operates, then, exclusively at the level of *narrative*, Duras's imaginary image 'captures' and 'stills' a scene in which her self-projective heroine journeys across the Mekong on a ferryboat, in order to return to school in Saigon after a holiday spent at home in Sadec: 'I think it was during this journey that the image became detached, removed from the rest. It might have existed, a photograph might have been taken, just like any other, somewhere else, in other circumstances. But it wasn't. [. . .] And it's to this failure to have been created that the image owes its virtue: the virtue of representing, of being the creator of, an absolute' (TL, pp. 13–14).[56] Incorporated into this scene is a primordial moment – that of the first look exchanged with her Chinese lover – as a result of which Duras's youthful protagonist will embark on a trajectory that breaks with the 'horror' of her family set-up and impels her into the domain of (non-familial) eroticism and, eventually, into that of writing. In her account of this centrally significant morsel of her past, and of the inexistent image within which it might have been, but missed being, embedded, Duras's adult narrator foregrounds her own, adolescent bodily appearance. Its nature and form – the essence of the phantasmatic photograph fabricated in the opening segment of Duras's story – merit precise attention.

The most striking things about the central, female, bodily entity 'snapped' by Duras's after-the-fact, narrativized photo-take are its artificial aspect and its *morcellement*, or fragmentation. Not unlike the text in which it/she features, the youthful Duras-self of *L'Amant*'s phantom-photo comes across less as a homogeneous, seamless, natural being than as a kind of constructed composite, made up of a series of diverse 'pieces'. The elements out of which this composite is created are sartorial. They include a sepia-coloured silk dress; a leather belt; a pair of gold lamé high-heeled shoes; and a man's flat-brimmed felt fedora, with a wide black ribbon (LA, pp. 18–21/TL, pp. 15–17). What is more, if viewed through the lens of the language of sexual fetishism, each of these vestimentary 'bits' can be read as manifesting an erotically resonant, fetishistic, phallicized/izable quality:[57] the most phallically significative, *punktum*-like of all of them, and the key source of Duras's image's 'crucial ambiguity' (TL, p. 16),[58] being the brownish-pink, height-enhancing *chapeau d'homme* that contrasts strikingly with the frailty of its owner's physique.[59] The sexually symbolic slant of the Durassian narrated photo-body represented in the *incipit* of *L'Amant* is inescapable. It invites Duras's reader to read the broader phenomenon of her 'photographic' self-narration in the context of fetishism, and through a consideration of the fetish object itself.

In 'Photography and Fetish', Christian Metz has the following to say about the way in which fetishes operate:

> [W]e can state that the fetish is taken up in two chains of meaning: metonymically, it alludes to the contiguous place of the lack [. . .]; and metaphorically, according to Freud's conception, it is an equivalent of the penis, as the primordial displacement of the look aimed at replacing an absence by a presence – an object, a small object, a part object. It is remarkable that the fetish – even in the common meaning of the word, the fetish in everyday life, a re-displaced derivative of the fetish proper, the object which brings luck, the mascot, the amulet [. . .] – it is remarkable that it always combines a double and contradictory function: on the side of metaphor, an inciting and encouraging one (it is a pocket phallus); and, on the side of metonymy, an apotropaic one, that is, the averting of danger [. . .].[60]

Metz's commentary on the double function of the fetish illuminates both of the texts dissected in the central sections of this chapter, and illuminates the unrealized photographs that inaugurate them. As I have already suggested, the *image fantôme* in which Guibert fails to represent his mother may be taken, as fetish object, to belong predominantly in the apotropaic sphere, in that its fabrication is inspired by Guibert's self-protective desire to distance a form of danger: namely, the threat posed to himself by the prospect/spectacle of maternal deterioration.[61] In contrast and, in view of her gender, curiously, we can read Duras's narrator's phantasmatic, verbalized self-image as adhering far more closely than Guibert's phantom-photo to the 'fetish = pocket phallus' paradigm Metz evokes. The reasons why Duras's imaginary, unmade image of her adolescent body can be taken to be (not unlike) a fetish governed by the phallic-substitute function, and to be fetishized as such by Duras's self-projective narrating persona, are complex. Bearing on more than just what is figured *within* the imaginary image's imagined frame, they require careful delineation.

The fact that its focus is a scene in which Duras's heroine features as a constella-tion of fetishizable items – hence as a conglomerate of phallic ciphers – cannot *per se* be deemed to 'prove' that the narrated photo-image of Duras's text functions as a phallic fetish object, or that Duras's narrator is a/its fetishizer. On one level, this simply suggests that in the existential instant 'captured' by Duras's phantom image (or, rather, envisioned in her phantasmic elaboration of its emergence), Duras's autoreferential protagonist – cast by her narrating counterpart, in Lacanian mode, as containing the site of *jouissance* (LA, p. 15/TL, p. 12) – performs in a way that invokes Lacan's apprehension of femininity as a phallic masquerade: a (fake) 'being of the phallus' that 'permits the imaginary phallus which both sexes want but neither sex has, to keep functioning as a *manque à être* ("lack in being") that generates desire'.[62] It *is* possible nonetheless to construe Duras's phantasmatic *autoportrait* as (resembling) a fetish that, fetishized by the narrating persona of *L'Amant,* works according to the 'phallic surrogate' model, and to read as at least *symptomatic* of its fetish-status the phallicity and *morcellement*[63] of the body it displays.

Fetishes of this type, Freudians contend, are made in the unconscious when the infantile gaze, faced with the spectacle of maternal Lack, fixes in fascinated distraction on substitute entities that come to replace the missing maternal phallus. Fetish objects that operate as substitutive phallic signs come into being, in other words, through a castration-anxiety averting, absence-disavowing 'stopping of the look'. As Metz suggests, a similar 'stopping of the look' occurs in the photographic act, when a 'cut inside the referent' is made and the object of the photo-take is targeted and reified, becoming at once static and separate from all the other entities the camera lens could have picked out.[64] What is more, says Metz, the photographic still, fixed as it is by the photographic gaze in the same way that the fetish is frozen, eternally, in the psyche, shares 'many properties of the fetish (as object)'.[65]

Because the phantasmatic image that initiates *L'Amant* issues out of Duras's narrator's verbal miming of the photographic gesture – a gesture that itself mimes the fixative, separating process whereby fetishization occurs – it seems reasonable to read this narrated self/photo-portrait as somehow impinging, along with the photographic artefact proper, on the space, and the nature, of the 'pocket phallus' fetish.[66] Moreover, because Duras's narrator is clearly intent on compelling a scene that failed in the 'real' either to hold the gaze or to be separated from a mass of potentially 'fixable' moments of being (TL, pp. 13–14/LA, pp. 16–17) or to achieve 'retinian permanence' to do so *retroactively*, in the 'photographic' realm of her *récit*, she in turn can be read as no less a fetishizing *agent* than the subject of photography him/herself. It is by virtue, then, of the fact that, textually and belatedly, it is made to be photographically immobile, to be 'removed from all the rest' (TL, p. 13)[67] and to 'stop the look', rather than simply as a result of the phallicized, fetishizable elements it contains, that Duras's inexistent, narrated image of her teen-aged body can be conceived as (being like) a phallically-surrogate fetish object, the source of whose fetishization is the 'photographic' narrator of *L'Amant*. This, though, poses certain problems, in that Duras's narrator's auto-fetishization/phallicization – achieved through the metamorphosis of her youthful self into an invented, fetish-like photo-image that figures the female-as-masquerading-phallus/fetish[68] ('Suddenly, I see myself as another, as another would be seen, outside myself, available to all, available to all eyes, in circulation for cities, journeys, desire' TL, p. 16)[69] – is, in the context of psychoanalytic thinking at least, highly unusual.

As Naomi Schor explains in her influential essay 'Female Fetishism: the Case of George Sand', psychoanalytic theory has been loath to recognize that women can fetishize. While individual Lacanian analysts – notably Gérard Bonnet[70] – have been willing to acknowledge that some female subjects may practise the fetishist's perversion in 'minor' mode, it is an article of faith with Freud and Freudians, Schor reveals, that 'fetishism is the male perversion *par excellence*. Traditional psychoanalytic literature on the subject states over and over again that there are no female fetishists; female fetishism is, in the rhetoric of psychoanalysis, an oyxmoron'.[71] Schor is evidently not at ease with the notion that fetishism, because it derives from a castration anxiety-inspired rebuttal of maternal Lack that girl-children, always already 'castrated', have no need to effect, must be the exclusive province of men. Neither, clearly, is she wholly happy with the related contention that pseudo-fetishistic practice is only pursued by those 'viriloid' women subjects who identify intensely with the phallic masculine position and partake in the unconscious fears its occupation entails. She herself seems keen to propose that female fetishistic activity – in whose existence she is inclined to believe – stems less from male-identifiedness than from a kind of 'perverse oscillation': a refusal by (bisexual) women to be anchored on any single side of the axis of castration.[72] Ultimately, however, she cannot bring herself entirely to demasculinize female fetishism. Her reading of manifestations of fetishistic eroticization in the 'bisexual' writings of George Sand leads her finally to frame fetishism-in-the-feminine – and, we sense, feminist attemps at theorizing it – as a 'perversion-theft' of a predominantly male disorder, and as a form of penis envy.[73] In the light of Schor's conclusions, I want in the following section of this discussion to think through the possible sources of Duras's female photo-fetishism, and to reflect on whether her narrator's fetishistic transformation of her adolescent persona into an imagined photo-entity that shares in the space of the phallicized fetish itself can be conceived as anything more than the mark of a masculinity complex. In order to do so, I shall elaborate on the kind of fetishistic function that Duras's invented photo-portrait may be taken to fulfil.

Photographs are revealed in *L'Amant* to be the fief of Duras's self-projective narrator's mother. Not only does she obsessively collect snapshots of her progeniture (LA, pp. 115–17/TL, pp. 99–101) but she also features prominently in the first *real* (hence contrapuntal) photo-image that Duras's narrative, labelling it 'la photo du désespoir', invokes (LA, pp. 21–3, p. 41/TL, pp. 17–19, p. 35).[74] Simultaneously, however, the photographs that the mother accumulates – and that, taken always by others, in fact elude her control – are established as resonant with the despairing impotence ('All around her are wildernesses, wastes' TL, p. 28)[75] that is her lot. By virtue of what they do and do not represent, these objects stand as testimony to her existential dejection, her impoverished, impossible lifestyle and her fruitless struggle to transcend it. Devoid of evidence that she enjoys a valorizing role as a player in the French subjection of Indochina, and imprinted with pointers to her despondency and poverty (LA, p. 21, p. 116/TL, pp. 17–18, p. 100), they intimate the *absence* of mastery that, as a racially privileged yet economically powerless white female subject, she both suffers and disavows under a patriarchal colonial order that thwarts her efforts to thrive.

Viewed through a Freudian optic, the photo-images that are associated with Duras's narrator's mother and that, in the face of others' disapprobation, she continues resolutely to show off (LA, pp. 116–17/TL, pp. 100–1) can be taken to symbolize a (refused) maternal 'castration' or failed female phallicity that is no less identifiable in *L'Amant* than it is in Leduc's *L'Asphyxie*. Read psychoanalytic-ally, in other words, these images can be translated as ciphers for a maternal Lack that is evoked, allusively, each time the mother is connected with (de)privation, whether of money, authority, sanity or, most especially, *jouissance*. This, in turn, suggests several things about Duras's autoreferential narrator's own, insistent creation of a verbally 'visual' image of her adolescent self that is made fetishistic – and hence semiotically/substitutionally phallic – by dint of its imaginary 'photographization'. One is that the textual existence of Duras's fetish-like *phantom* photo-portrait may likewise not be unrelated to the maternal phallic Lack that psychoanalysis cites as fetishism's stimulus, and that *L'Amant*'s evocation of *actual* photographs such as the 'photo du désespoir' tacitly points up.[76]

A second is that Duras's narrator's 'photographic', fetishizing, (self-)phallicizing production of her 'absolute' self-image may mesh somehow with the classic fetishistic move whereby the maternal 'wound' is masked and castration concealed by dint of the creation/cathexis of a phantasmatic entity that stands, phallically, for what the mother has never properly possessed. This latter point can be put another way. The verbalized emergence of Duras's imaginary photo-image – an image we can view as (resembling) a fetish that serves as a phallic proxy *and* as an object whose fetish-likeness secures the fetishization/phallicization of the Durassian subject it depicts – functions within *L'Amant* as a magnet for readerly attention, not to say fetishization. As readers attuned to the complexity of the desires that Duras's text bespeaks, we may opt to regard its narrative development as destined to occlude or even compensate a maternal phallic 'deficiency' that is itself implied in *L'Amant*'s references to despair-imbued, extant photographic artefacts and to the maternal impotence they betoken. If we choose to do so, then we need to ask ourselves: to what *specific* end, and for whose benefit, is the Durassian photo/auto-fetishism that *L'Amant* mobilizes effected?

By way of a response to this question, we can make two, related readings of the photographic, (self-)fetishizing activities inscribed in the opening segment of Duras's autobiographical novel. On the one hand, we can take them to signal that what the *incipit* of *L'Amant* dramatizes are 'the symptoms of [a] fetishism [that] only develops in females in whom the illusory phallus has gained such strength as to approach the delusional'.[77] This first interpretation is broadly neo-Freudian, foregrounds the phenomenon of female male-identifiedness and coheres in some ways with the elucidation of *L'Asphyxie*'s 'anxious' maternal substitutions I offered in Chapter 1. It rests on the notion that if Duras's narrator elects to invent, photo-graphically and fetishizingly, the phantasmatic, fetish-like *autoportrait* that *L'Amant* introduces, this is because her viriloid need to allay the threat of a castration she rejects as her own portion is such that it drives her to fabricate something that replaces, however obscurely, the phallus her mother has failed to manifest and whose absence, in the (m)Other, is too anxiety-inducing to bear.

Conversely, though, we can reckon with the possibility that if Duras's narrating persona photographically produces/'fetishizes' a 'visual' fetish-simulacrum that figures her adolescent body as phallicized and fetish-like, this is because she desires to fashion herself, retroactively and generously, into a consolatory surrogate for the phallus her mother did not have, and whose lack would appear to connect with the 'gothic' maternal madness that *L'Amant* chronicles (LA, p. 40/TL, p, 34).[78] This second reading coheres with the Lacanian stance on female fetishism, which casts the female fetishist as more concerned with being the (missing, desired) maternal phallus – hence with being a source of maternal *jouissance* – than with having/not having the penis.[79] It echoes Gérard Bonnet's argument (an argument that counters the credo that women are impervious to fetishistic desire) that if women fetishists fetishize, they do so for the mother. And it is consonant with the delight the mother of *L'Amant*'s diegesis displays as she witnesses her daughter's adolescent incursions into the domain of fetishistic performance: 'When my mother emerges, comes out of her despair, she sees the man's hat and the gold lamé shoes. [. . .] She looks at me, is pleased, smiles. [. . .] She doesn't ask if it's she who bought them, she knows she did. She knows she's capable of it' (TL, p. 27).[80]

Little concrete 'evidence' supports the first of the interpretations elaborated in the preceding paragraphs (save, perhaps, *L'Amant*'s occasional hints that its heroine employs the naked body of her Chinese lover as a phallic token that offsets a lack she disavows in herself (LA, pp. 46–9/TL, pp. 39–42)). The second, however – which intimates that there is indeed, as Schor suggests, 'more to female fetishism than the masculinity complex'[81] – is textually endorsed. It resonates with the nexus of bonds that Duras weaves between: (i) the narrative auto-phallicization that *L'Amant*'s adult daughter-narrator retroactively effects, by mutating her youthful persona into a fetish-like photo-object; (ii) the originary act of self-fetishization engendered by her adolescent performance as a sartorial fetish-composite; and (iii) her mother's collusion in the production of that act and her subsequent, vertiginous joy at it: 'My mother rattles on. She [. . .] laughs, at the scandal, the buffoonery, the funny hat, the sublime elegance of the child who crossed the river' (TL, p. 97).[82] My second interpretation spotlights, in essence, a kind of phantasmatic, reparative filial giving that, the reader senses, may relate to the human, absurd, valour-before-adversity (TL, p. 101)[83] that Duras's mature narrator, for all her maternally-directed hostility and fear of maternal madness, cannot help recognizing in her mother, or seeking belatedly to gratify. I want, now, to make two further points in connection with it.

Firstly, the reading I am privileging here problematizes the proposition, mooted in Maryse Fauvel's 'Photographie et autobiographie', that photography and (contra-) photographic writing are bound up in Duras's text with its author-narrator's antagonism towards her mother.[84] Fauvel's contention is that *L'Amant* turns on a photographic evacuation that emblematizes matrophobic rejection and generates an *écriture* that is no less maternally erasive than anti-photographic.[85] Working with the notion that the photo-image is the symbol *par excellence* of the Durassian mother's detested authority over her offspring, she argues that the unillustrated narrative space opened up by Duras's inceptive play with photographic stillbirth (LA, p. 16/TL, p. 13) attests to Duras's desire to repudiate the maternal by refusing to mimic her mother's fondness for photographic display. Fauvel's exegesis is not without interest. However, her analysis ignores the way in which the photograph-free but photographically-centred discourse that Duras's narrator evolves works to remedy, through the 'reparative' process of phantasmatic, photographic self-fetishization it pursues, the Lack that is imbricated in the Durassian mother's manifest defects.

The second thing I want to note *à propos* the treatment of Duras's narrative photographics offered above is that while it allows her narrator's engagement with (a form of) fetishistic activity to represent more than just a symptom of male-identifiedness, it in no way counters the phallocentric organization allotted to fetishism by psychoanalytic theory. But, if its failure to do so flies in the face of feminist efforts to free female fetishism, conceptually, from the confines of the phallic paradigm,[86] it nonetheless coheres with the particular preoccupations that *L'Amant* bespeaks. Most notably, my reading reflects *L'Amant*'s concern with a maternal 'castration' silhouetted in its narrator's summary of her mother's physical denudation: a summary that echoes, contrapuntally, the no less sartorially-focused rendition of the contents of Duras's absent, 'compensatory' fetish-photo provided in *L'Amant*'s *incipit*:

> My mother, my love, her incredible ungainliness, with her cotton stockings darned by Dô, in the tropics she still thinks you have to wear stockings to be a lady, a headmistress, her dreadful shapeless dresses, mended by Dô, [. . .] her shoes are down at heel, she walks awkwardly, painfully, her hair's drawn back tight into a bun like a Chinese woman's, we're ashamed of her, I'm ashamed of her [. . .](TL, pp. 26–7).[87]

The analytical 'take' on Duras's fetish-like 'absolute image' developed in Part II of this chapter coheres in several ways with the commentaries elaborated in relation to Guibert and Barthes in earlier sections of my discussion. First, it juxtaposes Duras's (m)Other-oriented photo/auto-fetishism with and against the self-protective Guibertian photo-fetishism highlighted by the failed photo-session recounted in *L'Image fantôme*'s opening essay, and by my reading of it. Second, my Durassian exegesis illuminates, as my exegeses of Guibert's 'phantom photo' and Barthes's Winter Garden Image likewise illuminate, the centrally significant role played in autobio/photographical narrative practice by the phenomenon of maternal *manque*. And, in so doing, it binds *L'Amant*, *La Chambre claire* and *L'Image fantôme* into an intertextual cohesiveness that transcends differences of textual genre and authorial gender. (We are prepared to pick up on this cohesiveness by the fact that Barthes's 'essential' 'Photographie du Jardin d'Hiver' is invoked in the writings of both Guibert and Duras.)[88] What my reading does not do, however, is explore the connection that obtains between, on the one hand, the fetishized aspect of the snapshot of *L'Amant*'s teenage heroine in her 'white slut's get-up' that Duras fabricates in the *incipit* of her story and, on the other, the broader lesson in female economic, erotic commodification in the colonial sphere offered by *L'Amant* as a whole.[89] In my next chapter, in compensation, some of the ways in which the relationships between gender, sexuality and the colonial context are adumbrated in the autobiographical work of André Gide and Marie Cardinal will constitute my object of scrutiny.

Notes

1. R. Barthes (1980), *La Chambre claire: Note sur la photographie*, Paris, translated as *Camera Lucida: Reflections on Photography*, trans. R. Howard, London, 1984.

2. For discussions of the theoretical shift Barthes effects in *La Chambre claire*, see V. Burgin (1986), 'Re-reading *Camera Lucida*', in *The End of Art Theory*, Basingstoke, pp. 71–92; W. J. T. Mitchell (1994), *Picture Theory*, Chicago, pp. 281–99.

3. See 'Re-reading *Camera Lucida*', p. 90.

4. 'la science impossible de l'être unique' (CC, p. 110). For a fascinating account of the role played by the Winter Garden Image in Barthes's embrace of an 'ontological' perspective on photographic representation, see Colin MacCabe (1997), 'Barthes and Bazin: The Ontology of the Image', in J.-M. Rabaté (ed.), *Writing the Image After Roland Barthes*, Philadelphia, pp. 71–6.

5. See Christian Metz (1990), 'Photography and Fetish', in C. Squiers (ed.), *The Critical Image: Essays in Contemporary Photography*, Seattle, pp. 155–64.

6. For details of Freud's discussion of the fetish as phallic substitute/metaphor, see S. Freud (1927/1977), 'Fetishism', in *On Sexuality*, Penguin Freud Library, vol. 7, pp. 344–57. For accounts of the role played in fetishism by disavowal – defined in psychoanalytic terms as that ego-splitting process whereby a belief in maternal 'phallicity' is both abandoned *and* retained – see E. Apter (1991), 'Fetishism in Theory', in *Feminizing the Fetish: Psychoanalysis and Narrative Obsession in Turn-of-the-Century France*, Ithaca and London, pp. 1–14; E. Grosz (1995), 'Lesbian Fetishism', in *space, time and perversion*, London and New York, pp. 141–54.

7. See Metz, 'Photography and Fetish', p. 158. I shall return to this issue, below.

8. Ibid., p. 161. Because, as Freud explains, a fetish not only masks maternal castration but also 'sets up a memorial to it' (cf. 'Fetishism', p. 353), the 'consolation' it offers is never unambiguous/total.

9. 'cette Photographie du Jardin d'Hiver était pour moi comme la dernière musique qu'écrivit Schumann avant de sombrer, ce premier *Chant de l'Aube* qui s'accorde à la fois à l'être de ma mère et au chagrin que j'ai de sa mort' (CC, p. 110).

10. For a reading of the role played in fetishism by the 'Je sais bien, mais quand même' paradigm, see Octave Mannoni's identically-titled essay in O. Mannoni (1969), *Clefs pour l'imaginaire*, Paris, pp. 9–33.

11. See Griselda Pollock (1996), 'Gleaning in History', in G. Pollock (ed.), *Generations and Geographies in the Visual Arts*, London and New York, pp. 266–88, p. 284.

12. Material contained in the discussion that follows first appeared in A. Hughes

(1998), 'Reading Guibert's *L'Image fantôme*/Reading Desire', *Modern and Contemporary France*, vol. 6, pp. 203–14, and features here in expanded form.

13. [L']image est l'essence du désir, et désexualiser l'image, ce serait la réduire à la théorie . . . (IF, p. 89).

  [C]e texte est le désespoir de l'image, et pire qu'une image floue ou voilée: une image fantôme . . . (IF, p. 18).

  No translation of Guibert's *L'Image fantôme* (Paris, 1981) exists; translations are my own.

14. Barthes (denoted as 'R. B.') and his mother make a brief appearance in Guibert's narrative, in a fragment entitled 'La Photo, au plus près de la mort' (IF, pp. 148–51). Insights into the intertextual relation between Barthes's and Guibert's photographic discussions feature prominently in Pierre Saint-Amand (1997), 'Mort à blanc: Guibert et la photographie', in R. Sarkonak (ed.), *Le Corps textuel d'Hervé Guibert*, Paris, pp. 81–95.

15. See Emily Apter (1993), 'Fantom Images: Hervé Guibert and the Writing of "sida" in France', in T. F. Murphy and S. Poirier (eds), *Writing Aids: Gay Literature, Language, and Analysis*, New York, pp. 83–97, p. 83.

16. 'Photobiographies' is a term used by Saint-Amand (cf. 'Mort à blanc', p. 82). On Guibert's diary as a source of *L'Image fantôme*, see R. Sarkonak (1994), 'De la métastase au métatexte: Hervé Guibert', *Texte*, vol. 15/16, pp. 229–59, pp. 230–1. Its incorporation of journal material supports our sense of the autobiographical foundation of *L'Image fantôme*. That said, as the introductory section of this chapter signalled, Guibert's text is elaborated less as an auto-biography 'proper' – like Leduc's *L'Asphyxie*, it favours a fragmentary structure over the linear organizational mode of 'classic' autobiography and opts not to identify, nominally, its author and narrator – than as a generically 'bastard', categorization-defying narrative artefact in which Guibert records his personal adventures in and engagements with the photographic realm.

17. On *L'Image fantôme* as 'virtual photography', see A. Buisine (1995), 'Le photographique plutôt que la photographie', *Nottingham French Studies*, vol. 34, pp. 32–41, p. 36.

18. 'images fantômes, images qui ne sont pas sorties, images latentes' (IF, p. 124).

19. See Buisine, 'Le Photographique', pp. 38–40. Buisine views Guibert's photo-graphic self-portraits as particularly indicative of (i) his vision of photography as an exercise in loss/disappearance and (ii) his desire that it should be so.

20. See for example the contents of the essay 'Photo-Souvenir' (IF, p. 28). This fragment resonates with Barthes's comments in *La Chambre claire* regarding the link between photography and death.

21. 'Il y avait, dans un de mes Bibi Fricotin, une invention fabuleuse qui me faisait rêver [. . .]: les lunettes à lire la pensée. Depuis, j'ai retrouvé dans des réclames

plus ou moins salaces l'existence de lunettes qui transpercent les vêtements, qui déshabillent. Et j'ai imaginé que la photographie pouvait conjuguer ces deux pouvoirs, j'ai eu la tentation d'un autoportrait . . .' (IF, p. 9).

22. See Guibert (1984), *Le Seul Visage*, Paris, p. 1.

23. 'Qu'Hervé Guibert ait intensément désiré l'image photographique pour autant qu'elle constitue à ses yeux l'essence, l'ontologie même du désir, pour autant qu'elle incarne, durcit, érige le corps de l'autre et fait irrésistiblement bander celui qui s'efforce de jouir de ce sex-appeal aussi intensément que désespérément mimétique, c'est absolument incontestable'. See 'Le Photographique', p. 32 (my trans.). The argument offered by Buisine in this section of his article and the reading I am offering here differ from that offered by Saint-Amand (cf. 'Mort à blanc', p. 89), which construes Guibert's photographic vision as founded on a sense of photography's 'metaphysical deficiency' and its inability to capture originary desire.

24. As I indicated above, Freud (cf. 'Fetishism', pp. 351–2) views the function of the fetish as, primarily, metaphorically substitutional, and consistently theorizes the fetish object as a symbolic representation of the maternal phallus.

25. In later writings (cf. 'An Outline of Psycho-analysis' (1940)) and, even, in 'Fetishism', Freud suggests that the fetish object may enjoy a metonymic as well as a metaphorical connection to the missing maternal phallus it replaces. He suggests in other words that a fetish may accede to fetish-status by virtue of having originally been somehow close to the 'castrated' female genitalia. Photography is certainly predicated on metonymy, replacing as it does real objects with filmic 'doubles' that relate 'contiguously' to them. This explains Metz's point (cf. 'Photography and Fetish', p. 164) that while film is capable of playing on fetishism, 'photography is capable itself of *becoming* a fetish'.

26. See H. Guibert (1986), *Mes Parents*, Paris, pp. 105–6. On the generic ambiguity of this work, see Marie Darrieussecq (1997), 'De l'autobiographie à l'auto-fiction', in Sarkonak (ed.), *Le Corps textuel d'Hervé Guibert*, pp. 115–30.

27. 'Je pris ma mère en photo: elle était à ce moment-là au summum de sa beauté [. . .]. [La séance finie] elle redevint la femme de son mari, la femme de quarante-cinq ans, alors que la photo, momentanément, comme par magie, avait suspendu l'âge [. . .]. Je voulus l'oublier, ne plus la voir, me fixer à jamais sur cette image qu'on allait extraire du bain révélateur' (IF, pp. 14–15). When a fetish comes into being, argues Freud (that is, when a (male) child, exposed to the spectacle of maternal 'castration', cathects a substitute object whose function will be to stand in for, and mask the absence of, the missing maternal phallus), it does so via a process of forgetting. This involves a forgetting of originary absence/Lack. It resembles the stopping of memory that occurs in traumatic amnesia (cf. 'Fetishism', p. 354). In seeking to take a photograph of his mother that will mask, and allow him to 'forget', the spectacle of her

diminishing beauty, Guibert is clearly pursuing the kind of self-protective *oubli* essential to fetishism as defined by Freud.

28. See 'Le Photographique', pp. 37–8.
29. Guibert views Kafka's diary as containing a form of writing that is as 'penetrative' as photography, offering a 'radiographic' take on its author's anguish ('un niveau presque radiographique de son angoisse'). See 'L'Ecriture photographique' (IF, pp. 73–7, p. 77). Other authors flagged here as producers of photographic writing are Peter Handke and Goethe.
30. 'l'image la plus intime de moi-même'. For an illuminating account of Guibert's use of the X-ray photograph as an analogy for the writing process, see J.-P. Boulé (1995), *Hervé Guibert: 'A l'ami qui ne m'a pas sauvé la vie' and Other Writings*, Glasgow, pp. 7–9.
31. 'La plupart de vos récits suintent l'homosexualité' (IF, p. 89).
32. See for example 'Premier Amour' (IF, pp. 19–21) and 'Photo Porno' (IF, pp. 100–1).
33. 'un second frère' (IF, p. 169).
34. Lee Edelman argues that the heterosexual cultural imagination cannot divorce the notion of male display from that of homosexuality: '[T]he textualized body that the régime of patriarchal heterosexuality compels us to recognize as "gay" enters the public imagination as a body that "flaunts" or advertises its difference.' See L. Edelman (1994), *Homographesis: Essays in Gay and Cultural Theory*, New York and London, p. 208. Since the gay male body *is* culturally coded as a body on display, I have no hesitation in reading the image dissected in Guibert's 'L'Image cancéreuse' as I do. For a fascinating analysis of the gay body as sign and 'reality', specifically in the age of AIDS, see L. Schehr (1996), 'Body/Antibody', *Studies in 20th Century Literature*, vol. 20, pp. 405–30.
35. See 'L'Image Erotique' (IF, pp. 25–7); 'Fantasme de photographie I' (IF, pp. 31–3); 'Le Scotch Rouge' (IF, p. 105); 'Danse' (IF, pp. 115–16).
36. See L. Edelman, *Homographesis*, pp. 3–23, p. 4.
37. Ibid.
38. Ibid., pp. 4–6.
39. Ibid., p. 9.
40. Ibid., p. 10.
41. Ibid., p. 12.
42. Ibid., pp. 12–13.
43. Ibid., p. 8.
44. See M. Pratt (1995), 'De la désidentification à l'incognito: à la recherche d'une autobiographie homosexuelle', *Nottingham French Studies*, vol. 34, pp. 70–81, p. 72. This article has compelling things to say about gay readability/self-definition, and Guibert's relation to it.

45. — A t'avoir raconté cette histoire ['L'Image cancéreuse'], je m'en sens com-
plètement vidé. Cette histoire est mon secret, tu comprends?
— Et après?
— A toi je ne veux pas dire: "je t'en prie, ne la répète pas" . . .
— Oui. Mais maintenant ton secret est devenu aussi mon secret. Il fait partie
de moi, et je me comporterai avec lui comme avec tous mes secrets; j'en
disposerai au moment venu. Et il deviendra le secret d'un autre.
— Tu as raison. Il faut que les secrets circulent . . . (IF, p. 170).

46. See Boulé, *Hervé Guibert*, pp. 31–9, on secrets and betrayals in Guibert's
oeuvre.

47. D. A. Miller (1988), *The Novel and the Police*, California, p. 207.

48. Ibid.

49. That avowal/confession constitutes an effect of power is a central tenet of
Volume I of Foucault's *Histoire de la sexualité*. I shall discuss this notion in
more detail, in connection with Guibert's work, in Chapter 4.

50. 'Cette image, cette photographie absolue non-photographiée est entrée dans
le livre [. . .] elle aura été et restera signalée, son existence, sa permanence
"*rétinienne*" auront été posées là.' See Duras, 'L'Inconnue de la rue Catinat',
interview with H. Le Masson, *Le Nouvel Observateur*, 28 Sept. 1984, pp. 52–
4, p. 52. Duras reveals here that the original title of *L'Amant* was *L'Image
absolue*.

51. M. Duras (1984), *L'Amant*, Paris, translated as *The Lover*, trans. B. Bray,
London, 1986.

52. While Duras avoids initiating a formal, name-based autobiographical 'pact'
in *L'Amant*, her narrative addresses an implied reader cast as someone who
has read her other texts (or texts like them) and is aware of a referential
connection between the author Marguerite Duras and the anonymous narrator/
protagonist of *L'Amant*. Yet, because her *opus* (i) eschews a canonical, linear
autobiographical format, privileging a fragmented organization and (ii)
oscillates, in terms of voice, between a predictable, autobiographical 'I' and a
third-person, novelistic narrative mode, it also smacks, disconcertingly, of the
postmodernistically fictional. Thus it is marked by a high degree of generic
'incoherence' reminiscent of that characterizing *L'Image fantôme*. For an
interesting discussion of Duras's relationship to autobiography, see A. Armel
(1990), 'Le Jeu autobiographique', *Magazine Littéraire*, no. 278, pp. 28–31.
On the autobiographical indeterminacy of *L'Amant*, see Lecarme and Lecarme-
Tabone, *L'Autobiographie*, p. 276.

53. 'Si le texte se retourne sur l'image [. . .], immédiatement ils ne manqueront
pas de se manquer, ils s'absenteront l'un à l'autre.' See A. Buisine (1988),
'Tel Orphée', *Revue des Sciences Humaines*, vol. 81, pp. 124–49, p. 124 (my
trans.).

54. For an account of the 'photographic' nature of Duras's writing in *L'Amant*, and of its connection with the 'écriture photographique' of Barthes, see M. Fauvel (1993), 'Photographie et autobiographie: *Roland Barthes* par Roland Barthes et *L'Amant* de Marguerite Duras', *Romance Notes*, vol. XXXIV, pp. 193–202.

55. Guibert employs this term as a title for several of the *récits* of his photo-essay. It usefully designates both the 'phantom photo' of *L'Amant* and what is going on, narratively, in the novel's opening segment.

56. 'C'est au cours de ce voyage que l'image se serait détachée, qu'elle aurait été enlevée à la somme. Elle aurait pu exister, une photographie aurait pu être prise, comme une autre, ailleurs, dans d'autres circonstances. Mais elle ne l'a pas été. [. . .] C'est à ce manque d'avoir été faite qu'elle doit sa vertu, celle de représenter un absolu, d'en être justement l'auteur' (LA, pp. 16–17).

57. For a useful account of sartorial fetishism and of the way in which objects of (female) clothing – high-heeled shoes, hats, ribbons, corsets and towering *coiffures* – can be presented by or function within the male imagination as fetishizable signs and as symbolic stand-ins for the (maternal) phallus, see Apter, *Feminizing the Fetish*, pp. 65–98. Apter's focus is the literature and fashion of eighteenth- and nineteenth-century France.

58. 'l'ambiguïté déterminante de l'image' (LA, p. 19).

59. For a fascinating account of the sexual symbolism of hats, see Briony Fer (1993), 'The hat, the hoax, the body', in K. Adler and M. Pointon (eds), *The Body Imaged: The Human Form and Visual Culture Since the Renaissance*, Cambridge, pp. 161–73. Fer notes how psychoanalysts and psychoanalytically-minded critics have, in fact, shifted between reading hats as symbols endowed with male/phallic significance and interpreting them as ambiguous entities capable of connoting both phallicity and (genital) femininity.

60. 'Photography and Fetish', p. 160.

61. In the concluding part of his discussion of 'L'Image cancéreuse', Saint-Amand (cf. 'Mort à blanc', p. 93) pertinently notes that when Guibert is drawn to/ presents photographs as fetish-objects, he foregrounds their conjuratory aspect.

62. See Apter, *Feminizing the Fetish*, p. 94. For Lacan's account of womanhood as phallic masquerade, see 'The Meaning of the Phallus', in J. Mitchell and J. Rose (eds), (1982), *Feminine Sexuality: Jacques Lacan and the Ecole Freudienne*, Basingstoke and London, pp. 74–85, as well as J. Lacan (1971), *Ecrits II*, Paris, pp. 103–15. Lacan's remark, here, that 'it is in order to be the phallus, that is to say, the signifier of the desire of the Other, that the woman will reject an essential part of her femininity, notably all its attributes, through masquerade' (cf. 'The Meaning of the Phallus', p. 84/*Ecrits II*, p. 113) meshes not only with the phallicized/fetishizable appearance of Duras's heroine but also with *L'Amant*'s inclusion of statements such as 'j'avais en moi la place du désir'/'the space existed in me for desire' (LA, p. 15/TL, p. 12).

63. As Apter explains (cf. *Feminizing the Fetish*, Chapter 2), various theorists of fetishism read the fetish object as partial. The fact that the body 'revealed' in Duras's imaginary photographic image appears as a fragmented *corps morcelé* enhances our sense of the fetishistic nature of the image itself.

64. See Metz, 'Photography and Fetish', p. 158. Jérôme Beaujour also links photography and fetishization, arguing that the fetish is above all separate from what it once formed part of ('le fétiche est ce qui est définitivement séparé de ce dont il n'est que partie') and suggesting that, since photography rests on a 'fonction séparatiste', the result of the photographic act (i.e. the photograph) may be viewed as fetish-like. Interestingly, Beaujour includes these observations in an article on the role played by photography and photographs in the work of Duras. See J. Beaujour (1990), 'L'Oubli de la photographie', *Magazine Littéraire*, no. 278, pp. 49–51, p. 50.

65. See 'Photography and Fetish', p. 161. Metz does not take the non-static cinematic image to be as fetish-like as the photo-image, which is permanently 'fixed' by/in the moment the camera shutter comes down. In view of Metz's sense that 'film is much more difficult to characterize as a fetish [than the photograph] (p. 161), it is significant that Duras chooses to create a 'photographic' rather than a 'filmic' image in the opening section of *L'Amant*; particularly since in many ways it would have been more appropriate to 'cinematize' the Mekong ferry episode.

66. Saint-Amand notes the fetish-like aspect of Duras's phantom-photo, without elaborating on it. See Pierre Saint-Amand (1994), 'La Photographie de famille dans *L'Amant*', in A. Vircondelet (ed.), *Marguerite Duras: Rencontres de Cerisy*, Paris, pp. 225–40, p. 227.

67. 'enlevée à la somme' (LA, p. 16).

68. In 'The Meaning of the Phallus', Lacan argues that when woman pursues that 'being of the phallus' he locates within femininity, she masquerades not only as the phallus *qua* signifier of desire but also as a fetish object. His characteristically hermetic account of this process certainly resonates with Duras's description of her heroine's 'performance' on the Mekong ferry, as does his conception of woman as the Other to, and the place of *jouissance* for, the male: 'Paradoxical as this formulation might seem, I would say that it is in order to be the phallus, that is to say, the signifier of the desire of the Other, that the woman will reject an essential part of her femininity, notably all its attributes, through masquerade. It is for what she is not that she expects to be desired as well as loved. But she finds the signifier of her own desire in the body of the one to whom she addresses her demand for love. Certainly, we should not forget that the organ actually invested with this signifying function takes on the value of a fetish.' See J. Lacan, 'The Meaning of the Phallus', p. 84; *Ecrits II*, pp. 113–14.

69. 'Soudain, je me vois comme une autre, comme une autre serait vue, au-dehors, mise à la disposition de tous, mise à la disposition de tous les regards, mise dans la circulation des villes, des regards, du désir' (LA, p. 20).

70. See G. Bonnet (1981), 'Fétichisme et exhibitionnisme chez un sujet féminin', *Voir Etre vu*, vol. I, Paris, pp. 79–109.

71. N. Schor (1985), 'Female Fetishism: the Case of George Sand', in S. R. Suleiman (ed.), *The Female Body in Western Culture*, Cambridge, MA. and London, pp. 363–72, p. 365.

72. Ibid., pp. 368–9. In this section of her essay, Schor acknowledges her debt to Sarah Kofman's work on female fetishism.

73. Ibid., p. 371.

74. For detail on the relationship between the real and imaginary photographs of *L'Amant*, see S. Cohen (1990), 'Fiction and the Photographic Image in Duras' *The Lover*', *L'Esprit Créateur*, vol. XXX, pp. 56–68, p. 61. For Duras's views on the 'photo du désespoir, see 'L'Inconnue de la rue Catinat', p. 52 (see Note 50).

75. 'Autour d'elle, c'est les déserts' (LA, p. 33).

76. Fauvel argues that the photograph represents, for the mother of *L'Amant*, (i) a substitute for happiness and power and (ii) the sole entity she can control ('un substitut de pouvoir et de bonheur, le seul object qu'elle est capable de dominer'). See M. Fauvel, 'Photographie et autobiographie', p. 197. While her remarks are pertinent, they obscure the way in which the actualized photo-image – emblematized by the *photo du désespoir* – incarnates also and above all maternal *powerlessness*.

77. Juliet Hopkins (1984), 'The Probable Role of Trauma in a Case of Foot and Shoe Fetishism: Aspects of Psychotherapy of a Six Year Old Girl', *International Review of Psychoanalysis*, vol. 11, pp. 79–91, p. 83, cited in Grosz, *space, time and perversion*, p. 149.

78. For an account of the mother's madness as emblematizing that of all the 'femmes folles' of Duras's creative universe, see J. Kristeva (1987), 'La maladie de la douleur: Duras', in *Soleil noir: dépression et mélancolie*, Paris, pp. 227–65, p. 249. For a psychoanalytic reading of the opening section of *L'Amant* that notes that Duras's protagonist's self-phallicization may compensate maternal castration but reads it primarily as a strategy adopted by Duras's heroine in order to afford herself a totalized identity that detaches her from the mother/daughter dyad, see S. Ferrières-Pestureau (1997), *Une étude psychanalytique de la figure du ravissement dans l'oeuvre de M. Duras*, Paris, pp. 27–34.

79. See Bonnet, *Voir Etre vu*, vol. I, p. 95. We need to note that while Lacanians such as Bonnet have acknowledged, albeit guardedly, the possibility of female fetishism (cf. Schor, 'Female Fetishism', p. 367), Lacan himself, although he

considered woman herself to take on the role of fetish, did not see fetishism as the province of the female.

80. 'Quand ma mère retrouve l'air, qu'elle sort du désespoir, elle découvre le chapeau d'homme et les lamés or. [. . .] Elle me regarde, ça lui plaît, elle sourit. [. . .] Elle ne demande pas si c'est elle qui les a achetés, elle sait que c'est elle. Elle sait qu'elle en est capable' (LA, p. 32).

81. 'Female Fetishism', p. 368.

82. 'La mère parle, parle. Elle [. . .] rit, du scandale, de cette pitrerie, de ce chapeau déplacé, de cette élégance sublime de l'enfant de la traversée du fleuve' (LA, p. 113).

83. 'cette vaillance de l'espèce, absurde' (LA, p. 117).

84. See 'Photographie et autobiographie', p. 198.

85. For the detail of Fauvel's arguments, see ibid., pp. 197–8. Without referring to the photographic dimension of *L'Amant*, Kristeva agrees that Duras's text is maternally obliterative, and relates this to Duras's fear of maternal madness. See *Soleil noir*, p. 250.

86. Apter's *Feminizing the Fetish* seeks to challenge the Freud-inspired phallo-centrism of fetish-theory, as does the work of Lorraine Gamman and Merja Makinen (cf. L. Gamman and M. Makinen (1994), *Female Fetishism: A New Look*, London).

87. 'Ma mère mon amour son incroyable dégaine avec ses bas de coton reprisés par Dô, sous les tropiques elle croit encore qu'il faut mettre des bas pour être la dame directrice de l'école, ses robes lamentables, difformes, reprisées par Dô, [. . .] ses souliers sont éculés, elle marche de travers, avec un mal de chien, ses cheveux sont tirés et serrés dans un chignon de Chinoise, elle nous fait honte, elle me fait honte [. . .]' (LA, pp. 31–2).

88. See Guibert, 'La Photo, au plus près de la mort' (IF, pp. 148–51); Guibert's review of *La Chambre claire* (cf. *Le Monde*, 28 Feb. 1980, p. 22); Duras (1987), *La Vie matérielle*, Paris, p. 42. Saint-Amand endorses my sense of the connection between the Barthesian, Durassian and Guibertian texts dissected here. See 'Mort à blanc', in Sarkonak, *Le Corps textuel*, p. 82.

89. For a useful 'postcolonial' reading of the link betwen narrative technique in *L'Amant* and the sexual dynamics of colonialism, see Suzanne Chester (1992), 'Writing the Subject: Exoticism/Eroticism in Marguerite Duras's *The Lover* and *The Sea Wall*', in S. Smith and J. Watson (eds), *De/Colonizing the Subject: The Politics of Gender in Women's Autobiography*, Minneapolis, pp. 436–57.

3

Imagining North Africa:
Sexuality, Gender and Colonial Space

In her introduction to *Sexuality and Space* (1992), Beatriz Colomina affirms that the 'politics of space are always sexual, even if space is central to the mechanisms of the erasure of sexuality'.[1] Colomina's sense of the pertinence of space-related issues to sexual politics, sexed subjectivity and sexual/gender representation finds an echo in all the texts I shall examine in this and my next chapter. In Chapter 4, I shall attend to the adventures in medical and narrative space inscribed in Hervé Guibert's AIDS-text *A l'ami qui ne m'a pas sauvé la vie* and Simone de Beauvoir's *Une mort très douce*. In the present chapter, colonial space – specifically, that constituted by 'French' North Africa – provides my focus. I want, here, to read autobiographical *récits* by André Gide and Marie Cardinal with a view to delineating the diverse ways in which, in relation to the Maghreb, two dissimilarly positioned French colonial subjects[2] narratively articulate the self/space/gender dynamic. My intention, in other words, is to explore the variant imaginary territories that come into being when the same geographical terrain is mapped within texts set apart by differences of sexual and cultural authorial identity, and to assess the nature of the individual contributions made by Gide and Cardinal, at a half-century's distance, to the discursive palimpsest formed by the canon of nineteenth- and twentieth-century French-authored narratives of colonial place.

André Gide's Paternal Africa

Published in 1926 and focused on its author's life-trajectory as it evolved between 1869 and 1895, Gide's *Si le grain ne meurt* (SLG)[3] offers the reader (at least) three visions of the North African environment. It goes without saying that in Gide's *récit* – the most 'formally' autobiographical of the exercises in auto-narration addressed in this study, and the one that promotes its referentiality most determinedly[4] – none of these narrative Africas is openly disassociated from the others. I want nonetheless to disentangle them here, in order to signal some tensions inherent in the representational treatment accorded to the Maghreb in Gide's first autobiography 'proper',[5] and to engage with existing interpretations of it. As my discussion will establish, the first of *Si le grain*'s North African visions posits the colonized Maghreb (especially Algeria)[6] as the site of a colonialist oppression that manifests itself, synecdochically, at the level of the sexual and is presented as a phenomenon in which Gide's autobiographical text-self remains largely unimplicated. In counterpoint, borrowing from an 'Orientalist' discursive model, the second casts North Africa as the utopic locale of a personal erotic awakening – the climax of Gide's confessional tale – whose imbrication in colonial politics goes broadly unacknowledged (or, at best, is communicated only tacitly). Finally, the third construes Algeria as the stage for a drama of gender (re)identification that has its roots in Gide's infancy, and connects with but also exceeds his adult embrace of the (homo)sexual.

The narratively inscribed André Gide whose youth and early adulthood *Si le grain ne meurt* chronicles first visits North Africa in 1893, aged twenty-three. This initiatory encounter – detailed in Chapter I of Part II of *Si le grain* – takes him from Tunis to the Algerian oasis resort of Biskra, where, dogged by ill-health, he encamps for the winter in the company of his fellow-traveller Paul Laurens. In 1895 he returns to Algeria, staying first in Algiers and Blidah, where he reacquaints himself with Oscar Wilde and meets Alfred Douglas ('Bosy'), then, later, with Bosy this time, in Biskra once again. It is during his second sojourn in the Maghreb, Gide's autobiographical narrator reveals, that his homoerotic, pederastic proclivities are confirmed as constituting his sexual *normale*.

Critics concur that Gide's *Si le grain* is far less openly critical of colonialism than his *Voyage au Congo*, published in 1927.[7] However, its 'apolitical' tenor notwithstanding, Gide's autobiography does, intermittently, inscribe North Africa as a space of racial disequilibrium, in which the Maghrebian Other's subjectivity is regularly exposed to violation by the white European male, by means of a practice/process of sexual commodification whereby Arab boys and women are made to function as objects for Western erotic consumption. That it does so cannot fail, moreover, to unsettle the Gidean reader. This is less, however, because *Si le grain*'s depiction of the Maghreb as a site of racial dominion is either unexpected or shocking than because it sits uneasily with that other, more powerful perception of North Africa as a locus of personal homoerotic epiphany proffered by the second part of Gide's self-history.

It is especially, then, in those sections of *Si le grain* where the sexual connections between Arabs and (other) Europeans are an issue that the first of the textual Africas invoked above – Africa-as-colonial-dystopia – is profiled. Gesturing tacitly towards their inegalitarian, economically transactive foundation, Gide's accounts of these connections evoke, variously, Daniel B's vampirical coupling with an absinthe-soaked adolescent musician (SLG, p. 345/IID [trans.], pp. 285–6); Douglas's licensed 'abduction' of Ali, a young Arab waiter (SLG, p. 335/IID, p. 278); and the horsewhipping the once-prized, not to say fetishized, Ali receives when Bosy discovers his 'infidelity' with an Oulad Naïl prostitute (SLG, p. 351/IID, p. 291).

In so doing, they cast into relief a Third World environment whose economic workings have been corrupted by the invasive influence of the West, and by the sexual politics of colonialism.[8] That Gide's solipsistic *récit* does not neglect to treat of this environment's existence is unsurprising, given the contestatory stance *vis-à-vis* the colonial enterprise its author came to adopt. Less predictable, perhaps, is the extent to which the Gide persona of *Si le grain* is figured by his older, narrating counterpart as almost entirely detached both from the colonialist sexual dominion that Gide's text illuminates and from the Africa that is its theatre.[9] His own, aborted plan to take his African teenage servant-companion home to France is flagged for instance (sincerely, we sense) as motivated by philanthropic instincts, rather than by the sexual voraciousness imputed to Bosy (SLG, pp. 353–4/IID, p. 293). His erotic dealings with the Oulad Naïl are presented not as evidence that he is no less willing to engage in consumerist sex tourism than any other Western traveller of his time, but instead as inspired by a therapeutically valid need to re-educate a sexuality warped by his puritanical background (SLG, pp. 306–9/IID, pp. 253–7).[10] The incongruity between the colonially-emblematic acts of (s)exploitation committed by European others and the African peripeteia of its autobiographical protagonist constitutes a key feature of *Si le grain*'s second part, and one that Gide's self-history foregrounds. It confirms our sense that if Gide was prepared to transcribe the Maghreb, in however piecemeal a manner, as a locus of colonial domination, his *récit* also strives to depict – and to privilege – another Africa, in which his narra-tive double/younger self is much more personally implicated, and in relation to which sexual practice and colonial politics are cast as potentially unconnected entities.

As Michael Lucey notes, *watching* sex is a significant facet of the trajectory traced within *Si le grain ne meurt*.[11] In Part II, for instance, we find Gide's André observing the 'colonial rape' inflicted by Daniel B. on a boy, Mohammed, who is manifestly construed as debauched by a European sexual/colonial culture symbol-ized, *inter alia*, by Wildean decadence and anal penetration (SLG, pp. 344–6/IID, pp. 286–7).[12] However, the same segment of Gide's *récit* also records two episodes during which his textual avatar manages to *have* sex – or, more precisely, *Si le grain* intimates, to indulge in the 'face to face, reciprocal and gentle' (IID, p. 287)[13] accompanied male masturbation he favours over the penetrative intercourse that he finds sexually unpalatable, and that Gide employs as a cipher for the colonialist ethos.[14] In the first episode, dazzled by the nubile anatomy of a young guide, André finally, after some ostensibly bemused hesitation, 'gives himself up' in the dunes at Sousse to the teasing boy's sexual sollicitations: '[Ali] stood up naked as a god [. . .] then, still laughing, he fell upon me. His body may well have been burning hot, but to me it felt as refreshing as deep shade. How lovely the sand was! In the glorious splendour of evening what radiance bathed my joy!' (IID, p. 249).[15] In the second, encouraged by Wilde, he enjoys an epic encounter with the same adolescent flute-player whose path later crosses Daniel B's:

[I]t was now that I found my normal. There was nothing constrained here, nothing precipitate, nothing doubtful; there is no taste of ashes in the memory I keep. My joy was unbounded, and I cannot imagine it greater, even if love had been added. How could love have entered into this? How could I have left my heart at the mercy of desire? My pleasure was quite free from ulterior motives and was not to be succeeded by any remorse. But then what name can I give to the transports with which I crushed in my bare arms [Mohammed's] perfect little body, wild, burning, sensual and mysterious (IID, p. 284).[16]

Gide's narrative renditions of these incidents represent the Maghreb as the site of a homoerotic awakening that, if it counters the heterosexual 'normalization' the Gide-self of *Si le grain*'s diegesis initially aspires to achieve there, is nonetheless celebrated as granting him access to his true sexual being.[17] As various critics indicate, his erotic recollections evince the presence, in *Si le grain*, of a second Gidean Africa, imagined as an ideal *lieu d'évasion* – and as a space of 'beckoning homosexuality'[18] – in which Gide's autobiographical *sosie* is profoundly invested, because it permits him to defeat both the sexual repression advocated by his protestant mother and the heterosexual orthodoxy it sustains.[19] This other Africa is conceived as a hypernatural, exotic realm:[20] a world of sunlit oases, hashish-enfumed cafés and musky nights in which the Western traveller – if he shares the Gidean hero's sexual sensitivities – can achieve a *jouissance* no less natural than the environment whereof it is born. It is an Africa signalled as a locus whose relative unadulteration by European 'civilization' permits those individuals attuned to its 'naturalness' to achieve a 'pure' eroticism (an *azur*) contaminated neither by the 'sinful', self-gratificatory practice (*vice ténébreux*) that constitutes Gide's sexual life in France nor by the spiritual complications of love nor, indeed, by that oppressive disregard for the Arab Other displayed by Bosy and Daniel B. It is, in other words, an Africa envisioned as a liberatory, pleasure-soaked terrain wherein, for all its thraldom to Europe (symbolized by the absinthe Mohammed is addicted to), interracial sex-acts, to paraphrase Lucey, need not always be despoiled by or complicit with the politics and power-relations of colonial mastery.[21]

Constituted as a personally emancipatory environment, in which a particular kind of politicized sex is (by and large) exceeded,[22] *Si le grain*'s second, utopic/erotic Africa is cast by Gide as a counterweight to the dystopic, colonially-political Africa mapped by certain of his more troublesome, troubling Maghrebian memories. His framing of it as such, and his idealized account of his own relation to it, have generated a good deal of critical debate. Amongst those who have dissected the erasures and illusions subtending Gide's autobiographical treatment of the Maghreb (specifically, his delineation of 'Africa 2'/erotic Africa), Lawrence Schehr stands out as an especially reproving voice.[23] Schehr levels two accusations at the author of *Si le grain*. First, he argues, Gide's narrative articulation of Africa-as-site-of-homosexual-liberation deliberately obscures the fact that the precondition of the individual emancipation celebrated in *Si le grain* is the continued non-freedom of the Maghrebian male. He contends, in other words, that key segments of Gide's *récit* fail properly to acknowledge that because the erotic epiphany achieved by its hero is ultimately founded on the economic and sexual subjection of the colonized Arab, it is no less inegalitarian or colonially-contaminated than the sexual consumerism practised by Bosy *et al.*[24] Second, Schehr suggests, Gide's construal of North Africa as a mysterious space of pure, homoerotic *jouissance*, characterized (cf. SLG, pp. 290–1/IID, pp. 240–2) by nature at its most primitively impressive and inhabited by a populace whose sexuality seems as natural as the land that spawned it, masks its own complicity with what Edward Said has termed 'Orientalist' or 'Africanist' discourse.[25] Gide's Maghrebian vision, then, occludes for Schehr the imbrication of its own representational codes within a 'systematic language for dealing with and studying Africa *for* the West' that employs concepts such as primitivism, vitalism and originality in order to affirm, in the service of European dominance, the alterity of Africa and its denizens.[26]

Schehr's crusade to expose Gide's colonialist blindspots is far from illegitimate. Gide's sexual utopianization of the Maghreb *is* flawed by a failure to reckon adequately and openly with the conjunction between the joyous erotic emancipation achieved in Africa by his textual persona/younger self and the geopolitical 'dialectic of proxemics, seductions, and exchange with the white men from Europe'[27] *vis-à-vis* which his autobiographical narrator/protagonist appears determined to signal/ keep his distance. Further (I shall return to this point below), his account of North Africa as a space of natural, primitive mysteriousness and smiling sexual promise, bursting with curious fauna and beckoning brown boys, does perpetuate – if not entirely unselfconsciously – standard tropes of an Orientalist discourse of/on non-Western exoticism that Said conceives as central to the control mechanisms of colonialism.[28] We should however be aware that Schehr's critique of Gide perpetrates its own form of 'blindspotting'. It does so by overprivileging one of the textual Africas represented in *Si le grain* – 'homoerotic' Africa – and by overlooking, concomitantly, a further, third Africa whose imagined presence in Part II of Gide's *récit* makes it into more than just a tale of inadequately acknowledged, imperialist sexual consumerism, posing as a flight from repressive Western heterocracy.[29] Schehr cannot be held entirely responsible for the erasure his reading effects.[30] Other critics (Lucey is a key exception here) who have focused on *Si le grain* and its treatment of the sexual likewise concentrate on the erotically liberating Africa envisioned in Gide's autobiography, partly because this is the Africa their knowledge of a canon of 'vacation cruise narratives' predisposes them to detect[31] and partly because 'Africa 2' is the Africa mapped most overtly by Gide's autobiographical account. Nonetheless, Schehr is wrong to neglect the third of *Si le grain*'s narrated Maghrebs, if only because its textual inscription, while it cannot be deemed (wholly) to palliate the political unpalatability manifest within Gide's

Orientalist narrative universe, at least extends the boundaries of the African geo-graphy *Si le grain* constructs, revealing it to be more complex, and less orthodoxly coded, than the reader might have supposed. With this in mind, I want to turn to the representation of 'Africa 3' that Gide's autobiography proffers, and to scrutinize those sections of *Si le grain* that cast it into relief. This will allow me to draw some conclusions concerning Gide's multiform discursification of the Maghrebian space.

During his early childhood, Gide's *récit* reveals, two father/son rituals took pride of place. The first involved a rite (cf. SLG, pp. 15–16/IID, pp. 14–15) whereby the normally distant Paul Gide would read to his child inside the sanctum of his library/study (off-limits to the intrusive Mme Gide), while the second turned on the strolls that father and son would take through the Parisian gloaming, initiated by the open-sesame paternal formula: 'Would my little friend like to come to come for a walk?' (IID, pp. 16–17).[32] Activities shared with M. Gide, *Si le grain*'s narrator suggests, afforded the boy he used to be a provisional purchase on a realm of male-centred community that excluded the mother (SLG, p. 17/IID, p. 15) and was otherwise not a feature of his female-dominated childhood, and on a masculine-identifiedness that was kept from being total by the sway exerted over his infantile world by the juridical Juliette Gide, but was deeply pleasurable nonetheless.[33] Once, however, Paul Gide's premature demise demasculinized and detriadized the Gide family unit, his ten-year-old self lost access, Gide's narrator implies, both to the homosocial realm that his father, the *Vir probus* of Paris's Law Faculty (SLG, p. 15/IID, p. 14), had hitherto epitomized and to the male identifications his own peripheral connection with it had permitted him to perform. Additionally, Gide's reader gathers, his father's death locked him into a de-genderizing, stifling symbiosis with his mother, emblematized in the constricting starched shirts that Juliette Gide obliged her son to wear and signalled by the *maternalized* identifications the young André would find himself effecting.[34] It ensured that he failed to achieve an easy capacity either for coexistence with his male peers (whence his *amitiés manquées* with Lionel de R. and Pierre Louis, and his tormented dealings with his Montpellier classmates (SLG, pp. 110–11/IID, pp. 93–4)) or, more broadly, for gendered allegiance. Further, *Si le grain* intimates, the loss of his father left André prey to a painfully 'queer' sense of his own gender insecurity, highlighted no less by the need to insist on his likeness to his dead male parent that was a feature of his formative years (SLG, p. 166/IID, p. 138) than by the curious, histrionic *schaudern* that caused him to weep, in the wake of Paul Gide's decease, over the differences dividing him from other boys (SLG, pp. 132–3/IID, p. 111).

If Part I of *Si le grain* signals Gide's adolescence to have been marked/marred by gender instability, then Part II suggests in a variety of ways that his early adulthood – as it evolves, at least, in the African context – incorporates a move towards a form of gender recuperation. It does so, most overtly, by charting a highly symbolic series of male–male promenades that emerge as as much a facet of Gide's North African adventures as of his earliest infancy. During the promenades in question, Gide's autobiography reveals, the Gidean avatar of *Si le grain*'s diegesis embarks on several sorts of Maghrebian excursion (these range from short walks to more protracted voyages) with, as his companions, the faithful Paul Laurens, his fellow 'argonaut' during his African initiation (SLG, pp. 286–7, p. 293/IID, p. 238, p. 243); Athman, his valet-factotum, with whom, every evening, he plays walking games (SLG, p. 355/IID, pp. 294–5); Dr Bourget of Lausanne, who refuses to enjoy the 'exotic' spectacle of the Oulad Naïl (SLG, pp. 304–5/IID, p. 253); Oscar Wilde, who leads him demoniacally through the streets of nocturnal Algiers to his meeting with Mohammed (SLG, pp. 337–41/IID, pp. 280–3); and, finally, Athman's older brother Sadek, with whom he wanders hand in hand in the Algerian twilight (SLG, p. 356/IID, p. 295).

A propos these various instances of (non-sexual) masculine, motile bonding – which regularly occur at or after dusk, and produce within *Si le grain* a racially fluid matrix of male-gendered pairings – we need to take cognizance of the following. First, because all of them come into being by virtue of the European colonial presence in nineteenth-century Africa, they clearly cannot be dislocated from the ambit of the white imperial enterprise, whose intrinsically masculinist – because territorially penetrative – character and androcentric organization they reflect, albeit in a complex, cross-racial manner.[35] Second, although manifestly colonially-anchored, they are nonetheless narratively *constructed* as less emblematic of colonialism's dominatory ethos, and less tainted by it, than some of the European–African sexual liaisons that Gide's self-history depicts. (Partly, this is because the *flâneries* they involve, when interracial, are shown to incorporate a mutuality absent from the Mohammed–Daniel B. penetrative encounter, as Gide's viscerally disgusted narrator remembers it. Partly, too, it is because if they take place in an African space that has been thoroughly colonially 'mapped' (that is, territorially penetrated and possessed), they are not on the whole presented as reproducing that process of invasive spatial appropriation that is the essence of the imperial project.)[36] Thirdly, and most importantly, Gide's North African, accompanied journeyings, as *Si le grain* reconstitutes them, function to intimate that his encounter with the space of masculinist hegemony and sanctioned male-relatedness that was the colonized Maghreb of the *fin-de-siècle* epoch – a space whose historiography documents it as 'the "imperial man's world" *par excellence*'[37] – permits him to overcome the gender insecurity provoked by his father's demise, and to re-embrace a masculine gender trajectory that has gone somewhat awry.

Included in the accounts of his African (co)ambulatory adventures that Part II of Gide's autobiography proffers are a number of narrative 'echoes' that pull the reader's attention back to the gender-formative, Parisian, evening promenades taken by André and Paul Gide in the 1870s and recorded in the opening part of the opening chapter of *Si le grain*'s first section (SLG, pp. 17–18/IID, pp. 15–17). The 'mysteriousness' that, stereotypically, the adult André is presented as discovering as he voyages in the African continent (SLG, p. 290/IID, p. 240) reminds us of that primordial *mystère* associated by *Si le grain*'s narrator with the forays into the urban Parisian environment that he and his father used to effect (SLG, p. 18/IID, p. 17).[38] Likewise, the receptivity to male–male ludic activity (SLG, p. 355/IID, p. 294) and the play of light, shade, silence and sound (SLG, p. 323, p. 337–8, p. 356/IID, p. 268, p. 280, p. 295) that Gide's *récit* ascribes to the Maghrebian space his text-self traverses recall phenomena first encountered by André in his boyhood, as he wandered with M. Gide through Paris's nocturnal streets (SLG, p. 18/IID, pp. 16–17). Finally, the quasi-filial position that the hero of *Si le grain* is portrayed as occupying *vis-à-vis* the mephistophelean Wilde and the infinitely protective Paul Laurens (SLG, p. 293/IID, p. 243), like the contrastingly 'paternal' stance he adopts during twilit strolls taken with his African boy-protégés Sadek and Athman (SLG, pp. 355–6/IID, pp. 294–5),[39] reproduces the father/son communitarian model foregrounded in *Si le grain*'s *incipit*.

In terms of Gide's Maghrebian gender peripeteia, the textual incorporation, in Part II of *Si le grain*, of 'echoes' such as these is highly significant. Their narrative inclusion suggests that, inside the androcentric realm of colonized Arab North Africa, Gide's autobiographical double contrives to re-enter a universe of maleness and masculine intersubjectivity from which his maternalized adolescence has alienated him. *Si le grain*'s textual mirrorings hint, concomitantly, that access to the Maghreb – revealed by Gide's memories of the Zaghouan army camp (SLG, pp. 293–5/IID, pp. 244–5) as governed by a paternalistic order whose interpellations compellingly call the European male into the collective masculine[40] – allows the post-adolescent André Gide to enjoy not only a liberatory release into *sexual* 'abnormality' but also a *gendered* 'renormalization' that counters the truncated paternal identification of his childhood years. (This renormalization is announced as central to his African trajectory as early as Part I of Gide's *récit*, once Algeria is connected with Albert Démarest, his surviving male familial role-model and, arguably, his father-surrogate (SLG, p. 229/IID, p. 190).) Finally, the 'echoes' of *Si le grain*'s second section help to place Africa as the site, within Gide's narrative, of a drama of gender (re)allegiance whose evolution turns on a movement out of a space of (relative) genderlessness associated with the Juliette–André mother–son dyad and with metropolitan France and into a realm of gendered being that is dominated by male–male relationality, and that, consequently, it is tempting to perceive as somehow 'post-oedipal'.

As his description of his interaction with Laurens, Wilde and his African 'sons' implies, Gide's colonial gender-adventure unquestionably involves a sort of 'being like' as well as a 'being with' the father. That it is also coloured by an oedipalized aspect must be acknowledged as less certain. Because we cannot straightforwardly

locate, in Gide's autobiography, the tropes and trappings of the oedipal narrative –
Si le grain does not, for instance, dramatize father–son desiring rivalry or constitute
its principal actor as subject to the particular type of primary repression that the
paternal/oedipal castratory menace produces[41] – we might opt simply to dismiss
the notion that the Maghreb in any way represents an oedipally-inflected or 'post-
oedipal' Gidean 'place'. Yet it is difficult not to detect, in Gide's account of his
African engagement with the domain of male intersubjectivity, evidence of an at
least partial pull towards precisely the kind of masculine identificatory relatedness
that Freud cites as the hallmark of the male, post-oedipal, psychosexual moment
(normally marked, Freud affirms, by an intensification of the son's identification
with the father, and by a consolidation of his masculine gender-situation).[42]

The contention that Gide's African trajectory, as *Si le grain* reproduces it,
incorporates a by no means straightforward shift into a gendered realm of paternally-
identified, 'oedipalized' masculinity (enabled, the reader senses, by the 'castratory'
voyage into colonial Africa and out of mother France that the Gide-self of *Si le
grain* embarks on in 1893)[43] is given credence by two events detailed in the
concluding chapter of his autobiographical *opus*. The first is his 'paternal' attempt
to keep Athman – the Arab youth who assumes the *petit ami* function that he himself
has previously performed *vis-à-vis* his father – by his side, by taking him back to
Paris.[44] The second is his formal engagement to Emmanuèle, the object of his
ascetic devotions and a woman who manifestly resembles Juliette Rondeaux, Paul
Gide's consort and his own mother. (Once, Freud asserts, his oedipal development
has run its course and his paternal identification is secure(d), the male subject can
and does take as his love-object a woman who is not the mother but is like her.)[45]
And there are three further, final things that I want to say about the reidentificatory
gender-transition that Gide's autobiography reconstructs.

First, and most obviously, it attests to a belated opposition to his mother's
dominion on Gide's part: an opposition that resonates with the resistances Paul
Gide is cast as having opposed to his wife in the early days of their union (SLG,
pp. 162–3/IID, pp. 135–6) and works in counterpoint to the covert struggle against
her son's entry into paternally-inflected maleness that Juliette Gide is consistently
presented as mounting. (This struggle is emblematized in Juliette's reluctance (SLG,
pp. 197–202/IID, pp. 164–8) to allow André full, unsupervised access to his father's
books, whose role in the gender-rituals played out by Paul and André Gide during
the latter's childhood was not insignificant.)[46] Second, the textual manifestations
of Gide's Maghrebian gender-recuperation problematize the proposition, mooted
in Lucey's elegant exegesis of *Si le grain*, that Gide's desire to go to North Africa
– and, indeed, to write about North Africa – bespeaks his will to escape into, and
to narrate himself as/into escaping to, a 'marginal' colonial locus where the dominant, linear, oedipally-grounded sexed structures of European patriarchy may be
evaded.[47] Third, the narrative record of Gide's African (re)insertion into the

masculine that *Si le grain* includes suggests that what his account of his voyages in the Maghreb invokes, ultimately, is his recourse to a 'both/and' strategy that colonial Africa puts within his reach, and that allows him to embrace the gendered normativity required by European civilization even as he defies its (hetero)sexual conventions.[48]

In terms of *Si le grain*'s discursification of the North African environment, the both/and paradigm is likewise unquestionably pertinent. As well as profiling Algeria as an erotically liberating locus, Gide's autobiography clearly also charts the contours of a Maghreb conceived not as a realm of homosexual revelation nor as a theatre of sex tourism but, rather, as a profoundly *homosocial* domain.[49] Further, this domain ('Africa 3') is construed as the cradle for a kind of (prelapsarian) gendered community that is presented also as a matrix of engenderment, and is emblematized as much in the hand-to-hand connection Gide's text-self enjoys with the African Sadek as in the 'fraternal possibilities' *Si le grain*'s narrator associates with adventures shared in Algeria with his fellow Frenchman Laurens (SLG, p. 286/IID, p. 238). It would be simple enough, in a critical move reminiscent of that operated by Schehr, to do no more than detail the delusions and *non-dits* intrinsic in *Si le grain*'s homosocializing construction of 'Africa 3'. Gide's reader could, for instance, elect just to decry the wilful blindness to race hierarchy that his vision of Africa as a site of cross-cultural gender-bonding entails, or to condemn his failure openly to critique either the (white, imperialist) androcentrism of the colonial enterprise or his own (historically produced, culturally inevitable) complicity with it. To do so is not however my intention here. I want, rather, to move beyond the political pitfalls inherent in Gide's representation of 'Africa 3', in order to assess what its narrated existence within *Si le grain* may be taken to signal about his effort to map the Maghrebian space, and about its 'contestatory' potential.

In *Si le grain ne meurt*, by dint not only of delineating 'Africa 2'/homoerotic Africa but also of illuminating its emancipatory influence, André Gide constructs a vision of the Maghreb mirrored *ad infinitum* in a corpus of modern Western travel narratives that commonly (and regardless of the sexual orientations of their authors) cast the Arabic Orient as a 'psychic screen on which to project fantasies of illicit sexuality and unbridled excess'.[50] In consequence, he must be recognized as endorsing on one level an enduring, exoticizing discursive mode that (i) perpetuates an imperialist association between the Orient and erotic escapism rendered standard by the writings of Gide's nineteenth-century predecessors;[51] (ii) produces 'knowledge' about the colonized world that works in the service of European hegemony;[52] and (iii) belongs, by virtue of its de-individualized character, to the 'public' as well as to the 'Orientalist' representational spheres. Yet, by counterposing against his institutionalized rendition of North-Africa-as-realm-of-erotic-liberation another, more private vision of Africa-as-theatre-of-gender-reintegration,[53] and by creating thereby a significant degree of internal representational 'incoherence' in

Si le grain, Gide permits his autobiographical *récit* to discursify the Maghreb in a manner that departs from the 'uniform' Orientalist model invoked by critics such as Said, Boone and Schehr. And in so doing, I would argue, he allows his narrative to interrogate the validity of those more predictably coded, colonially-inflected representations of the sexualized, erotically libertine non-West proffered by the textual productions of post-1800 French and British literary tourists – representations that are 'inseparable from deeply rooted standards of white [. . .] racism and political and cultural imperialism'.[54]

We must be careful not to overstate the radicalism of the discursive challenge presented by Gide's autobiography. *Si le grain*'s African vision is, after all, haunted by the spectre of an ultra-masculinist, imperialist discourse on/of male camaraderie and adventure in the colonial context to which its author has partial if by no means wholehearted recourse. But because this latter discourse is commingled with a discourse on/of homosexual colonial experience that is dissonant with it and cannot coexist alongside it without producing tension, it is left no more intact, in Gide's self-history, than the 'Orientalist', eroticizing take on Africa whose presence in *Si le grain* Schehr detects and deplores.[55] It is certainly not the case that the multiform North Africa imagined in Gide's autobiographical tale can be placed unproblematically in the same geotextual camp as those narratively re-territorialized, politically resistant, (de)colonized spaces charted in the writings of more contemporary post-colonial authors.[56] Nevertheless, Gide's multilayered autobiographical African mapping must be acknowledged as one that reminds us that narratives of colonial space should strive always to break imaginative ground. In framing the Maghreb as a gendered and an engendering as well as an erotic realm, *Si le grain*'s Maghrebian geography is certainly richer than some of its readers have allowed. And it cannot, in sum, be taken simply to shore up the kind of monolithic, colonialist spatiosexual fantasies whose proliferation naturalizes what are deeply pernicious modalities of 'seeing' place.

Les Mots pour le dire: Marie Cardinal's 'Maternal' Maghreb

While it is no less intimate a narrative than *Si le grain*, Cardinal's *Les Mots pour le dire* (MPD),[57] published in 1975, could hardly be more dissimilar, in terms of its content and tenor, to the *récit de vie* Gide wrote half a century earlier. For one thing, Cardinal's text addresses the youthful experiences of a female *pied-noir*[58] settler, rather than those of a male French colonial traveller. Further, in its account of its heroine's relation to the cultural, class and gender codes of the colonial bourgeoisie that formed her, *Les Mots* is at once more overtly 'political' and less openly autobiographical than Gide's confessional *opus*.[59] However, these differences aside, Cardinal's autobiographical novel can be taken, like Gide's self-history before it, to imag(in)e Algeria – specifically, the Algeria of the 1930s-1950s – in a manner that simultaneously deconstructs and underwrites established colonialist representational paradigms. Indeed, as the next section of this chapter will suggest, its Maghrebian mappings may be regarded as more profoundly – if less conspicuously – eurocentrically inf(l)ected than those of its 'Orientalist' predecessor. They can be read, in other words, as countering the convention according to which female-authored tales of colonial life, by virtue of their creators' cognizance of gender inequality, fall less easily than their male-authored counterparts into complicity with discursive practices coloured by the geopolitics of racial/cultural dominion.[60] That this is the case must, moreover, be acknowledged as ironic, given the consciously denunciatory stance that, in *Les Mots* and elsewhere, Cardinal adopts with regard to colonial paternalism.[61]

Les Mots pour le dire deals with the protracted psychoanalysis that Cardinal's anonymous narrator embarks upon in order to overcome the mental and emotional disequilibrium and attendant somatic trauma to which she succumbs in her thirties. A key feature of her *cure* – the central focus of Cardinal's tale – is a lengthy rememoration of her *pied-noir* girlhood, her psychologically harmful dealings with her distant, damaged mother and the play of passionate idealization and semi-acknowledged loathing that characterized her evolving relation to her genetrix. It is in the context, then, of an analytically-induced, narratively reconstructed disinterment of the past of a troubled female subject whose experiences mirror Cardinal's own that the colonized mid-century Maghreb comes to be profiled in *Les Mots*. And it is certainly the case that the manner of its profiling – which is patently 'sexed' – owes much to specific, gender-related facets of its creator's personal history, as Cardinal's *roman autobiographique* reworks it. That said, as I indicated above, *Les Mots*'s Maghrebian representations form part of the discursive palette generated by the French colonial enterprise, and must also be elucidated and understood as such.

Critics who have dissected Cardinal's textual treatment of the Maghreb (whether in *Les Mots* or in her more recently published travel narrative, *Au pays de mes racines*)[62] have signalled issues of sexual difference to be no less pertinent to it than to the accounts of 'Africa 2' and 'Africa 3' furnished by *Si le grain*.[63] More specifically, confronted with Cardinal's vision of Algeria as a lost source of origin and as a realm ravaged by imperialism and patriarchy, with *Les Mots*'s narrator's nostalgia for a Maghreb perceived (MPD, p. 112/WSI [trans.], p. 88) as her *vraie mère* and with her equation of her mother's physical decline and the collapse of *L'Algérie française* (MPD, p. 111, p. 317/WSI, p. 87, p. 270), individual readers, familiar with Cardinal's familial baggage, have elaborated 'maternalized' interpretations of her North African imaginings. These interpretations affirm, amongst other things, that Cardinal's writing casts Algeria as an ideal mother-surrogate; as an antidote to difficulties engendered by mother–daughter *déréliction*;[64] as an emblem of the semiotic (the presymbolic space Kristeva associates with the mother–child dyad and the experience of *jouissance*);[65] or as a mirror for her mother's repressed, oppressed body, caught in a matrix of power-relations she colludes with but cannot control.[66]

In addition, they commonly imply that the affective privations marking Cardinal's earliest connection to the female colonial subject who gave her life powerfully inflect her creative constructions of the colonized Maghreb. Some of these critical readings betray however a greater sensitivity to the nuances of Cardinal's maternalized North African representations than others. Of particular interest, as far as this discussion is concerned, is that proposed by Marie-Paule Ha. Ha contends, convincingly, that *Les Mots*'s Algeria constitutes a privileged textual locus posited less as a maternal *extension* than as a '(M)Other' territory set in *opposition* to that 'Me(re)tropolitan' spatial entity created by Cardinal's conflation of her protagonist's biological mother, the space she inhabits/represents and mainland, colonizing France, whose values the mother incarnates.[67] In so doing, she opens Cardinal's Maghrebian textual geography up to an analysis that keeps its gendered aspect in view, but admits readings of it that are not exclusively gender-focused. It is my intention, here, to develop an analysis of this type, counterposing against the interpretation of the discursive and structural bases of *Les Mots*'s narrative mappings that I would wish to privilege other possible exegeses of the novel's oppositional, maternalized Algerian constructions. But, before I can perform my readings, the detail of these constructions requires further attention.

As Ha's essay reveals (without, however, dissecting the cultural and ideological import of this phenomenon), Cardinal's Maghrebian imaginings are fundamentally reliant on the figure of antithesis.[68] Specifically, across the 17-chapter spread of *Les Mots*, and, more especially, within a narrower narrative field composed of Chapters 3–15, four key oppositions ground its author's engendering representations of North Africa, and of the dynamic binding it to its (m)Other(s): Cardinal's geotextual *Me(re)tropole*. The first of these oppositions features in Chapters 3, 4, 5, 11, and 15, and makes extensive use of natural reference. It sets Algeria up as a space of sensual provocation (MPD, p. 59/WSI, p. 45) and, more particularly, as a space resembling a sexually excited, exciting female body (MPD, pp. 88–9, p. 105/WSI, p. 69, p. 83). This space is set against a sphere of frigidity associated with the streets of France (MPD, p. 63/WSI, p. 48), with the moral strictures its Catholic faith imposes and with Cardinal's narrator's sexually self-denying mother, in whom such strictures are emblematized (MPD, p. 237, pp. 302–5/WSI, p. 201, pp. 256–9). The second opposition is introduced in Chapter 5, and dominates Chapter 7. It establishes the Maghreb — cast as a fecund, edenic garden, teeming with and beneficent to the good things of the earth (MPD, pp. 106–9/WSI, pp. 84–6) — as a protective, fertile, 'uterine' realm. Concomitantly, it invokes as this environment's 'other' a deficient womb-space whose facets are (i) the unwelcoming uterus from which Cardinal's heroine's mother sought to eject her unwanted daughter, conceived during the death-throes of her marriage (MPD, pp. 164–5/ WSI, pp. 135–6) and (ii) the 'French' colonial interior – the *salon* of the mother's family farm, with its *feu de bois* and leather armchairs – that fails, its superficially sheltering aspect notwithstanding (MPD, p. 132/WSI, p. 106), to safeguard Cardinal's self-projective protagonist (MPD, pp. 160–1/WSI, pp. 131–2) against exposure to her mother's *saloperie* (that is, her decision to inform her resented child of her unsuccessful efforts to abort her). 'Opposition 3' figures Algeria as a bountiful breast, and as the source of a spiritual and material sustenance that the 'bad breast' constituted by Cardinal's heroine's repressive maternal parent, her detested French 'motherland' and its desiccated cultural and religious traditions cannot provide. This third opposition is central to Chapter 6 of *Les Mots*. It emerges out of contrasts between, on the one hand, the dripping honey-pastries, spicy stews and colourful Arab folktales that Cardinal's narrator's child-self enjoyed in the company of Daïba, an elderly family retainer (MPD, pp. 123–4/WSI, pp. 98–9), and, on the other, the stultifying religious rituals and improving historical and moral narratives she was introduced to by the formal, French, Catholic upbringing her mother determinedly imposed (MPD, pp. 122–3/WSI, pp. 97–8).[69] Resting as it does on a dynamic of positive/negative nurturance, 'antithesis 3' likewise makes its mark on Chapter 11, which records an episode during which the Cardinal child-persona of *Les Mots* is forced by her mother to ingurgitate 'bad' French (rather than 'good' Arabic) food – specifically, some *potage de légumes* she has previously vomited up (MPD, pp. 214–17/WSI, pp. 179–81). 'Opposition 4' – which both recalls and counter-mands Gide's vision of 'Africa 3' as a site of gender formation – plays off an Algeria envisioned as a presocial, rural 'outside' where gender constraints and behavioural rules do not necessarily prevail (MPD, p. 141/WSI, p. 114)[70] against the constrictive European environments in which, amongst other things, Cardinal's heroine receives the social and sexual training her mother insists upon (MPD, p. 107, pp. 141–2/WSI, p. 85, pp. 114–15). These include the 'civilized', highly regulated bourgeois spaces her family inhabit or create around themselves in their metropolitan *terre d'origine* (MPD, pp. 179–80/WSI, p. 148).

Cardinal's matrix of gender-inflected representational antitheses is elaborated extremely carefully. And it manifestly valorizes, to the detriment of its Other(s), the North Africa her narrative reconstructs. Because, moreover, Cardinal's network of contrastive mappings issues out of an insistent play of reiterated, good/bad, Maghreb/*Me(re)tropole* juxtapositions that echoes the good/bad maternal dialectic of *L'Asphyxie*, it would appear that her autobiographical novel is no less narratively 'compulsive' than its Leducian predecessor. If, though, *Les Mots*'s repeated narrative antitheses reveal the existence, in Cardinal's text, of a mode of figuring the Maghreb that smacks of the obsessional, then what does this signal about its author's repre-sentational motivations? And what does Cardinal's play with contrast suggest with regard to the discursive allegiances that can be ascribed to, or detected within, the

North African constructions her self-referential fiction contains? With a view to addressing these questions, I want to elaborate three, necessarily brief, critical diagnoses of *Les Mots*'s Maghrebian representational economy, concluding with the one I find to be the most enlightening.

In his psychoanalytically-oriented evaluation of the relevance to Cardinal's writing of oedipal processes, Phil Powrie uses the work of Melanie Klein to contextualize the splittings and remouldings of (m)Other and self that, he suggests, *Les Mots*'s narrator effects. He argues that the dichotomizations and semiotic manipulations to which Cardinal's *récit* subjects its central maternal persona, Cardinal's heroine's loved/loathed genetrix, and the associated guilt that it conveys constitute clues to the fact that what the 'unconscious' textual space of *Les Mots* configures are the 'principal positions within the splitting mechanism of the pre-Oedipal phase: the paranoid-schizoid position where the [. . .] subject hates the mother and accommodates this hate by splitting the mother figure into good and bad, followed by the depressive position where the mother is made whole'.[71] A Kleinian perspective likewise illuminates Cardinal's oppositionally-grounded African representational practice.[72] Recourse to it encourages the reader to construe the 'good'/'bad' Maghreb/*Me(re)tropole* dichotomies that Cardinal's novel incorporates as so many signals that the African realm that *Les Mots* envisions, and its European other(s), partly function in Cardinal's narrative, and are figured by it, as (coloured by) maternally-related unconscious phantasms. A Kleinian approach allows us, in other words, to read Cardinal's beneficent Maghreb and the alien, privatory Me(re)tropolis she plays off against it as the phantasmic creations of a (narratorial? authorial?) psyche that is not only governed by an infantile ambivalence towards the mother, but is also divisively at work in *Les Mots*'s narrative fabric. It permits us to view this textual psyche as one that projects onto the external environment (colonial Algeria-plus-France) the imprint of a dynamic of nurturance-plus-denial familiar to every neonate, transmuting it into a maternal avatar and a site of displaced maternal splitting. A reading of the Kleinian type is endorsed by the centrality accorded by those segments of *Les Mots* dominated by the Maghreb/Me(re)tropolis opposition to issues of protection, persecution, ('good'/ 'bad', oral) gratification and deprivation. Such a reading cannot however be taken to be comprehensive or wholly satisfactory, in that it entirely disregards the 'political' dimension of *Les Mots*'s North African mappings.

An interpretation that does address the ideological aspect of Cardinal's Maghrebian vision is one that connects *Les Mots*'s gendered African/Me(re)tropolitan antitheses to a politics of representation centred on a deconstruction of standard tropes produced by the (male) French colonial imagination. As Winifred Woodhull's *Transfigurations of the Maghreb* convincingly demonstrates,[73] on a number of levels, including the cultural, colonial Algeria came to be profoundly feminized by and in the minds of its colonizers, and feminized, in the service of colonialist exploitation, as a possessed, dominated, uncivilized woman whose Other was the developed French *Métropole*. Its *sexuation* is moreover, Woodhull argues, no less evident in the writings of its colonial administrators than in Orientalist painting and photography. As readers of *Les Mots*, *Autrement dit* and *Au pays de mes racines* cannot help but recognize, Cardinal's stance *vis-à-vis* French colonialism has been consistently critical. Moreover, she published *Les Mots* during an era of sociosexual contestation when French feminist authors, inspired by the theoretical work of such as Hélène Cixous, were pursuing representational strategies aimed at 'stealing', and redeploying ironically, the 'objects' of patriarchal culture.[74] These factors suggest that we can construe the hyperbolically positive feminizations of the Maghreb that *Les Mots* incorporates – feminizations that countermand the demeaning feminizations privileged by French colonialist discourse – as evidence of an attempt on Cardinal's part to resist the limitations of an imperialist, patriarchally-marked cultural paradigm, by plundering and reworking some of that paradigm's more hackneyed modes of African discursification. Cardinal's manipulations of what is a personally significant geotextual representational opposition – Maghreb = a good mother/Me(re)tropole = its bad Other – can be read in other words, albeit not unproblematically,[75] as emblematizing her rejection of a parallel, colonialist, 'orthodox' practice of gendered mapping that cast Algeria as France's supine houri. What is more, the extensive use that *Les Mots* makes of its 'deconstructive', good/bad Maghreb/*Me(re)tropole* dynamic can be taken to attest not only to its author's disapproval of the colonial scene but also, we sense, to her personal culpability at having been culturally implicated in it.[76]

The Kleinian and feminist treatments of Cardinal's antithetically-oriented African representations summarized above are not unilluminating. But it is possible to construct a supplementary interpretation of *Les Mots*'s Maghrebian mappings that produces a clearer picture of their discursive foundation and, in addition, uncovers the occluded ideological, eurocentric bias that subtends them. In his dissection of the workings of colonialist discursive practice, 'The Economy of Manichean Allegory', Abdul R. JanMohamed isolates a Manichaean paradigm as a central axis of the colonialist cognitive framework, and of colonialist literary representation.[77] Defining this eurocentric paradigm as predicated on a 'field of diverse yet interchangeable oppositions between white and black, good and evil, superiority and inferiority, civilization and savagery, intelligence and emotion, rationality and sensuality, self and Other, subject and object',[78] he notes, further, that it not only functions in colonialist texts to validate colonial occupation, but also incorporates a fixation on the savage, all-too-feminine 'otherness' of the non-european native that produces a kind of fetishization of it.[79]

On a surface level, to suggest that *Les Mots* might have any kind of truck with the paradigm JanMohamed delineates might appear nonsensical. For one thing, Cardinal's narrative can scarcely be deemed to privilege European 'superiority' at the expense of the 'inferiority' of the North African Other and/or his/her homeland. Further, *Les Mots* is a female-authored colonial tale; and female-authored colonial writing, produced as it is by subjects whose subjectivity is split by the contrapuntal experiences of racial empowerment and gender subordination, tends generically, so the critical credo goes, to challenge rather than uphold the fixed, subject–object antitheses and stable modalities of othering that are essential to the Manichaean discursive model.[80] That said, the structural fundament of *Les Mots*'s maternalized Algerian mappings does rely – albeit 'in reverse' – on precisely the kind of antithetical, positive/negative dichotomies that JanMohamed associates with the colonialist discursive machinery. Equally, *Les Mots*'s play with gendered, geotextual opposition generates a form of fetishization that may take as its object the maternal, nurturing beneficence of Cardinal's North African (m)otherland instead of the irrational, sensual savagery of the colonized Algerian subject, but that recalls, nonetheless, that other form of denigratory, femininizing fetishization to which, JanMohamed's essay suggests, colonialist literature insistently subjects the racial(ly) Other.

It would seem, then, to be the case that her anti-colonial intentions and manifest efforts to turn colonialist paradigms around notwithstanding, Cardinal cannot keep from resorting to a mode of Maghrebian representation that is, after all, intrinsically – if not superficially – bound up with the ideology of colonialism. The key indication that she succumbs to its lure (*Les Mots*'s culturally predictable, if individualistic, *sexuations* of the Maghreb constitute a further, lesser 'clue') is her employment of a representational organization whose inverted, politicized Manichaean dynamic (Africa = good/Me(re)tropolitan space = bad) serves in the end, paradoxically, to support the standard, Manichaean, colonialist discursive strategy that JanMohamed addresses. The structural basis of its contrastively-grounded African imaginings can be taken, in sum, to signal the presence within *Les Mots* of a kind of 'return of the (colonial) repressed'.

A *mise-en-abyme* of this phenomenon is provided by Cardinal's brief and unexpectedly denigratory depiction, in Chapter 7 (MPD, pp. 160–4/WSI, pp. 131–5), of urban Algiers. Cardinal's narrator strongly implies that if she offers, here, a description of the North African space that spotlights its 'savage' aspects (leprous beggars and screeching street hawkers included) and, for once, is less than edenic, this is because her memories of the Maghrebian city environment – an environment she intuits as 'French' in a way that the countryside of occupied Algeria is not (MPD, p. 105/WSI, p. 83) – have been polluted by the fact that her mother chose it as the setting for her horrific revelations regarding her attempt at miscarriage, and for the particularly deformative lessons on/in womanhood she used those revelations to impart. However, what the short – and inferiorizing – account of the sordid *rue méditerranéenne* proffered by *Les Mots* encapsulates, arguably, is the temporary, *overt* emergence, in Cardinal's narrative, of a colonialist angle of vision that may appear not to be manifest within it, but can in fact be viewed as imbricated in, even as it is masked by, all the hierarchized Maghreb/*Me(re)tropole* antitheses mobilized within Cardinal's autobiographical fiction.

In Chapter 4 of *Transfigurations of the Maghreb*, 'Out of France', Winifred Woodhull suggests that André Gide and Marie Cardinal may be viewed as equally guilty of constructing Algeria, textually, as the cipher for an ahistorical, acultural paradise; of supporting, however inadvertently, the stereotypes of eurocentric discourse; and of failing to work effectively against the structures of colonial dominion. That Woodhull focuses, in the section of her study devoted to a comparison of the North African narratives of Gide and Cardinal, on Gide's *L'Immoraliste* (and on Cardinal's *Au pays de mes racines*) is not insignificant, as far as my own assessment of the relation between the Maghrebian writings of these authors is concerned.[81] My particular object of interest, here, has been Gide's *Si le grain ne meurt* – a *récit* that is not only more 'properly' autobiographical than *L'Immoraliste* but is also characterized neither by the excessive lyricism that *L'Immoraliste*'s narrator Michel brings to his account of his encounter with the natural realm of Africa, nor by the irony that Gide, as (detached) author, infuses into it. Its Orientalist dimension notwithstanding, it is not in my view the case that *Si le grain* can be taken to represent as ideologically-implicated a textual production as that constituted either by *L'Immoraliste* or, more pertinently, by Cardinal's *Les Mots pour le dire*, my other key focus in this discussion. It is certainly true that in his autobiography, by imagining North Africa as a 'good', emancipatory erotic space whose other is the sexually repressive realm constituted by 'maternal' metropolitan France, Gide recurs, like Cardinal after him, to a sort of reverse Manichaean strategy. It is true, too, that by virtue of so doing he can be similarly charged with underwriting, by simply inverting them, oppositional paradigms peculiar to the colonialist representational optic. Yet, the both/and, multilayered model of Maghrebian mapping contained in *Si le grain* ultimately strikes the (this) reader as less *straightforwardly* a product of the eurocentric, colonial imagination and the power-relations that feed into it than the antithetically-grounded African vision proffered by Cardinal's more openly contestatory *Les Mots*.

Clearly, to speculate on why this might be the case constitutes an exercise of limited value. However, it is hard to resist the temptation to wonder to what extent Gide's ability to envision the racially/culturally 'other' space of the Maghreb in a manner that seems less unimaginatively circumscribed by a colonialist, inegalitarian representational ethos than that exploited by the ex-colonial Cardinal relates to his experience, in his own culture, of homosexual minoritization. Equally, given the myriad ways in which, under patriarchy, the female/maternal body is made into a 'colonized' territory (and is acknowledged as such in *Les Mots pour le dire*), it is hard not to wonder, Cardinal's colonial formation notwithstanding, at the role played in the production of *Les Mots*' female-authored North African inscriptions by the discursive tools of the colonizer.[82]

Notes

1. B. Colomina (ed.) (1992), *Sexuality and Space*, Princeton, Introduction.
2. In their Introduction to *De/Colonizing the Subject*, Sidonie Smith and Julia Watson use the term 'colonial subject' to denote the marginalized subject/oppressed object of colonial rule. See *De/Colonizing the Subject*, pp. xiii–xxxi, p. xvi. I am using the term more broadly, to signal any subject implicated in colonialism.
3. A. Gide (1955), *Si le grain ne meurt*, Paris, translated as *If It Die*, trans. D. Bussy, Harmondsworth, 1977.
4. This is not to say that *Si le grain* neglects to raise the issue/problem of 'total' autobiographical truth, or to question the possibility of its realization. That it does so is made most apparent in the concluding paragraph of the first of its two parts.
5. For an account of (i) Gide's wariness regarding the phenomenon of the totalizing autobiographical self-portrait; (ii) the relationship between this reluctance and his own, lengthy narrative engagement with a kaleidoscopic, multiform *espace autobiographique* that includes the autobiographical novel *L'Immoraliste* (1902); and (iii) the reasons that led him finally to produce in *Si le grain* a canonical, confessional autobiographical *opus* focused around the emergence of his homosexuality, see P. Lejeune (1975), 'Gide et l'espace autobiographique', in *Le Pacte autobiographique*, pp. 165–96.
6. Gide began his North African travels, charted in *Si le grain*'s second part, in Tunisia; his Maghrebian experiences related mostly, however, to Algeria. Unlike Tunisia and Morocco (French protectorates), Algeria was colonized as a French territory, and assimilationist policy was practised there more thoroughly than in other French colonies. Invaded in 1830, Algeria only gained independence in 1962.
7. See J. Dollimore (1991), *Sexual Dissidence: Augustine to Wilde, Freud to Foucault*, Oxford, p. 337; E. Marty (1994), 'Le Poète sans livre', *Bulletin des amis d'André Gide*, vol. XXII, pp. 219–26; M. Lucey (1995), *Gide's Bent: Sexuality, Politics, Writing*, New York and Oxford, pp. 13–14, p. 17. We should note that while *Si le grain* was published in full in 1926, extracts from it appeared in the *Nouvelle Revue Française* between 1920 and 1921. That Gide was far less concerned, in *Si le grain*, to decry Africa's colonial travails than to highlight the role played by the Maghreb in the sexual illumination he was afforded in the 1890s reflects the resolutely confessional character of his narrative enterprise.
8. For a discussion of this environment, and of the role played within it by North Africa's economics of boys, see J. Boone (1995), 'Vacation Cruises; or, The Homoerotics of Orientalism', *PMLA*, vol. 110, pp. 95–107.

9. It is worth noting in this context that, as Dollimore argues (cf. *Sexual Dissidence*, pp. 337–8), the account Gide's autobiographical narrator offers of the Ali/horsewhipping episode and his own spectatorship of it does signal his sense of personal involvement in, as well as distaste for, colonial dynamics.

10. As Lucey notes (cf. *Gide's Bent*, pp. 60–1), Gide also seems reluctant to construe these women simply as common prostitutes whose trade is intimately imbricated with the French colonial presence.

11. See 'Watching Sex in *Si le grain ne meurt*', in Lucey, *Gide's Bent*, pp. 21–41.

12. Ibid., pp. 36–7. See also p. 39 for a discussion of how Gide connects sodomy, decadence and colonial politics. I am most grateful to Judith Still for signalling that Lucey's assumption (which I endorse) that the Mohammed/Daniel B. encounter involves anally penetrative sex is borne out only implicitly in *Si le grain*.

13. 'face à face, réciproque et sans violence' (SLG, p. 346).

14. For a reading of the link between Gide's dislike of fucking and his resistance to 'colonial' sex, see Lucey, *Gide's Bent*, p. 37. For an interesting, contrasting analysis of how Gide's depictions of non-penetrative, non-relational cross-racial sex in the colonial context can be read as indicative of a Gidean failure to recognize the Arab Other as an autonomous subject, possessed of meaningful otherness, see Bersani's discussion of *Si le grain*'s 'pre-text', *L'Immoraliste*, in L. Bersani (1995), *Homos*, Cambridge, MA. and London, pp. 113–29, p. 122.

15. '[Ali] se dressa nu comme un dieu [. . .] puis, en riant, se laissa tomber contre moi. Son corps était peut-être brûlant, mais parut à mes mains aussi rafraîchissant que l'ombre. Que le sable était beau! Dans la splendeur adorable du soir, de quels rayons se vêtait ma joie! . . .' (SLG, p. 299).

16. '[A] présent, je trouvais enfin ma normale. Plus rien ici de contraint, de précipité, de douteux; rien de cendreux dans le souvenir que j'en garde. Ma joie fut immense et telle que je ne la puisse imaginer plus pleine si de l'amour s'y fût mêlé. Comment eût-il été question d'amour? Comment eussé-je laissé le désir disposer de mon coeur? Mon plaisir était sans arrière-pensée et ne devait être suivi d'aucun remords. Mais comment nommerai-je alors mes transports à serrer dans mes bras nus ce parfait petit corps sauvage, ardent, lascif et ténébreux?' (SLG, p. 343). *Ténébreux*, we should note, is inadequately rendered in Bussy's translation. For interesting analyses of Gide's 'erotics of the skin', manifest in both of the passages I have just cited, and of its relationship to colonial sexual politics, see K. Kopelson (1994), 'Pederastic Trappings: Gide and Firbank', in *Love's Litany: The Writing of Modern Homoerotics*, Stanford, pp. 49–73, pp. 62–3; Naomi Segal (1998), 'André Gide and the Niece's Seduction', in M. Merck, N. Segal and E. Wright (eds), *Coming Out of Feminism?*, Oxford, pp. 194–213, pp. 197–8.

17. Sheringham (cf. *French Autobiography*, pp. 183–93) rightly notes that this celebration is not devoid of ambiguity.
18. See L. Schehr (1995), 'On Vacation with Gide and Barthes', in *Alcibiades at the Door: Gay Discourses in French Literature*, Stanford, pp. 113–54, p. 121.
19. See Dollimore; Lucey; Schehr; Sheringham; also J. Delay (1956/7), *La Jeunesse d'André Gide*, 2 vols, Paris; E. Apter (1987), *André Gide and the Codes of Homotextuality*, Stanford.
20. For an account of (i) the naturalness attributed to Africa by Gide; (ii) the way the body of the Arab male Other is made to symbolize it and (iii) its problematic implications, see Schehr, *Alcibiades*, pp. 120–1.
21. In *Gide's Bent* (cf. pp. 26–40), Lucey offers an intricate dissection of Gide's efforts to write (colonial sexual) politics out of his renditions of his own, liberatory African homosexual experiences. He also details the ways in which the spectre of that politics unfailingly, for all Gide's will to efface it, writes itself back into them. As Lucey suggests, in his treatments of his (textual counterpart's) sexual encounters with Ali and Mohammed, Gide is keen to emphasize their 'mutual', politically 'innocent' character – by, for example, underplaying the role played in them by payment, and by retrospectively contextualizing them as instances of 'reciprocal','gentle' pleasure. Yet, elements of these treatments – their account of the predatory curiosity with which Gide's textual *sosie* observes Ali's advances, and of the pleasure he takes in the dusky (*ténébreux*) hue of Mohammed's naked body – betray the inevitably politicized hue of the sexual exchanges they transcribe (cf. *Gide's Bent*, pp. 30–4). I am most grateful to Naomi Segal for drawing my attention to this aspect of Gide's descriptions of his African sexual adventures, and for alerting me to the fact that the key phrase Gide employs in order to underline their 'mutual', anti-exploitative aspect – that pertaining to the 'reciprocal', face-to-face pleasure they introduce him to – was added belatedly to *Si le grain*, in 1935, on Malraux's advice.
22. See Lucey, *Gide's Bent*, p. 30. In invoking Gide's (self-deconstructive) utopic vision of the Maghreb as a place where the burden of a certain sort of sexual politics may be evaded, Lucey's analysis is specifically concerned with Gide's account of his laughter-filled exchange with Ali.
23. Lucey (cf. *Gide's Bent*, Chapter 1) is far less antagonistic towards Gide's utopic imagining of a politics-free African homosexual space than Schehr, suggesting that our readings of Gide should 'go beyond merely noting the dishonesty and/or ideological blindness of various forms of nostalgia for pure sexual apoliticality' (p. 27). And, as I have already indicated, he is willing to view *Si le grain* as a text that remedies its own 'erasures', up to a point, by tacitly illuminating the political colour of that which it overtly presents as somehow outside the political – i.e. its hero's African sexual adventures. Eric Marty (cf. 'Le Poète sans livre', pp. 219–20) also urges us, less persuasively than Lucey,

not to condemn out of hand Gide's depoliticized/depoliticizing or politically disingenuous treatment of his North African experiences.

24. See *Alcibiades*, pp. 116–27.
25. Ibid., p. 116, p. 127. Schehr's criticisms pertain also to *L'Immoraliste*.
26. See E. Said (1993), *Culture and Imperialism*, London, p. 233.
27. Schehr, *Alcibiades*, p. 125.
28. When Gide evokes the Maghreb as a space 'straight out of the Arabian Nights' (cf. SLG, p. 290/IID, p. 241), full of camels, lightening-streaked horizons and flamingo-infested lakes and peopled by crafty traders, exotic houris and ardent adolescents, we sense that we are being offered the kind of literary discourse that colludes, however undeliberately, with the Orientalist move to transform Africa into an exotic *topos* (as opposed to a real place) that is represented/representable by standard, hackneyed discursive codes and, in consequence, is knowable and eminently masterable. Yet we cannot help but feel that Gide does not use these codes wholly unawarely. Two features of Part I of *Si le grain* – its account of the elephant, camel and mosque-bestrewn 'paysage oriental de Tournemine' the young André comes upon in the Louvre (SLG, p. 167/IID, p. 139) and its description of the Tuareg spears Dr Brouardel uses to threaten him with after his masturbatory activities are discovered (SLG, pp. 66–7/IID, p. 57) – are significant here. These preposterous symbols of the exotic East constitute, arguably, 'clues' that signal to the reader Gide's cognizance of (i) the impossibility of representing North Africa in ways that wholly elude an Orientalist, ideological narrative mode marked by what Said describes as 'a sort of regimented antiquarianism by which the exotic and the strange get formulated into lexicons, codes, and finally clichés' (cf. E. Said (1995), *Orientalism*, London, p. 177); (ii) the (inevitably) Orientalist, exoticizing tenor of his own text; and (iii) the problematic character of this aspect of it.
29. See Schehr, *Alcibiades*, p. 127.
30. It is not in any case total, given that the narrative Africa I am about to dissect *is* touched on in the latter stages of Schehr's account of Gide's African tourism.
31. This term is borrowed from Boone, whose 'Vacation Cruises; or, the Homoerotics of Orientalism' offers an illuminating survey of the canon in question.
32. 'Mon petit ami vient-il se promener avec moi?' (SLG, pp. 17–18). *Si le grain*'s account of the father–son rituals performed by André and Paul Gide is initiated by Gide's memory of flying paper dragons with his father.
33. For an account of the incompleteness of the young Gide's paternal/masculine (oedipal) identification, see Delay, *La Jeunesse d'André Gide*, vol. I, p. 79, p. 265. Delay's psychobiographical *opus* constitutes an essential companion-piece to *Si le grain*. Gide's depiction of reading-with-father as a route into masculinity both recalls and countermands the vision of reading-as-route-into-female-pleasure that Sartre adumbrates in *Les Mots*.

34. That Gide's autobiographical avatar's adolescence is characterized by a maternally-oriented identification is indicated by Lucey (cf. 'The Place of the Oedipal: Gide Writing Home from North Africa', in *Gide's Bent*, pp. 42–67, p. 59), who detects evidence of it in the 'Passage du Havre' episode of *Si le grain* (SLG, pp. 191–3/IID, pp. 159–61). A rich account of Gide's maternal identifications and of their multifaceted basis is also offered by Catherine Millot. See Millot (1996), 'Un hybride de bacchante et de Saint-Esprit', in *Gide Genet Mishima: Intelligence de la perversion*, Paris, pp. 19–79, pp. 40–1.

35. There is insufficient space, here, for a detailed analysis of the gendered, androcentric architecture of imperialism. For a reading of the colonial enterprise as a mechanism whereby white men ruled in the male interest, assuring a (white) male patrimony and homosociality, see A. McClintock (1995), *Imperial Leather: Race, Gender and Sexuality in the Colonial Contest*, New York and London, Chapter 1; C. E. Gittings (ed.) (1996), *Constructions of Masculinity*, New Lambton and Hebden Bridge, pp. 1-8. For an account of the colonial realm as a context wherein white male travellers could legitimately find access to a space of exclusively masculine sociality, see M. L. Pratt (1992), *Imperial Eyes: Travel Writing and Transculturation*, New York and London, p. 240. For a summary of the complex process whereby colonialism generates homo-social, albeit unequal/hierarchical, mirror-relations between colonizing and colonized male subjects, see G. Bergner (1995), 'Who is that Masked Woman?, or, The Role of Gender in Fanon's *Black Skin, White Masks*, *PMLA*, vol. 110, pp. 75–88, pp. 80–1. All these studies illuminate *Si le grain*.

36. The Gide/Wilde urban promenade is a possible exception here, since its description, unlike that of Gide's other strolls, incorporates a 'penetratory' aspect mirrored in the textually proximate account of Daniel B.'s penetration of Mohammed. McClintock (cf. *Imperial Leather*, pp. 27–8) offers a useful discussion of the relationship between the 'penetrative' act of mapping and the colonialist impulse toward territorial control.

37. On 'French' Algeria as a space demarcated in history/by historiography as the epitome of imperial masculinism, see Julia Clancy-Smith (1992), 'The "Passionate Nomad" Reconsidered: A European Woman in L'Algérie Française', in N. Chauduri and M. Strobel (eds), *Western Women and Imperialism: Complicity and Resistance*, Bloomington and Indianapolis, pp. 61–78, p. 61. Clancy-Smith's sense of the extremely masculinist character of France's colonial occupation of the Maghreb is endorsed by Alain Ruscio's account of how nineteenth-century Algeria was conceived, notably by the French educationalist Paul Bert, as a space to be 'penetrated' and 'impregnated' with 'l'esprit de la France'. See A. Ruscio (1995), *Le Credo de l'homme blanc*, Brussels, p. 101. Elsewhere in his study (cf. pp. 249–52), Ruscio offers further examples of the masculinist language employed by proponents of French colonialism.

38. For an account of Gide's association of mysteriousness with the paternal sphere, see Delay, *La Jeunesse d'André Gide*, Vol. I, pp. 73–5.

39. It is clearly possible to read this stance through and in terms of Gide's 'pedagogical' pederasty; however, lack of space prevents me from doing so here. My sense of his 'filial' connection to Laurens is reinforced by the fact that the latter shares a common first name with Gide's father.

40. As I indicated above, the colonial economy is theorizable as one in which a homosocial order prevails, especially between white male colonizing subjects but also (cf. Bergner, 'Who is That Masked Woman?', pp. 80–1, p. 85), albeit in a different form, between the white colonizers and the black male colonized. In view of this, it is clearly less than straightforward, in the colonial environment, for normative gender interpellation – conceived by Judith Butler as a call performatively to repeat the binary law of sexual difference (cf. J. Butler (1993), *Bodies that Matter: On the Discursive Limits of Sex*, London and New York, Chapter 4) – to be resisted, by the white European male subject at least. The black male subject, under colonial rule, is however arguably interpellated into a different, and in Butlerian terms far more 'abject', kind of gendered being: one marked by a gender ambiguity generated by racial objectification (cf. Bergner, ibid., p. 80). I shall look at Butler's account of gender performativity in more detail in Chapter 5.

41. Gidean critics generally concur that Gide 'misses' effecting a positive oedipal integration. For a fascinating reading of how Gide's autobiography – and, more especially, the 'Tuareg Spears' episode of Chapter III Part I – illuminates its chief player as a desiring subject who, when faced with the menace of castration and the call to oedipalization that it incorporates (cf. SLG, pp. 66–7/IID, pp. 56–7), struggles to *resist* both the oedipal progressive trajectory and the acknowledgment of the possibility of castration on which it is grounded, see Lucey, *Gide's Bent*, pp. 48–52. In this section of his monograph, Lucey suggests, further, that the young Gide of *Si le grain* associates with his oedipally-oriented resistance an Africa that not only is conceived as a place where the sexual rules of bourgeois Parisian families such as his can be refused but also finds its emblem in the spears Dr Brouardel employs in order to *threaten* him with castration. I shall return, below, to a discussion of Lucey's propositions.

42. See S. Freud (1923), 'The Ego and the Id', Chapter III, *Standard Edition*, vol. 19, pp. 28–39, p. 32, and S. Freud, (1924/1977), 'The Dissolution of the Oedipus Complex', in *On Sexuality*, *Penguin Freud Library*, vol. 7, pp. 313–22, pp. 318–19.

43. That his gender-shift *is* a focus of Gidean ambivalence is conveyed by the unease his textual duplicate is represented as experiencing in the androcentric universe of the Zaghouan camp. Telling, also, is the fact that, in January 1895, before setting off on his *second* Maghrebian trip, the Gide-self of *Si le grain*

makes a curious stab at 'depaternalizing/de-oedipalizing' colonial Africa, by inviting his mother and *her* substitute, his future fiancée Emmanuèle, to join him there (cf. SLG, p. 325/IID, p. 269). That he does so confirms the/this reader's sense of the uncertainties he harbours with regard to his African embrace of the 'post-oedipal'.

44. In *Gide's Bent* (cf. pp. 63–7), Lucey offers a reading of the Athman episode that argues, convincingly, for its *anti*-oedipal aspect, and consequently counters the reading constructed here.

45. See, for example, Freud (1931/1977), 'Female Sexuality', in *On Sexuality*, *Penguin Freud Library*, vol. 7, pp. 369–92, pp. 374–5. It is *not* the case that the Gide persona of *Si le grain*'s diegesis does not love Emmanuèle before he goes to Africa: however, it is only after his 'masculinizing/paternalizing' African experiences have occurred (and once Emmanuèle has overcome her reluctance to accept him) that his affection is *formalized*. On Emmanuèle's status as Juliette's 'double', see Millot, *Gide Genet Mishima*, p. 45.

46. Basing his reading on Gide's correspondence with his mother as well as on *Si le grain*, Lucey (cf. *Gide's Bent*, pp. 52-3) construes Mme Gide as representing a sort of oedipalizing gender regulator. On the evidence of Gide's autobiography alone, I would view her rather as a force that works against Gide's effort to emerge into gendered 'normality', even though she appears to endorse it. Her long-lasting refusal to sanction her son's gender-conventional marital projects (a refusal tempered only by her need, when on the point of death, to leave him 'in safe hands') confirms my sense of this.

47. See Lucey, *Gide's Bent*, Chapter 2, especially his reading of the 'Tuareg Spears' episode.

48. Schehr addresses this phenomenon (cf. *Alcibiades*, p. 125), noting that 'in *Si le grain ne meurt*, Gide discovers a Maghreb where the possibility exists of liberating the self from the weight of a binary system that imprisons a man in the dualities that confuse male, masculine, and heterosexual'. We must recognize that Gide's sexual 'defiance'/'deviance' is not as contestatory as all that. As Boone explains, (cf. 'Vacation Cruises', p. 92, pp. 99–100), the Maghrebian cruising ground in which it takes place and that enables its existence is (i) itself a kind of European 'product' (i.e., a product of the economic and sexual consequences of European colonialism) and (ii) the theatre for an 'exotic' (homo)sexual experimentation that was an institutionalized facet of nineteenth- and twentieth-century Western colonial tourism. Further, since the Napoleonic Code contained no provision for punishing homosexuality, homosexual practices were not actually illegal in France during the period covered by Gide's narrative.

49. On the complex, potentially continuous relations between the homosexual and the homosocial, see E. K. Sedgwick (1985), *Between Men: English Literature and Male Homosocial Desire*, New York, pp. 1–20.

50. See Boone, 'Vacation Cruises', p. 89. Authors cited include Gide, Flaubert, Durrell and Orton. On Gide's own encounters with Orientalist writing, see M. Sagaert (1994), 'Exotisme, métissage et écriture', *Bulletin des amis d'André Gide*, vol. XXII, pp. 173–87. In the latter article, and in line with the argument developed at some length in the concluding part of my discussion of *Si le grain*, Saegert suggests that Gide does more than exploit, blindly or exclusively, an Orientalist, exoticizing perspective on North Africa.
51. See Said, *Orientalism*, pp. 188–90. Authors associated by Said with the construction of the Orient as a place where sexual experience unavailable in Europe could be enjoyed include Flaubert, Nerval, Gide, Conrad and Maugham.
52. For a useful account of the connection between (i) travel writing; (ii) the production of knowledge about colonized countries; and (iii) the exercise of colonial power, see Sara Mills (1994), 'Knowledge, Gender and Empire', in A. Blunt and G. Rose (eds), *Writing Women and Space: Colonial and Post-colonial Geographies*, New York and London, pp. 29–50, pp. 34–5.
53. Given the markedly psychological aspect of Gide's rendition of his Maghrebian gender-trip, it is not unjustifiable to deem this latter vision a 'private' one, even though it is not wholly dissimilar to that contained, according to Mills (cf. ibid., p. 37), in various male-authored travel/adventure narratives that, produced in the context of British imperialism, connect travel in colonial space to '[the] proving [of] individual manhood'.
54. M. Bronski (1984), *Culture-Clash: The Making of Gay Sensibility*, Boston, pp. 26–7, cited in Dollimore, *Sexual Dissidence*, p. 338.
55. For a useful reading of the incompatibility of homosocial and homoerotic models of/discourses on colonial masculinity, see Gittings, '"What are soldiers for?" Re-Making Masculinities in Timothy Findley's *The Wars*', in *Imperialism and Gender*, pp. 184–91.
56. For a discussion of the phenomenon of post-colonial literary remapping, see Graham Huggan, 'Decolonizing the Map', in B. Ashcroft, G. Griffiths and H. Tiffin (eds) (1995), *The Post-Colonial Studies Reader*, London and New York, pp. 407–11.
57. M. Cardinal (1975), *Les Mots pour le dire*, Paris, translated as *The Words To Say It*, trans. P. Goodheart, London, 1993.
58. The *Pieds-Noirs* came first from France, then later from other parts of Southern Europe, and settled as colonists in Algeria after the 1830 invasion. They formed an established society by the end of the last century. Cardinal's maternal family were *pieds-noirs* of French origin, while her father was from metropolitan France.
59. For a useful description of Cardinal's evolving views on/recognition of her text's autobiographical status, in which no formal 'pact' is established but which records experiences that parallel Cardinal's own and is acknowledged by its author as incorporating many elements of her personal history, see Phil Powrie

(1993) 'Foreword', in M. Cardinal, *Les Mots pour le dire*, Bristol, pp. xix–xxiii. By 'political', I mean denunciatory both of French colonialism and of the sociosexual practices of the French Catholic bourgeoisie.

60. For a discussion of this issue and related questions, see Chauduri and Strobel, 'Introduction', in *Western Women and Imperialism: Complicity and Resistance*, pp. 1–15.

61. See for example M. Cardinal (1977), *Autrement dit*, Paris, pp. 16–17, pp. 168–76.

62. M. Cardinal (1980), *Au pays de mes racines*, Paris.

63. These critics include M. Le Clézio (1981), 'Mother and Motherland: The Daughter's Quest for Origins', *Stanford French Review*, vol. V, pp. 381–9; F. Lionnet (1989), 'Privileged Difference and the Possibility of Emancipation', in *Autobiographical Voices: Race, Gender, Self-Portraiture*, Ithaca and London, pp. 191–206; C. Durham (1992), *The Contexture of Feminism: Marie Cardinal and Multicultural Literacy*, Urbana and Chicago; L. Cairns (1993), 'Roots and Alienation in Marie Cardinal's *Au pays de mes racines*', *Forum for Modern Language Studies*, vol. XXIX, pp. 346–58; W. Woodhull (1993), 'Out of France', in *Transfigurations of the Maghreb: Feminism, Decolonization and Literatures*, Minneapolis and London, pp. 154–71; and M.-P. Ha, (1995), 'Outre-Mer/Autre Mère: Cardinal and Algeria', *Romance Notes*, vol. XXXVI, pp. 315–23.

64. As Whitford explains (cf. Margaret Whitford (1989), 'Rereading Irigaray', in T. Brennan (ed.), *Between Feminism and Psychoanalysis*, London and New York, pp. 106–26, p. 112), this phenomenon, discussed at length in the work of Luce Irigaray, embraces the state of trauma-inducing non-individuation to which mothers and daughters are consigned within the patriarchal symbolic order. For an account of its relevance to Cardinal's *Les Mots*, see S. Haigh (1994), 'Between Irigaray and Cardinal: Reinventing Maternal Genealogies', *Modern Language Review*, vol. 89, pp. 61–70. I shall return to the issue of mother/daughter (con)fusion in Part II of Chapter 4.

65. See Woodhull, *Transfigurations*, pp. 154–5. Woodhull's focus is *Au Pays de mes racines*.

66. See Le Clézio, 'Mother and Motherland', p. 385; Lionnet, *Autobiographical Voices*, p. 205; Woodhull, *Transfigurations*, pp. 156-7.

67. See Ha, 'Outre-Mer/Autre Mère', pp. 315–19 (Ha plays here with a pun on the French words 'Mère' and 'Métropole' that I shall also exploit). In her discussions of Cardinal's Algeria, which relate also to *Au pays de mes racines*, Ha notes (cf. p. 317) that 'in more ways than one, the maternal space overlaps with the me(re)tropolitan space. The mother's world is dominated by bourgeois values imported from France.' It is true that Ha's account skates somewhat hastily over the parallels that *Les Mots*, and Cardinal's work more generally,

establishes between Cardinal's mother and the Algerian space. However, she is in my view right to foreground the stronger connection between the mother and the French *Métropole* that Cardinal's work stages.

68. Critics who note the centrality of opposition to Cardinal's Algerian representations but neglect to engage analytically with this phenomenon include Cairns and Durham.

69. Phil Powrie makes some interesting observations regarding the Daïba episode and its relation to Cardinal's novel's use of opposition. See Phil Powrie (1990), 'Reading for pleasure: Marie Cardinal's *Les Mots pour le dire* and the text as (re)play of Oedipal configurations', in M. Atack and P. Powrie (eds), *Contemporary French Fiction by Women*, Manchester, pp. 163–76, pp. 171–2. I shall return to Powrie's argument below.

70. Chapter 7 of *Les Mots* establishes rural Algeria as a place where Cardinal's youthful protagonist could cross gender-borders. However, in Chapter 6 (cf. MPD, pp. 125–7/WSI, pp. 100–2), the same rural space is presented as a milieu where Cardinal's heroine may have played transgressively with gender roles but where other children – the Arab children living on her family estate – maintained gender-boundaries. We need also to remember that urban Algiers – the environment in which Cardinal's heroine's mother traumatizingly informed her of her attempts at amateur abortion, *and* of the 'realities' of womanhood – is not cast as a space where gender constraints fail to be imposed. I shall discuss Cardinal's depiction of the urban Maghrebian space below.

71. See Powrie, 'Reading for pleasure', p. 170.

72. On the key tenets of Kleinian psychoanalysis, see Mitchell, 'Introduction', in *The Selected Melanie Klein*.

73. See *Transfigurations*, pp. 1–49, especially pp. 1–4 and pp. 16–24.

74. For a summary of Cixous's views on this practice, see H. Cixous (1977), 'Entretien avec Françoise van Rossum-Guyon', *Revue des sciences humaines*, vol. 44, pp. 479–93, p. 485.

75. As Woodhull notes (cf. *Transfigurations*, p. 165), Cardinal's possibly ironic re-use/reversal of cultural stereotypes in fact involves a kind of valorization of them that 'leaves the structure of colonial domination in place, provisionally inverting its terms'. I shall return to this issue, and discuss it at length, below.

76. This guilt, evident in the opening segment of Chapter 6 of *Les Mots*, is doubtless intensified by the fact that the time with which Cardinal's text deals with was one that was especially strained in terms of *pied-noir*–Algerian relations.

77. See A. JanMohamed (1985), 'The Economy of Manichean Allegory: The Function of Racial Difference in Colonialist Literature', *Critical Inquiry*, vol. 12, pp. 59–85. In line with JanMohamed's work, Alain Ruscio (cf. *Le Credo de l'homme blanc*, p. 89) likewise notes the Manichaean nature of French colonialist discourse. JanMohamed's essay elaborates on different 'categories'

of colonialist literature and on their specific narrative workings; I shall focus here, however, on his assessment of its key structures.

78. JanMohamed, 'The Economy of Manichean Allegory', p. 63.

79. Ibid., pp. 62–3. We should note that the colonialist texts/discourse JanMohamed concentrates on in his essay relate to what he labels (cf. pp. 61–2) the 'dominant' phase of colonialism; that is to that period between Europe's conquest of its colonies and their independence.

80. For a discussion of female-authored colonial writing and its relation to colonialist literary paradigms, see Suzanne Chester (1992), 'Writing the Subject', in S. Smith and J. Watson (eds), *De/Colonizing the Subject: The Politics of Gender in Women's Autobiography*, Minneapolis, pp. 436–57. This critiques JanMohamed for failing to recognize the specificity of women's colonial textuality.

81. See *Transfigurations*, p. 165.

82. The work of Luce Irigaray, especially *Ethique de la différence sexuelle* (Paris, 1984), compares the female body to a space that, because it is built upon, penetrated and exploited by the male subject and has its specificity erased, is made by the patriarchal economy into a 'colonized' realm. For a discussion of this comparison, see Grosz, 'Women, *Chora*, Dwelling', in *space, time and perversion*, pp. 111–24.

—4—

Configuring the Clinic: Medical
Geographies in Guibert and Beauvoir

As I indicated in my Introduction to Chapter 3, in the texts addressed in the discussion that follows, medical space – the space of the diagnostic and therapeutic environment – is not only mapped, but is mapped in a manner that invokes issues of narrative and sexual politics and sexual/gender identity. The first of the narratives selected for dissection here is Guibert's *A l'ami qui ne m'a pas sauvé la vie*,[1] the opening volume of an AIDS-trilogy also comprising *Le Protocole compassionnel* (1991) and *Cytomégalovirus* (1992). The second is Beauvoir's (auto)biographical account of her mother's agony, *Une mort très douce*.[2] Published not long before Guibert's death, *A l'ami* at once constitutes a more easily identifiable instance of life-writing than the photo/autobiographical *L'Image fantôme* and embraces the 'disidentificatory' practice of autofictional self-representation far more radically than, for instance, Sartre's *Les Mots*.[3] *Une mort*, on the other hand, departs from the classic autobiographical model, in that it is other-oriented, but privileges at the same time a semi-documentary, memorialist style also in evidence in Beauvoir's earlier, more canonical *récits autobiographiques*. In reading these narratives, I shall seek to elucidate what each conveys about the medical environment, and about the (gendered) subject's experiences within it. Concomitantly, I will explore the ways in which *A l'ami* and *Une mort* can be viewed as spaces of resistance to the power dynamics of the medical arena, and as sites where practices of writing with/ towards the same-sex Other come into play.

Hervé Guibert's Medical Mirrors

In the history of the advent of disciplinary power elaborated in *Surveiller et punir* (SP) (1975),[4] Michel Foucault privileges the concept of the 'docile' – the product-ive, trained, publicly viable, pliable – body (SP, pp. 159–99/DP [trans.], pp. 135–69). And, in his dissection of the practices whereby the *corps docile* is produced and manipulated by the disciplinary society – practices that evaluate bodies and behaviours against Norms, impose performance-standards, correct non-conformity and attach individuals to identities – he highlights the regulatory role played by observation, spatial distribution and identificatory classification.[5] All these phenomena, Foucault's text affirms, are mutually implicated, and implicated in the exercise of a power centred in/on the individual, individualized body. Achieved via activities such as surveillance, normalizing judgement and the (medical) exam-ination, observation locates the individual in a field of compulsory visibility, exposing him to objectifying operations of knowledge and technologies of domina-tion (SP, pp. 200–27/DP, pp. 170–94).[6] Spatial distribution (the distribution of bodies in environments, and the disposition of environments themselves) organizes individuals so that they become optimally supervisable and useful, and enables masses to be carved up and controlled. Intrinsic in it are tactical partitioning and enclosure – modes of spatial and human organization that allot individuals to cellularized, codified places, defuse the threat the plurality poses and permit the 'deficient' (the sick, the mad, the delinquent) to be separated from the normal, measured, observed, and, eventually, reintegrated into the community of the produc-tive (SP, pp. 166–75, pp. 228–33/DP, pp. 141–9, pp. 195–200). Classification – an essential facet of disciplinary power, and one enabled by the observational examination and by spatial/human segmentation alike – is inextricably imbricated in procedures of identificatory individua(liza)tion, objectification and subjection. It works to differentiate and identify individuals, and to produce them as such, as correlative elements of *savoir* and *pouvoir*. The classificatory process involves techniques of codification, registration and taxonomic organization. It ranks subjects *vis-à-vis* the Norm (on a valid>invalid continuum), and forms them as entities possessed of particularized, value-laden identities (that can nonetheless be under-stood in terms of broader corpora of knowledge). It constitutes them as describable, analysable, knowable objects whose need for specific modalities of discipline can be quantified and acted on, and whose potential for manipulation, training and dominion is maximal (SP, pp. 212–27/DP, pp. 180–93).[7]

Grounded in a genealogical analysis of the eighteenth-century and its institutions, and focused on the relations of power and knowledge generated by the emergence of the disciplinary social order, *Surveiller et punir* could hardly be more different from *A l'ami qui ne m'a pas sauvé la vie* (ALA), the work of self-inscription under scrutiny in Section I of this chapter. Yet Guibert's AIDS narrative, in its transcription of its moribund narrator's relationship with Parisian medical spaces of the late twentieth century,[8] echoes sections of Foucault's 1975 essay so self-consciously as to function as a text that manifests and pursues a kind of mirror-connection with Foucault's exegesis of disciplinary practice. An intimate of Guibert's and a secondary player in various Guibertian writings, Foucault himself features promi-nently in *A l'ami*'s cast of characters, in the fictionalized and referentially ambiguous but, equally, in the 'condensed', recognizable, not to say hyper-identifiable guise of the HIV+ philosopher Muzil (a guise that readers, and even Guibert himself, were quick to dis-guise).[9] Foucault's 'presence' in Guibert's text and its (brief) iteration of 'Foucault/Muzil''s perspective on the grip institutional power exerts on the pliable, medicalized body (ALA, p. 32/TTF [trans.], pp. 23–4) dispose us to intuit the reflective status that *A l'ami* enjoys *vis-à-vis Surveiller et punir*, even though the latter *opus* is not, unlike Foucault's *Histoire de la sexualité*, extensively alluded to in *A l'ami* (ALA, p. 35/TTF, p. 26). I shall address the significance of *A l'ami*'s intertextual inflection below. First, though, I want to illuminate the Foucauldian foundation of Guibert's narrative treatment of the medical arena.

In the chronologically elusive account of Guibert's narrator's experiences during the 1980s offered in *A l'ami* – a text whose narrative 'present' begins in late 1988 and moves diaristically into the future, but whose broader structure eschews the developmental organization of canonical autobiography, commingling present-oriented and diversely-focused retrospective narrative segments[10] – two types of medical space are mapped. Deriving their salience from their relation to the point in time at which its narrator opts to seek formal confirmation of his seropositivity (January 1988), the medical environments of Guibert's *récit* can be qualified, broadly, as pre-diagnostic or HIV-functional. Although they increasingly become so, as its protagonist's illness progresses, the therapeutic loci charted in Guibert's account are not always as obviously institutional as the disciplinary locales evoked in *Surveiller et punir*. But the way in which both pre-diagnostic and HIV-oriented milieux are portrayed in *A l'ami* certainly coheres with Foucault's vision of power-knowledge and its disciplinary workings, mirroring, particularly, the emphasis that vision places on corrective training, surveillance, spatial disposition and individual-izing, hierarchical classification.[11] The Foucauldian aspect of Guibert's tale is in evidence throughout *A l'ami*. It is especially identifiable, however, in narrative tableaux (nos. 15–18) that follow those (5–14) in which the Foucault-figure of *A l'ami*, Muzil, enters the space of Guibert's story.

In the narrative segments of *A l'ami* in which pre-diagnostic medical topography features centrally (tableaux 15, 16, 17 and 25), it is mapped in a manner that is blackly humorous, as well as textbookly Foucauldian. These tableaux introduce us to the consulting rooms of two Parisian GPs, Drs Nocourt and Aron; the *cabinet* of a society homeopath, Dr Lérisson; and the acupuncture clinic at the Falguière hospital.[12] And, in recording Guibert's hero's adventures in these loci, they cast the contemporary medical environment as one where the individual who has not been relegated to the realm of the corporeally 'invalid' (by, for instance, the abjecting effects of a positive HIV-test result) is subjected, simultaneously, to the disciplinary force of the normative, classificatory gaze and to a degree of coercive correction reminiscent of that bodily *dressage* initiated, *Surveiller et punir* suggests, at the dawn of the classical age.

In its depiction, then, of the medical spaces its narrator encounters in the early 1980s, before his HIV-status is established, *A l'ami* is doubly indebted to its Foucauldian pre-text. On the one hand, as it presents them as milieux in which its protagonist is scrutinized and identified as renally malformed, 'spasmophilic', 'dysmorphophobic' and eminently in need of (re)normalization, *A l'ami* dramatizes *Surveiller et punir*'s account of the power-dynamics of the diagnostic examination. It echoes Foucault's thesis (evoked in Muzil's assessment of how the medicalized body, caught in the maw of the clinical mill, is disgorged as a number-coded lump of testable flesh (ALA, p. 32/TTF, pp. 23–4)) that the examinatory procedure 'makes each individual a 'case': [. . .] an object for a branch of knowledge and a hold for a branch of power' (DP, p. 191).[13] Concomitantly, as Guibert's *récit* renders its prediagnostic environments as spaces where his textual double confronts the homogenizing, correctional power of the Norm (cf. SP, p. 216/DP, p. 184), and encounters apparatuses and therapies (ALA, p. 44, p. 46, p. 49, p. 78/TTF, pp. 32–3, p.35, p. 37, p. 66) that mechanically manipulate the ailing body or perforate its skin, miming that mode of bodily inscription-correction imagined in Kafka's *In the Penal Settlement*,[14] *A l'ami* plunders the vision of the *corps docile* on which *Surveiller et punir*'s third part opens – a vision that casts the disciplined body as one that submits mechanistically to transformation, improvement and normalizing reintegration.

In transcribing the HIV-functional spaces its narrator is introduced into after he decides to go through with an AIDS-test (a test that proves positive), *A l'ami*'s tone and emphasis change: however, the manner in which these more institutional milieux are portrayed remains resolutely Foucauldian. The milieux in question include Paris's Claude-Bernard hospital (dedicated, by December 1988, solely to the care of AIDS patients) and the Institut Alfred-Fournier, formerly the site of research into VD. They are depicted in Guibert's narrative as establishments whose imbrication in processes of knowledge-generating surveillance and spatial segregation, construed by *Surveiller et punir* as equally power-imbued, is profound. At the same time, they are configured as loci that work to 'produce' Guibert's HIV+ hero – to visibilize and single him out – as a being whose relation to norms of healthiness and humanity is definitively flawed. In other words, they are constructed as environments whose workings and effects confirm Foucault's contention that, in a disciplinary order, certain types of individual are more thoroughly subjected to individualizing, identificatory, classifying mechanisms than others (SP, pp. 225–6/DP, pp. 192–3).

Surveillance and self-surveillance (construed by Foucault as no less an effect of power's policing aspect than surveillance itself) are presented in *A l'ami* as enduring features of its central character's dealings with doctors (ALA, p. 143/ TTF, p. 122). However, the kind of surveillance he encounters in the medical environments he finds himself in once his seropositivity is assessed is shown to be intensive. By emphasizing the enhanced, qualitatively different degree of observation his textual counterpart is exposed to in such spaces, and by casting it as research-oriented, Guibert proffers a vision of them consonant with the dissections of power/ knowledge contained in *Surveiller et punir*. The *hôpital Claude-Bernard*, for instance, is depicted as a place in which Guibert's protagonist's blood samples, ostensibly taken so that his T-cell count can be tested, are smartly dispatched to researchers to be experimentally 'transformed into gamma globulin, into the deactivated material of a vaccine that will save others after [his] death, or to be used to infect a lab monkey' (TTF, p. 41).[15] It is conceived as a 'public health institution', whose procedures are investigative rather than therapeutic, and as a cog within a system of state medical regulation and scrutiny whose puppet Guibert's hero becomes (ALA, pp. 58–60/TTF, pp. 47–8). In envisioning Claude-Bernard and the techniques of examination/observation practised there in these politically-inflected terms, Guibert's narrative strives unmistakably to echo Foucault's account of how disciplinary surveillance functions in 'laboratory' settings to constitute bodies of knowledge that nourish technologies of control. And it works, thereby, to endorse a key tenet of *Surveiller et punir* (cf. SP, pp. 218–19, pp. 237–9/DP, pp. 185–7, pp. 203–4).

As it maps the spatial situation of its HIV-functional medical environments, and the disposition of spaces and subjects within them, *A l'ami* maintains its Foucauldian tone. Disciplinary power, Foucault contends, requires spatial division or enclosure (SP, p. 166/DP, p. 141) in order to be deployed. Spatial cellularization allows environments to be rigorously segmented, rendering individuals controllable and useful. It functions to contain threats of epidemic and rebellion, to segregate the normal from the abnormal, and to create conditions in which delinquency can be studied, measured and used to extract *savoir*.[16] Historically, Foucault suggests, it was clearly in evidence in milieux such as the Rochefort naval hospital and the plague-stricken city, that hyper-segmented entity where the sick were involved in meticulous tactical partitioning yet, unlike the lepers of the medieval age, were kept within the communal group, undergoing endless inspection (SP, p. 169, pp. 228–33/DP, p. 144, pp. 195–200).

The cellularization of space/subjects is more than manifest in *A l'ami*'s depictions of the clinical milieux to which its narrator and his fellow PWAs are exposed once their seropositivity is verified. Consistently, these milieux – the clinic where Guibert's hero and his lover, Jules, receive formal confirmation of their HIV+ status (ALA, p. 156/TTF, p. 133); the Pitié-Salpêtrière hospital where Muzil is taken to die (ALA, p. 108, p. 113/TTF, p. 92, p. 95); the *hôpital Claude-Bernard* (ALA, pp. 51–60/TTF, pp. 40–49) – are revealed as partitioned, partitioning loci. They are cast as segmented spaces where the AIDS-victim enters so many *cellules*, *cabines*, specially dedicated *pavillons barricadés* and *boxes de ponction du sang* that isolate him from the community of the well whilst keeping him in proximity to it, expose him to codifying operations of knowledge/research, and/or regulate and contain the contagion – and the medical challenge – intrinsic in his condition. In particular, Claude-Bernard (more specifically, its Chantemesse pavilion, the hospital's 'sole illuminated cell still humming behind its frosted glass' TTF, p. 45)[17] is represented as emblematic of Foucault's conception of the disciplined, cellularizing environment. Located in Paris but situated on its periphery (ALA, pp. 54–5/TTF, pp. 43–5), and dedicated to the observation of only one category of disease (ALA, pp. 52–6), its cellular, segregating situation resonates powerfully with *Surveiller et punir*'s accounts of spatial and human disciplinary – and identificatory – organization.

Throughout *A l'ami*, Guibert portrays his HIV+ narrator/protagonist as a being who, in the institutional spatial 'cells' he is obliged to visit post-diagnostically or by dint of his encounters with them, is singled out as marginal to the community of the normal and is visibilized and codified as a defective denizen of the fringe.[18] Guibert's rendition of the visibilization of the PWA (cf. ALA, pp. 54–5, p. 56, p. 57, p. 154/TTF, pp. 43–4, p. 45, p. 46, p. 130) reaches its apogee in his account of how, in the *pavillon Chantemesse*, his textual counterpart is compelled to acknowledge the wholly appropriate nature of his personal presence within an establishment reserved solely for AIDS patients, by laying claim, publicly and 'confessionally', to his name: 'Three nurses were [. . .] flipping frenetically through the pages of a record book, calling out the names written there, and then they called out mine, but there's a stage in this sickness when keeping it secret just doesn't matter any more, it even becomes hateful and burdensome' (TTF, p. 46).[19]

Guibert's description of this painful episode presents his textual double as a subject whose post-diagnostic insertions into the power-saturated domain of medicine involve him in a process whereby he must not only submit to an individuating classification that isolates and constructs him as an (assessable, codifiable) individual, by isolating him as an individual 'instance' of seronormative transgression, but must himself *partake* in that classification, performatively, by means of an act of constrained avowal or open self-identification/individualization that is far more definitively identifying than the codifications imposed upon him, externally and pre-diagnostically, by Drs Nocourt, Aron and Lérisson. And it represents the medical realm inhabited by the AIDS-sufferer – i.e., by the patient gripped by a condition that itself eludes classification – as one in which the self-codifying, self-identificatory, self-individualizing act is unavoidable.[20] In so doing, Guibert's narrative engages twice over with Foucault's take on the workings of power. On the one hand, it upholds the proposition proffered in *Surveiller et punir* that, under a disciplinary régime and in its environments, individua(liza)tion works in a 'descendingly' intensifying manner, so that the unhealthy patient is more strongly individualized than the healthy man, the madman and the delinquent more individualized than the normal/non-delinquent, etc. (SP, p. 226/DP, p. 193). Concomitantly, *A l'ami* endorses the argument elaborated by Foucault in *La Volonté de savoir* (VDS) (1976) that avowal, or self-decipherment/classification, is inscribed at the heart of procedures of individualization by power and its agents (VDS, pp. 78–9/HOSI [trans.], pp. 58–9).[21]

In his 'De la métastase au métatexte', in the context of a discussion of the debt that Guibert's AIDS-writing may or may not have owed to Foucault's reflections on authorship, Ralph Sarkonak suggests that it is productive to view the work of Guibert and Foucault as including texts that interpellate each other mutually, rather than to qualify elements of Guibert's *oeuvre* as Foucauldian 'borrowings'.[22] Analogously, in 'Cippus: Guibert', Lawrence Schehr affirms that while the reader might elect to construct a critical scenario in which 'the matters Foucault discusses function as interpretemes' for *A l'ami*, it is ultimately unnecessary to do so, because Guibert's story itself, proffering its own form of 'philosophical' discourse, 'tells us all we need to know'.[23] These (convincingly argued) contentions notwithstanding, and by virtue, especially, of its diverse configurations of medical loci and their disciplinary dynamics, I wish, here, to situate Guibert's first AIDS narrative 'proper'[24] as a work that not only reproduces facets of the analysis offered in *Surveiller et punir*, but does so in such a way as to leave the reader in no doubt as to its deliberately Foucauldian hue.

This, of course, poses the question of why, in a text in which Foucault figures in a 'borrowed' guise, Guibert chooses to borrow from (a key element within) Foucault's theoretical corpus quite so extensively and specularly. The 'mirror-bond' that connects Guibert's *A l'ami* – specifically, its map of medical geography – to Foucault's seminal dissection of discipline and its mechanisms can be understood in a number of ways. We may construe it simply as a gesture of homage to a philosopher who, Guibert states in an interview given in March 1990, was his *maître* as well as his close friend.[25] Equally, we can interpret *A l'ami*'s Foucauldian aspect as incorporating a form of apology to the profoundly private individual who shared its author's thanatological fate (cf. ALA, p. 107/TTF, p. 91), whose own death foretold it, and who, critics have claimed, would have been shocked, as French readers were shocked, by the exposures and betrayals woven into *A l'ami*'s discussions of his fictionalized-but-identifiable life and demise.[26] In this discussion, however, I want to work with the notion that if, in *A l'ami*, Guibert privileges a vision of medical topography that chimes with Foucault's exegesis of disciplinary power/knowledge, this is in part at least a function of the fact that (a tiny aspect of) Foucault's own dream of medical space – as it is creatively refashioned in Guibert's AIDS-text, via an observation of Muzil's – holds a reflexive clue to the resistance *A l'ami* mounts against the power-saturated practices its narrator is subjected to in the medical realm. In the section of this chapter that follows, I shall engage with this notion at some length, addressing three key questions. These are: (i) What kind of resistance inheres in Guibert's narrative? (ii) How does it relate to the 'Foucauldian' *vorstellung* of the medical environment that that narrative proffers? and (iii) What type of dynamic prevails between the Guibertian–Foucauldian and 'Foucauldian'–Muzilian visions of medical space in evidence in *A l'ami*?

In 'Autobiographie/vérité/psychanalyse' and 'L'Autofiction, un genre pas sérieux', essays united by a common will to qualify *autofiction* as a narrative mode that flags itself as fictional whilst featuring a first-person narrator/protagonist possessed of a name and stock of life-experiences identical to those of its author, Serge Doubrovsky and Marie Darrieussecq offer parallel perceptions of auto-fictional practice. Doubrovsky defines the narrative activity whose label he coined as involving the production of a story that, 'whatever the accumulation of referential details and whatever their accuracy, has never "taken place" in "reality", whose only real situation is the discourse in which it operates', and that constitutes the 'fiction that I have decided, as a writer, to make of myself and for myself'.[27] Likewise, he construes the self-truth that *autofiction* produces not as a carbon-copy of its author's existential 'meaning' – a meaning that 'doesn't exist anywhere; doesn't exist' – but rather as an artificial graft (*implant fictif*) that, having engendered it discursively, the author assumes.[28] Pursuing the implications of Doubrovsky's observations, Darrieussecq casts *autofiction* as a narrative form that works at once, and openly, with the act of enunciating the real/true that governs the autobiographical enterprise and with the impossibilities intrinsic therein, in order to generate definitively 'undecidable' texts that simultaneously, and in contrast to 'classic' autobiographical works, ask to be believed and to be not believed, to be taken 'seriously' and to be read as 'feigned' self-representations.[29]

Darrieussecq's and Doubrovsky's analyses illuminate the situation in which readers of autofictional narratives must find themselves. When we read an auto-biography of the canonical type (Rousseau's *Confessions*, for instance), we are confronted, as Darrieussecq affirms, with the declaration/demand 'here is the sincerely recounted story of myself and my life, please accept it as faithful and veracious'.[30] Concomitantly – that is, guided by the appeal to belief and the claim to visibilizing truthfulness that a work of this kind presents – we are encouraged to partake, as readers, in a 'disciplinary' process of individualizing identification whose target is the autobiographical author. It is almost impossible, when reading 'classic' autobiography, not to engage, however unwillingly/unwittingly, in a mode of reading whereby we read in such a way as to (endeavour to) produce, in an identificatory, 'classifying' manner, an image of the individual reality of the writer behind the text. This is because, as instances of a self-identificatory discourse predicated on an avowal of sincerity and truthfulness, canonical autobiographies both indulge in the confessional, self-deciphering activity that Foucault construes as compelled by power, and constitute us as conduits of power: that is, as textual receivers who react to their confessional aspect, or 'truth effect', by evaluating and individuating – by attaching, in other words, a specific identity to – the authorial subject (object) their narrative weave 'visibilizes'.[31]

Autofiction does not, however, generate an analogous mode of reader-response. The autofictional text, as Doubrovsky and, especially, Darrieussecq assert, is a text that has deliberate, overt recourse to a recognizable ambiguity centred in the truth–falsehood relation.[32] Located in the interval between fictional and (self-)

referential, 'objective' writing,[33] the autofictional *opus* preserves authorial identity, because it protects the name in which that identity is cradled, yet reinvents it, precluding identitarian certainty (or, at least, declining openly to invite it). The autofictional work, then, is a generically 'bastard' narrative artefact that, in contrast to the classically autobiographical confessional *récit*, refuses to incite or allow us to exploit it in order to seek definitively to know, to decipher the existential 'truth' about, to pin down the particuliarity of, and thus to individualize (and objectify), its 'real-life' creator. *Autofiction*, in short, is a narrative practice whose immersion in generic undecidability shields its practioners from the identifying, knowledge-seeking, would-be-classificatory, power-imbued lectorial gaze. It constitutes an ultimately 'disidentificatory' – and hence paradoxical – self-referential narrative form that denies the reader the opportunity to indulge, in disciplinary mode, in what Darrieussecq describes as the *plaisir identificateur*.[34]

Through the self-designatory signals it emits, *A l'ami* displays a marked reluct-ance definitively to establish the Guibertian self and self-history it presents us with as either wholly veracious or purely fictional – a reluctance that, Darrieussecq claims, is the hallmark both of the autofictional act and of the writing of Guibert's postdiagnostic maturity.[35] Guibert's text introduces us, on the one hand, to a narrator/protagonist whose name is given, belatedly and somewhat obliquely, as 'Hervé Guibert' (ALA, p. 73/TTF, pp. 60–1) and whose writing career (ALA, p. 35/TTF, p. 26), relationships and HIV-status we can equate with Guibert's own. In so doing, *A l'ami* associates itself with the autobiographical, referential, truth-telling discurs-ive process. But, simultaneously, via its generic peritextual designation (*roman*),[36] it posits/dereferentializes 'Hervé Guibert' as a literary signifier whose reality is sited in the fictional, thus undercutting its own status as an exercise in truthful life-writing. Its antiautobiographical, generically subversive fictionalization of 'Hervé Guibert' is endorsed in the back-cover blurb of its sequel, *Le Protocole com-passionnel*,[37] a paratextual fragment in which Guibert (H.G.) tells us that, in *Le Protocole*, we will meet the same 'personnages' as in *A l'ami*, notably one 'Hervé Guibert, écrivain malade du sida'.[38]

Intradiegetically, too, *A l'ami* destabilizes the referential, biographical standing of 'Hervé Guibert', destabilizing its own relationship to the truth-telling, mimetic autobiographical enterprise. It places him at the centre of a circle of friends, lovers and relatives that we can qualify as neither squarely located in, nor entirely dislo-cated from, the real. (Some of its members – Great Aunts Louise and Suzanne – can be read referentially, inasmuch as *A l'ami* accords them names identical to those possessed by personae in texts within Guibert's corpus (*Mes Parents*, *Cytomégalovirus*) that are not flagged as fictions.[39] Others, though, (Jules, Berthe, Muzil) are inserted into the 'fictional' by virtue of the fact that Guibert's narrative denies them both the appellations (T., C., M.) his overtly non-fictional life-writings protectively allot to textual players who appear to be their homologues *and* the nominal identities we can calque onto the latter.)[40] Similarly, *A l'ami* casts 'Hervé Guibert' as the author of published novels (ALA, p. 22/TTF, p. 13) that certainly resemble those extant works Guibert dedicated to Foucault, his neighbour and his *ami mort*, but that, dedicated as they are revealed to be to an imaginary-but-decipherable individual named 'Muzil', must also be recognized as no less imbricated in a (con)fusion of the real/invented than their creator.[41]

Finally, Guibert's narrative abstracts 'Hervé Guibert' from the order of (pure) reference by constituting him the architect of an AIDS-narrative – a book whose construction is a key focus of *A l'ami* – that clearly enjoys a connection with Guibert's own, real *sidaautofiction*, *A l'ami*, but that, unlike Guibert's *A l'ami*, would seem to be motivated, predominantly, by the confessional, truth-telling impulse (cf. ALA, p. 15, p. 264/TTF, p. 7, p. 228). (When we read the opening, diaristic sections of *A l'ami*, which include the statement 'On this twenty-sixth day of December, 1988, as I begin this book' (TTF, p. 2),[42] we initially assume that 'Hervé Guibert''s book *is A l'ami*, or is consubstantial with it. As we read on, however, encountering pointers to divergences between 'Hervé Guibert's' narratively-evoked, self-revelatory *récit d'aveu* and Guibert's self-dereferentializing, concrete equivalent (the former, for instance, is recorded as complete in tableau 78 of *A l'ami*'s 100 segments, though its completion is called into doubt in tableau 94), our readiness simply to equate book and book – and to identify, unproblematically, their authors – gradually and inevitably diminishes.)[43]

Refusing as it does to offer us an autoreferential tale that we can securely anchor in the factual/biographical/existential, *A l'ami* situates itself as a work of Guibertian self-inscription *and* self-*deinscription* in which the self of the real is textually 'treated' and reborn in the realm of fiction. It situates itself as a work that does not evacuate referential material, but works with it and reworks it in order to generate a story – a self-history – whose relation to the act of veridical self-representation is as free as it could possibly be within the confines of a narrative whose author and narrator are onomastically identified. And it situates itself, above all, as a powerfully *resistant* text. By virtue of its unwillingness to posit itself as a 'case' of transparent, (wholly) truthful, self-deciphering autobiographical writing,[44] *A l'ami* deters its readers from using its contents to subject with any certainty its author Hervé Guibert to the kind of objectifying, evaluative scrutiny[45] that would construct and produce him as an individual, judgeable *cas*, possessed of identifiable, particu-larized features open to knowledge and qualificatory assessment. In devisibilizing his existential reality, by means of its generic imbrication in autofictional practice and the 'assertively ambiguous' discourse of selfhood it engenders,[46] Guibert's text protects him from processes of individualizing, identificatory classification that operate in the lectorial sphere, and are cast in *A l'ami*'s pre-text *Surveiller et punir* as controlling mechanisms whereby the subject is inserted (*qua* judged, described, measured object) into the realm of discipline. In other words, *A l'ami*'s status as a 'texte indécidable en bloc' (Darrieussecq's term)[47] preserves its creator against a practice of readerly power that is precisely that to which his autofictional counterpart 'Hervé Guibert' is exposed in all the medical spaces, pre-diagnostic and HIV-functional, mapped within *A l'ami*: spaces in which he is 'read', identified, fabricated and forced to 'produce' himself as a deficient individual on whose 'abject' body scientific knowledge/power can work. It undermines an objectifying modality of discipline that Hervé Guibert himself would undoubtedly have encountered, as an HIV+ subject, in the real.

In sum, the resistance that Guibert's *autofiction* proffers, by dint of its play with self-inscription/self-deinscription, is reader-related. It involves a resistance to the disciplinary function of identificatory, evaluative individualization – a function at stake in autobiographical reading and medical diagnosis alike – and reminds us of that resistance to (homo)sexual codification woven into *L'Image fantôme*. It coheres with Foucauldian notions of what resistance to power entails in the same way that Guibert's treatment of medical space coheres with Foucault's genealogical conception of discipline and its technologies.[48] The narratively- and generically-sited resistance that Guibert's *sidaautofiction* presents turns on a textual practice of authorial self-occlusion that parallels that favoured by the Foucault-figure of *A l'ami*, Muzil (ALA, p. 26/TTF, p. 18).[49] This practice, which we can read as a primary facet of Guibert's self-representational project, is internally mirrored in *A l'ami*, in a series of reflexive *mises-en-abyme* that encapsulate and signal the autodisidentifying impulse behind Guibert's tale. What is more, the majority of *A l'ami*'s microcosmic mirror-fragments are centred around phenomena related to the medical sphere, or to the writings/pronouncements of 'Foucault/Muzil', or both.

A l'ami includes (at least) four key textual *mises-en-abyme*.[50] It incorporates, in other words, four diegetic elements in which the resistant, self-(de)scriptive, disidentificatory path that Guibert pursues within it – a path not pursued, apparently, by his narratorial double, in the 'confessional' AIDS-narrative that tableaux 2–78 of *A l'ami* record him as writing – is metaphorically emblematized and identified. One such is a segment of tableau 18 that recounts 'Hervé Guibert's' sighting, in the cellular, 'visibilizing' environment of Claude-Bernard, of a speeding, helmeted biker, whose 'unidentifiable face, like that of a fencer' (TTF, p. 48)[51] defies detection and observation. Another derives from a set of references to texts produced by 'Foucault/Muzil' – his pseudonymically-signed article on criticism (ALA, p. 26/ TTF, p. 18); his unsigned will (ALA, p. 115–16/TTF, p. 97) – in which identity is rendered elusive.[52] A third is generated by *A l'ami*'s evocation of the AIDS virus itself, and the decoy operation it effects – an operation that contrives to mask its core, and to protect it against discovery/isolation by the body's immune system (ALA, p. 276/TTF, p. 239).[53]

Each of the above-mentioned features of *A l'ami* symbolically illuminates the anti-identificatory strategy built into its self-inscriptive/deinscriptive narrative fabric.

But the central *mise-en-abyme* that Guibert's *sidaautofiction* includes and exploits in order to point this resistant strategy up is locatable in a section of tableau 9 in which 'Foucault/Muzil' imagines what an 'identity change' death-clinic might be like. This narrative fragment records Muzil's dream of perfect, identity-masking medical-therapeutic space. And it offers, I would argue, significant clues to the self-metamorphotic 'slippage' Guibert realizes inside the devisibilizing autofictional space of *A l'ami*, as well as to the resistance to (readerly, disciplinary) processes of individualizing detection, identification and evaluation that that slippage produces and permits:

> Once Dr. Nacier had left, [Muzil] said to me, 'This is what I told your little chum: that nursing home of his, it shouldn't be a place where people go to die, but a place where they pretend to die. Everything there [. . .] would all be just camouflage for the real mystery, because there'd be a little door hidden away in a corner of the clinic [. . .], and to the torpid melody of a hypodermic nirvana, you'd secretly slip behind [a] painting, and presto, you'd vanish, quite dead in the eyes of the world, since no [witness] would see you reappear on the other side of the wall, in the alley, with no baggage, no name, no nothing, forced to invent a new identity for yourself' (TTF, pp. 16–17).[54]

This spatially-oriented passage can be taken to pick up, in a kaleidoscopically allusive fashion, on the identitarian veiling that autofictional writing operates, and on its 'protective' effects. It proposes a vision of clinical space focused on a clinical institution that facilitates an identity-shift *and* safeguards its perpetrator from the isolating gaze of the Other. The vision that it proffers metaphorizes and replicates both the identity-mutations that *autofiction* allows, and the manner in which autofictional narrative screens its author-subject against readerly interpretation/ judgement and 'fixative' identification. Hence, it may be deemed to relate, as an emblematic *mise-en-abyme*, to *A l'ami* as a self-reinventive, 'resistant' narrative whole. Additionally, however, by virtue of its clinical spatial focus and its 'Foucauldian' status (bestowed by the fact that it issues from the mouth of Muzil, Foucault's fictional/identifiable 'double'), the key textual mirror-segment cited above also enjoys a mirror-connection with those elements of Guibert's text in which medical space is plotted in a Foucauldian fashion. *A l'ami* establishes, in other words, a specular, circular, complementary relation between, on the one hand, the 'Foucauldian'/Muzilian, clinical *mise-en-abyme* that features in its ninth tableau as an indicator of the power-related resistance it incorporates and, on the other, its disseminated Foucauldian mapping of the medical milieu. Further, the reflexivity on which this latter relation hinges partakes of a mirror-paradigm that likewise marks multiple aspects of Guibert's *autofiction*,[55] ensuring that *A l'ami* works as a narrative construct whose textual personae (Jules/Hervé; Marine/Hervé; Thomas Bernhard/Hervé; Muzil/Hervé; Muzil/Bill) and narrative segments (notably, its opening, 'Muzil' section and its closing, 'Bill' phase)[56] emerge as either paralleled/ identifiable or antithetical/opposed.

The central role that mirroring is granted in *A l'ami*, the primary mirror/emblem-function that Guibert's text accords to the 'Foucauldian'/Muzilian vision of clinical space that it includes, and the reflexive connection that links that vision to Guibert's broader, Foucauldian 'take' on the medical realm help us to recontextualize Guibert's decision to reflect Foucauldian theoretical insights (specifically, those rendered by *Surveiller et punir*) in his narrative elaborations of medical geography. These phenomena, taken in conjunction, allow us to draw two inferences with regard to *A l'ami*. The first is that if Guibert chooses to map medical space in a Foucauldian manner, inside a text that also employs a 'Foucauldian' conception of the ideal clinic as a key internal metaphor, this may well be because he seeks to remain true to, or enhance, the 'mirror logic' that generally inflects his *autofiction*. The second is that if he opts to draw as extensively as he does, in his depictions of medical loci, on Foucauldian conceptualizations of the disciplinary environment, this is conceivably because he seeks actively, by directing our attention towards its primary, 'Foucauldian' *mise-en-abyme* and the signifying signals sited in it, to encourage us to read *A l'ami* as a 'resistant' *opus*.

Confronted with *A l'ami*'s explicitly Foucauldian treatment of the power-imbued medical domain, and aware of the 'treated' role that Foucault plays within its pages, the reader instinctively understands as significant and takes heed of the 'Foucauldian'/Muzilian comments regarding the medical arena it likewise contains – notably, those observations relating to the 'identity change' institution offered in tableau 9. Once focused on them, provided that s/he reads perceptively, with a sense of what Guibert's narrative says about power's identificatory impact, the reader stands every chance of recognizing the pointers to the disidentificatory stakes behind Guibert's autofictional project that these observations vehicle, and of consolidating an awareness of the power-related resistance they confirm as intrinsic in *A l'ami*. In other words, *A l'ami*'s determinedly Foucauldian delineation of the disciplinary medical milieu can be taken to function as a clue to reading, and as a textual stratum that helps to alert us to what, as an exercise in self-(de)representation, Guibert's *autofiction* is 'doing'. By virtue of its account of the workings of (medical) power, and by virtue, especially, of the way in which its Foucauldian slant compels our readerly antennae towards that key 'Foucauldian' fragment of Guibert's text where *A l'ami*'s anti-identificatory aspect is clinically emblematized/identified for the reader, this stratum works as a kind of lectorial indicator. And it must, I would suggest, be understood as such, rather than simply as a narrative element in which Guibert makes intertextually manifest his personal loyalty and indebtedness to his *maître* Michel Foucault.

This is not to say that Guibert's recourse to a Foucauldian perspective, or his elaboration of a 'doubling' dynamic that 'twins' his own Foucault-inspired construction of the (disciplinary) medical realm with a textually-emblematic 'Foucauldian' conception of (liberatory) therapeutic space, are devoid of personal investment. It would be a mistake, certainly, to regard *A l'ami*'s inclusion of the latter phenomenon – which turns on a reflexivity grounded in likeness *and* contrast – merely as a function of the narrative mirror-games that Guibert's *opus*, like much experimental fiction, insistently plays. The dynamic in question only exists because Guibert takes a piece of *authentic* Foucauldian discourse, 'Un plaisir si simple' (an account of Japanese love hotels that recasts them as suicide-sites where gay men elude identitarian determination), turns its vision of (ideal) space into a facet of Foucault's vision of clinical spatiality by weaving a medicalized version of it into comments made by a figure we unfailingly read as Foucault-in-disguise, and affords it a textual 'reflection'/counterpoint by incorporating into *A l'ami* his own, narratively-evolved Foucauldian discursification of the medical environment.[57] Guibert's spatially-focused Foucauldian narrative mirror-dynamic is, in other words, both painstakingly and artificially engineered. This aspect of it is telling. It suggests that one of the things that Guibert works to do in *A l'ami* is to produce a specular connection between himself and his (fictionally refashioned) mentor that does not derive simply from sexual sameness or from the mortal, seropositive situation in which he and Foucault found themselves, but is born instead out of a process of discursive paralleling – a process that is itself born out of Guibert's conjunction of his personal-but-Foucault-indebted discourse on/of medical space and a clinical vision that is not properly Foucauldian but is remade as such in Guibert's alchemical text.

In his essay 'Une entreprise qui n'eut jamais d'exemple . . .', Raymond Bellour speaks movingly of the 'twin souls' union Guibert and Foucault enjoyed in the real, before the latter's death.[58] In elaborating his medical/spatial 'doubling' dynamic, within his autofictional *récit*, Guibert certainly shores up, *post mortem*, this lost existential relation (Foucault died a half-decade before *A l'ami* was published). Simultaneously, though, by creating a narrative phenomenon that brings himself and his philosophical *ami* together as participants in a discursive encounter,[59] he also distances it from paradigms of male same-sex relationality that construe that relationality as grounded in passive, self-fixated, specular narcissism or as predicated on a shared pathology.[60] The mirror-bond that Guibert establishes between his own, Foucauldian map of medical space and the (alternative) 'Foucauldian' dream of the clinical environment he also integrates into *A l'ami*, like his account of the parallel paths their common seropositivity compels 'Hervé Guibert' and 'Foucault/Muzil' to follow, buys, indubitably, into an economy of self–other reflexivity. On one level, moreover, the specularity it evinces invokes that static, imaginary specularity that the heterosexual and psychoanalytic imaginations detect and deplore in gay intersubjectivity. But at the same time, the discursively-sited, complementary reflexivity on which Guibert's carefully crafted medical/spatial narrative dynamic turns is of a quite different order from the passive, entrapping, undifferentiated reflexivity that heterosexual culture pathologizingly construes as the hallmark of gay self–other relations. And we can read its difference as sexually/politically significant.

In his polemical discussion of gay activism in the face of AIDS, 'The Mirror and the Tank', Lee Edelman suggests that, confronted with heterosexist constructions that stigmatize gayness as a specular, imaginary, ultimately lethal modality of self-investment and stigmatize gay 'imaginary intersubjectivity' as AIDS's root cause, it is vital for those individuals who are and invest in gay people not to leave the mirror behind. Rather, Edelman affirms, it is necessary and expedient to foreground mirrors, mirror-paradigms and mirror-relations that are politically and personally powerful and constructive.[61] This, I would argue, is what Guibert may be deemed to do in *A l'ami*. His narrative mirror-play with parallel, different-but-complementary medical/spatial visions implies that, faced with the culturally sanctioned option of figuring himself (*qua* 'Hervé Guibert') and Foucault (*qua* 'Muzil') as doubles or mirror-selves whose connection rests uniquely – and predictably – on seropositive and sexual identifiability, he elects also to privilege a different, less obvious intersubjective filiation: one that does not deny a specular tie between himself and his mourned HIV+ *maître*, but allows it not (just) to be (read as) 'imaginary', 'narcissistic' or entrenched in diseased mortality.

In *A l'ami*, then, as he plays with narrative articulations of medical space, Guibert does not simply focus solipsistically on his individual experiences of medicalization and incipient mortality. He also writes with and towards the (dead, male) Other, engendering a discursive 'communion' – one, admittedly, that is solely his own creation – that we can view as operating outside the imaginary sphere. In *Une mort très douce*, a much more overtly other-oriented, biographical/autobiographical *opus*, Simone de Beauvoir pursues a not dissimilar writerly course.[62] In so doing, however, I shall suggest in what follows, she unseals an imaginary self–other space pathologized and refused elsewhere in her autobiographical corpus: a space whose topography is always traceable in female-authored renditions of mother–daughter relationality.[63]

Beauvoir's Maternal/Medical Mappings

In contrast to *A l'ami*, *Une mort très douce* (MTD) elaborates a clinical geography centred on a single therapeutic milieu – the private Parisian *clinique de luxe* where Beauvoir's mother Françoise is taken with a fractured femur, where her intestinal cancer is diagnosed and operated on, and where she dies, some thirty days later.[64] Moreover, in delineating this environment (characterized, as Nancy Miller contends, by a 'bizarrely Aristotelian unity of place'),[65] Beauvoir's text is less concerned with the disciplinary dimension of the medical milieu (a prominent focus of Guibert's

AIDS-writing) than with the body – more precisely, the bodies – that medical power/ space brings into being.

Her account of her mother's clinical peripeteia introduces us to two key types of body, both of which can be designated as 'docile': that is, as open to external manipulation and regulation, to transformation and subjection and to normative constraint. Both of these narratively-inscribed bodies are located in the physical, declining body of Françoise de Beauvoir, and both are presented as 'produced' in the clinical institution where Françoise's agony plays itself out (itself depicted, in Foucauldian mode, as a spatial 'cell' that imposes identifications and identities, and compels its denizens to assume an ethos consonant with them).[66] The first of the bodies in question, like a number of the bodies profiled in *A l'ami*, is a pliable, 'medicalized' body that manifests its docility by dutifully refusing to die and by offering up its moribund flesh to its doctors' investigative manipulations. The second – which interests me especially here – is a particular kind of female, aged, docile body: one that obediently recognizes its failure to remain within the realm of female bodily (re)productivity and viability and performs itself, accordingly, as 'redundant'.[67]

Beauvoir's memoir, or *récit-reportage*,[68] is divided into eight unnumbered chapters. These give rise to a deeply moving four-part text that documents, cathartic-ally but not unclinically, her mother's accident, operation and diagnosis (Chapter 1); the pre-history of Françoise's largely unsatisfactory life (Chapter 2); the stations of her descent into death (Chapters 3 and 4); and its aftermath (Chapters 5–8). In its third and fourth chapters, especially, *Une mort* proffers a bleak vision of the *clinique C.* as a place where the ailing body comes to function as a live-but-failing fleshly object, on which medical knowledge/power – embodied in Dr. N., a specialist 'infatuated with technique' (VED [trans.], p. 46)[69] – can freely exercise itself, in pursuit of 'therapeutic' triumphs (MTD, pp. 42–3, 64, 73, 108/VED, pp. 27, 40, 46, 67). It maps the medical environment it illuminates as an increasingly segrega-tional, cellularized *mouroir* where 'flawed' bodies are preserved beyond their natural timespan (MTD, pp. 64, 108, 118/VED, pp. 40, 67, 73) – as reprieved corpses, living dead and ghouls sucking at life (MTD, p. 28, p. 103, p. 110/VED, p. 19, p. 64, p. 68) – by surgical procedures and mechanical apparatuses destined to further or abet the operations of medical know-how. And it constructs the clinic as a site where the delinquent, declining bodily entity is compelled to envision itself and play itself out as moribund, undead and abject:

> And I said to her 'You don't have to bother about a bed-pan. They will change the sheets – there's no sort of difficulty about it.' 'Yes,' [my mother] replied. And with a frown and a look of determination on her face she said, as though she were uttering a challenge, 'The dead certainly do it in their beds.' This took me aback. [. . .] Maman, who had lived a life bristling with proud sensitivities, felt no shame. In this prim and

spiritualistic woman it was also a form of courage to take on our animality with so much decision (VED, p. 48).[70]

The inscription of medical space as a realm of technico-scientific 'conquest' and imposed abjection included in *Une mort*'s central parts is extremely poignant; it is by no means, though, unpredictable. More individualized and unexpected, however, is the account *Une mort* offers of the medical realm as a space of geronto-logical gender-regulation. In its first chapter, particularly, Beauvoir's *récit* represents the *clinique C.* as a place where the aged female body is construed and constructed as a body that is less than wholly viable/valuable (because 'functionless', and in (re)productive atrophy),[71] and as a body that must, with a *docilité désolée* (MTD, p. 38/VED, p. 25), publicly acknowledge itself as outworn. The opening section of Beauvoir's text presents Françoise's hospital habitat as one in which her medical-ized body, as needy as a neonate's and as desiccated as a cadaver's, is openly reduced to a 'remnant' (*dépouille*) and to a shrivelled, wizened piece of vine (MTD, pp. 27, 34, 39/VED, pp. 18, 23, 25). This segment of *Une mort*, in other words, configures Françoise's clinical asylum as a site where her body is 'visibilized' in counterpoint to, and as the ('useless') antithesis of, that healthy, fecund, alimentary female (re)productive body that disciplinary patriarchy and its reproductive tech-nologists normatively valorize and cultivate in the interests of species-productivity.[72]

Concomitantly, Chapter 1 of Beauvoir's narrative conveys the inciting role that the clinic and its clinicians play, its health-farm aspect notwithstanding (MTD, p. 18/VED, p. 13), in Françoise's fabrication as a 'redundant' embodied/gendered subject. It does so, notably, in its rendition of the denigratory, identificatory fashion in which Françoise's doctors – cast as 'judges' in whom sexism and ageism combine – read her formatively and relegatingly as an ill-kempt old woman and an elderly potterer, capable only of producing old-lady food-treats-for-one and of pursuing her own, purposeless '*petite* vie' (MTD, p. 29/VED, pp. 19–20).

Finally, Beauvoir's memoir's *incipit* signals how her mother's new, medical environment compels her to comport and codify herself in a manner consonant with the bodily (re)productive non-viability it helps to establish as her 'ethos' and her lot. In other words, *Une mort*'s introductory section posits the *clinique C.* as a disciplinary, 'docilizing' locale where the aged female post-menopausal body is made actively and obediently to act in accordance with its gendered 'truth' (bestowed by normative, value-laden cultural criteria of female procreative utility).[73] *Une mort* evokes the docile twilight gender-identity performance into which Françoise is impelled by (her admission to) the clinic – and, especially, by Dr N., whose hostile stance on abortion marks him out as a prime agent of gender-regulation (MTD, p. 113/VED, p. 70) – in two ways. First, it spotlights her inhabitual readiness to designate herself, overtly, as a *vieille femme* who must abandon all pretensions to youthfulness and usefulness (MTD, pp. 23–4/VED, p. 16). (In so doing, we should note, Beauvoir's text stages a classic instance of how the subject beholden to discipline polices him/herself against performance-standards and norms of functionality and reports on his/her deviations from them.)[74] Secondly, and more shockingly, *Une mort* charts Françoise's uncharacteristic willingness to put herself on display as a non-fecund female body whose potential for reproductive, fruitful productivity is long gone:

> The physiotherapist came to Maman's bed, turned down the sheet and took hold of her left leg: Maman had an open hospital nightdress on and she did not mind that her wrinkled belly, criss-crossed with tiny lines, and her bald pubis showed. 'I no longer have any sort of shame,' she observed in a surprised voice (VED, p. 18).[75]

The vision of the obsolescent, elderly female body that dutifully 'performs' its own non-viability with which *Une mort très douce*'s first chapter presents us is unsettling. It unsettles its author/narrator Beauvoir, who records her own inability to confront it: 'I turned away and gazed fixedly into the garden. The sight of my mother's nakedness had jarred me. [. . .] My mother's indifferent acquiescence made it worse' (VED, p. 18).[76] The body that this vision delineates – a body we can liken to a ruined production-plant, or a long-disused machine[77] – is manifestly 'other' to the life-giving, nurturing maternal body that biopower (the power over life and populations dissected by Foucault)[78] pivotally targets and technologizes in the service of social reproduction. Equally, though, the non-(re)productive, 'acquiescent' body profiled in *Une mort*'s *incipit* has its own other, constituted by a third body treated in Beauvoir's grief-stricken memoir.

The clinically-moulded, self-identifyingly 'dysfunctional', waning maternal body depicted in Beauvoir's opening chapter ('[Maman] leaned back against her pillows, looked straight at me and said very firmly, "I have been overdoing it, you know. I tired myself out – I was at the end of my tether. I would not admit I was old. But one must face up to things [. . .]"' VED, p. 16)[79] is a very different body from that delineated in those sections of *Une mort* centred on Françoise's preclinical, post-menopausal, postmarital existence. The female body envisioned in these latter parts of Beauvoir's narrative, if increasingly physically enfeebled, is vital, defiant, autonomous and open to new experiences and pleasures (MTD, p. 21, pp. 24–6/ VED, p. 15, pp. 16–17). It is a body in its Indian summer: a body that reads as a site of that insubordinate freedom to which, Beauvoir suggests in *Le Deuxième Sexe* (1949), women potentially accede once their reproductive usefulness is exhausted.[80] Clearly, its ghost endures in Françoise after she is admitted to the *clinique C.* (MTD, pp. 99–100/VED, p. 62). But its obstinate resistance to redundancy is crushed, through her immersion in the clinical environment, not only by the destructive tentacles of her cancer, but also by the abjecting manipulations and deviabilizing interpretations to which her bodily being is exposed in the medical arena her daughter's narrative meticulously maps.

It is by no means the case that Beauvoir's *récit* reproduces the space constituted by the *clinique C.* in a dispassionate manner. Rather, as elements of the foregoing discussion have revealed, her memoir adopts a critical, resistant stance focused less on the careless inhumanity of its practices and practitioners (broadly speaking, Beauvoir accepts Françoise's doctors' decisions, whilst loathing the consequences they entail) than on the various modalities of 'docilization' to which her mother's body is subjected within its confines.[81] Confirmed by the emotionally charged lexis that Beauvoir employs in order to invoke her mother's hospitalized anatomy, diminished into a 'dépouille sans défense, palpée par des mains professionnelles' and a 'morceau desséché de sarment rosâtre', the denunciatory tenor of her narrative, and the target of its denunciations, are announced in the epigraph she chooses for *Une mort*. Taken from Dylan Thomas, the citation that provides it ('Do not go gentle into that good night/Old age should burn and rave at close of day/Rage, rage against the dying of the light . . .') patently foregrounds the phenomenon of geriatric bodily docility, and illuminates its tragic undesirability.

Beauvoir's denunciatory discourse on/rendition of clinical space can be viewed as a function of the filial compassion that explodes, unexpectedly, into her consciousness as she watches her mother die and is dissected at length in her *récit* (MTD, p. 44, pp. 146–51/VED, p. 28, pp. 89–92). (As Marks observes, *Une mort* communicates a sense of solidarity with the Other-who-is-not-Sartre that is otherwise largely absent in Beauvoir's extensive corpus.)[82] Likewise, this discourse may be construed as a by-product of Beauvoir's effort textually to 'rescue the lost Other from the "scandale" of physical disintegration and death'.[83] But, equally, we can read Beauvoir's condemnatory 'take' on the docilizing medical milieu as deriving from a culpability inspired not by her unavoidable collusion in her mother's clinical calvary (MTD, p. 80/VED, p. 50) nor by her failure to apprise Françoise of her imminent death (MTD, p. 150/VED, p. 91)[84] but, rather, by a daughterly desire that Beauvoir's narrative imputes to its author, without, however, doing so wholly overtly.

In *Une mort très douce*, it appears, Beauvoir generally elects to articulate the conflictual nature of her bond with her mother, the gamut of emotions she felt for Françoise in the various phases of her existence and the mutations they admitted during Françoise's decline with transparent, analytical honesty.[85] In other words, she opts in *Une mort*, the reader senses, to inscribe her experience of mother–daughter relationality in a manner that is at once more open and more 'interpretative' than that employed in her *Mémoires d'une jeune fille rangée* (1958), a work in which she eschews extended narrative commentary and leaves the 'facts' of her youthful dealings with Françoise largely to speak for themselves.[86]

One facet, though, of Beauvoir's connection to Françoise that *Une mort* profiles but neglects explicitly to unpack pertains to her adult need to perceive her genetrix as, indeed to transmute her into, a 'docile' aged female body of the kind Françoise is finally reduced to incarnating in the early days of her stay in the *clinique C.*

(a stay her daughter finances). That the middle-aged Simone de Beauvoir wanted her mother to function, in her third age, as a 'redundant' bodily Other and to acknowledge herself as non-viable and outworn is tacitly conveyed in elements of *Une mort*'s first chapter that detail Françoise's preclinical life and/or focus on particular, non-clinical spatial environments. This phenomenon is hinted at, for instance, in Beauvoir's suggestion that she would have been willing to see her mother spend her summers in rural hotels or convents open to boarders: that is, in exemplary (female) geriatric vacation-sites (MTD, p. 13/VED, p. 10). It is evinced by Beauvoir's account of the plans she formed (thwarted by the gravity of Françoise's sickness) to find her mother a suitable rest-home after her release from hospital (MTD, p. 22/VED, p. 15). It is intimated by her reference to the dislike she felt for the studio-flat her mother took on at her widowhood and held onto in the teeth of encroaching feebleness: a flat that, open to all comers and filled with the furnishings of Françoise's choice (these do not include her marriage-bed), was the locus and emblem of the post-marital/menopausal independent existence she came to enjoy, and of her defiant rejection of inactive obsolescence (MTD, pp. 21–2, 25/VED, pp. 15, 17). It is implied, finally, in Beauvoir's inference that she found the determinedly vital pursuit of gratification her mother embarked on in her twilight years somewhat comic: '[W]hen friends or cousins invited her out of Paris or into the country, nothing would stop her: she would have herself hoisted into the train by the guard without a second thought' (VED, p. 17).[87]

The features of *Une Mort*'s *incipit* cited above – and the adult filial desire they silhouette – sit ambiguously with those parts of Beauvoir's memoir where she seems straightforwardly to celebrate Françoise's refusal dutifully to 'act her age': that is, to act in accordance with culturally-inscribed notions of female viability/obsolescence.[88] They mesh, on the other hand, with elements of *Une mort*'s second chapter that hint at a resentment harboured by its author's childhood self, targeted at Françoise's failure, as a youthful mother, to play out wholly 'properly' her role as maternal, nurturing carer (MTD, pp. 47–8, 52–3, 55/VED, pp. 30, 33, 34–5).[89] On one level, the features in question can be read as attesting, simply, to Beauvoir's daughterly *caritas*. Carefully scrutinized, however, they quietly signal that maternal geriatric docility constituted in fact (before, at least, her mother's hospitalization) a desideratum for the mature Simone de Beauvoir. They imply that the gendered, bodily 'docilization' Françoise succumbs to in the *clinique C.* – manifest in her readiness to comport and categorize herself as a worn-out *vieille femme* – furnishes Beauvoir with a form of wish-fulfilment, betokened by the pleasure she records herself as feeling at her mother's post-operative willingness to turn herself into the likeness of a da Vinci drawing of a serene old lady (MTD, pp. 68–9/VED, p. 43). They indicate, likewise, that Françoise's abjecting encounter with medical space, far from wrenching her out of the framework/role in which her daughter has habitually situated her (cf. MTD, p. 28/VED, p. 19), inserts her into an identitarian situation Beauvoir has somehow willed her to embrace. And the 'message' that they communicate enables us to understand why Beauvoir elects to represent the clinical environment, and the docilizing influence it exerts on Françoise, in such a condemnatory fashion. It encourages us to view the denunciatory discourse she evolves in *Une mort* in the aftermath of her mother's death – a discourse whose object is geriatric docility, and the milieu that produces it – as a function of a belated, regretful guilt inspired by Beauvoir's sense of her own implication in Françoise's fate, and epitomized in her reluctance to gaze upon her mother's newly docile, self-denotingly obsolete body.

If, as I have suggested here, remorseful personal culpability of a very particularized kind subtends Beauvoir's critical elaboration of medical space and its docilizing effects, then we can construe the condemnatory narrative in which that elaboration inheres as one that is not only guilt-imbued but seeks also, indirectly, to make amends. *Une mort*'s closing chapters tell us that, in the wake of her mother's demise and as a result of the evolution her filial feelings undergo after Françoise's clinical incarceration, Beauvoir comes to need to confront and make reparation for 'crimes' perpetrated against the parent who poisoned periods of her youth (MTD, p. 135, pp. 147–8/VED, p. 83, pp. 89–90). Her desire to do so is evinced by her denunciatory treatment of the docilizing medical milieu: a treatment that attests, implicitly, to her will to atone for her own wish to see Françoise assume, in old age, a bodily docility/redundancy she spends at least part of her life stubbornly resisting.

A text that works, however obliquely, to effect a discursively-sited expiation of daughterly 'sins' committed against the mother is a text that effects, concomitantly, a move back towards the mother, and towards mother–daughter (re)connectivity. A move of this kind, even when pursued *post mortem*, exposes its perpetrator to a possible reimbrication in a realm of unmediated, imaginary identity (con)fusion that mother–daughter relationality renders all too accessible, and that Beauvoir evokes, pathologizes, and writes in order to put behind her in *Mémoires d'une jeune fille rangée* (a *récit* where, as I have argued elsewhere, she strives to realize, through a process of narrative substitution, a displaced discursive 'matricide' rooted in her rendition of the death of Zaza Mabille).[90] In *Une mort très douce*, Beauvoir explicitly addresses the problems that being in the mother's orbit poses.[91] Yet, she manifestly uses her narrative creation in order to reconnect with her dead maternal parent. She does so not only by producing a record of her trajectory towards renewed mother-love that acknowledges, belatedly, a kinship between Françoise's elderly 'indocility' and her own, life-long rejection of convention, but also by writing in a manner that, in decrying her mother's clinical docilization, atones for (one of) her own destructive filial desires, redeems daughterly dereliction and reduces the gulf between herself and her genetrix.

Should we conclude, then, that Beauvoir utilizes her (auto)biographical *opus* in order somehow to write herself back into the imaginary sphere, and into an imaginary, undifferentiated union with Françoise? As Nancy Miller remarks, in *Une mort très douce*, Beauvoir endeavours on the one hand to 'keep the story of her disconnection from her mother straight'.[92] At the same time, however, as I have signalled here, she pursues a 'reconnective' writerly practice apparent, *inter alia*, in her negative discursification of the docilizing medical arena and in the self-culpabilizing, reparative personal stakes subtending it. That she does so suggests that what she seeks to create in *Une mort* is a narrative construct that refuses to regenerate or re-embrace wholesale a mother–daughter 'indistinction' at odds with the subjective autonomy other of her autobiographical (and fictional) writings work to produce and protect,[93] but that, concomitantly, refuses also to 'write against', or foreclose, the peculiarly close intersubjective tie constituted by the mother–daughter connection.

In this context, it is worth remembering that *Une mort* incorporates two, key, passages where the phenomenon of mother–daughter imbrication is explicitly treated. The first chronicles Beauvoir's sense of how despair at Françoise's ineluctable death compels her to 'become' her mother: 'I talked to Sartre about my mother's mouth as I had seen it that morning [. . .]. And he told me that my own mouth was not obeying me any more: I had put Maman's mouth on my own face' (VED, p. 28).[94] The second reproduces an anxious, recurrent dream of Beauvoir's in which she sees herself as re-imprisoned in her mother's sphere of influence, and in a daughterly dependency she has fought to resist (MTD, p. 147/VED, p. 89). These passages contrast markedly with a trio of micro-narratives integrated into her *Mémoires* in which, as she re-narrates narratives encountered in her childhood, Beauvoir articulates in a covert, metaphorical fashion the fear that mother–daughter (con)fusion inspired in her and the intensity of her will to elude it.[95] As critical essays on *Une mort* have demonstrated, they invite a plethora of readings. My own sense is that their *overt* inclusion in Beauvoir's *récit* emblematizes her (tardy) readiness to cease to fear mother–daughter relationality, and to cease to write in a matrophobic manner informed by a determination to keep it – and the mother – firmly at bay.

The texts I have addressed in this chapter were written by authors of different generations, as well as genders. At their moment of production, these authors enjoyed dissimilar relationships to bodily well-being, to autobiographical and textual practice and to literary reknown. (When Beauvoir published *Une mort*, in 1964, she was already in her fifties, was an established practitioner of realist, politically-committed writing and was a doyenne of the French cultural firmament. Conversely, until he published *A l'ami* in his mid-thirties, Guibert's status remained that of a 'minor' writer, known, primarily, as an avant-garde literary stylist.) For all that, *A l'ami* and *Une mort* configure the medical environment in parallel ways, depicting clinical space as an arena in which the sick subject is not only abjected and marginalized, but is also exposed to productive modalities of identification that s/he must performatively endorse.

That Beauvoir and Guibert do not diverge, dramatically, in their portrayals of the clinical realm is not in fact surprising. The medicalizing experience, for men and woman alike, *is* potentially abjecting, and lends itself to a restricted range of representations (which is not to say that differently sexed diseased bodies are not the object of different disciplinary technologies and (ab)normalizing codifications). Less predictable, though, is the way in which both of these authors, as they narratively map the medical milieu, adopt discursive strategies destined to bring them close(r) to the (same-sex) Other. The intersubjective connections that they establish, as they do so, are by no means identical. (The discursive encounter into which Guibert writes himself and Foucault, his *ami mort*, as he plays with conceptions of clinical space stands, we sense, outside the imaginary realm. On the other hand, the reconnected relation with the lost (m)Other that Beauvoir produces by evolving her reparative – because (self-)denunciatory – medical-spatial discourse revives the possibility/menace of unmediated, imaginary self–other entanglement, even if it does not actually regenerate it.) That said, Guibert and Beauvoir clearly share a kindred desire to use medically/spatially-oriented writing to 'relational' ends. As my discussion has demonstrated, we can read their will to do so as differently motivated. Ultimately, however, we must recognize it as produced, at least in part, by the fact that, as they turned the clinical environment into text, Guibert and Beauvoir were both writing from a position of loss: a position that appears to have created as its corollary a need for a *post mortem* self–other relationality realizable uniquely in narrative space.

Notes

1. H. Guibert (1990), *A l'ami qui ne m'a pas sauvé la vie*, Paris, translated as *To The Friend Who Did Not Save My Life*, trans. L. Coverdale, London, 1995.
2. S. de Beauvoir (1964), *Une mort très douce*, Paris, translated as *A Very Easy Death*, trans. P. O'Brian, Harmondsworth, 1969.
3. *Les Mots* does of course 'treat' the raw material of its author's boyhood in a manner that allows us, according to Doubrovsky at least, to read it as 'auto-fictional'; it does not, however, embrace strategies of self-fictionalization of the kind deployed in *A l'ami*. I shall address *A l'ami*'s generic status in detail, below. For now, though, I want to flag Guibert's text up as more self-denotingly

autofictional than either *Les Mots* or *L'Amant*, a work that, as Chapter 2 established, is generically very slippery but that, because it does not constitute its narrator/protagonist as a persona who is the chief player of a novel but possesses nonetheless its creator's *name*, eschews the specific form of ambiguity intrinsic in the autofictional enterprise.

4. M. Foucault (1975), *Surveiller et punir: naissance de la prison*, Paris, translated as *Discipline and Punish: The Birth of the Prison*, trans. A. Sheridan, London, 1977. Foucault's conceptualizations of power shifted as his career/thinking progressed: in this chapter, however, it is that elaborated in *Surveiller et punir* that concerns me.

5. For excellent summaries of Foucault's account of discipline, on which I have drawn here, see B. Smart (1985), *Michel Foucault*, Chichester; J. Sawicki (1991), *Disciplining Foucault: Feminism, Power and the Body*, New York and London; J. Ransom (1997), *Foucault's Discipline: The Politics of Subjectivity*, Durham, NC and London.

6. On this aspect of Foucault's treatment of disciplinary practice, see Smart, *Michel Foucault*, pp. 85–7.

7. On Foucault's views on the relations between classification, identification, individualization and disciplinary control, see R. Diprose (1994), *The Bodies of Women: Ethics, Embodiment and Sexual Difference*, London and New York, pp. 22–5.

8. In the section of *A l'ami* that Guibert confirms as having been added to his text after it was submitted to his publisher (cf. 'Hervé Guibert: Foucault a été mon maître, je devais écrire sa mort . . .', *L'Evénement du jeudi*, 1–7 March 1990, pp. 82–5, p. 84), an Italian medical environment – Rome's Spallanzani hospital – is also evoked. I shall concentrate here, however, on *A l'ami*'s treatment of Parisian medical space.

9. In 'Hervé Guibert: Foucault a été mon maître, je devais écrire sa mort . . .', Guibert exposes 'Muzil' as a screen for Foucault fairly comprehensively. On the impossibility of not discerning Foucault as the reality behind Muzil, on Muzil as a condensation of Foucault-as-philosopher and on the implications of the Muzil/Foucault imbrication, see Schehr, 'Cippus: Guibert', in *Alcibiades*, pp. 155–96, pp. 182–5. For helpful discussions of (the ambiguity intrinsic in) Guibert's depiction of Foucault/Muzil in *A l'ami* and his comments regarding it, see Sarkonak, 'De la métastase au métatexte', especially pp. 229–30, p. 247, and R. Bellour (1995), 'Une entreprise qui n'eut jamais d'exemple . . .', *Nottingham French Studies*, vol. 34, pp. 121–30, pp. 122–3. Bellour argues that in *A l'ami*, Foucault is accorded exactly the kind of veiled identity his knowledge of Guibert's work would have led him to suppose that his friend would have ascribed to him. I shall discuss Guibert's veiling of Foucault in terms of *A l'ami*'s autofictional aspect, below.

10. For a helpful account of the temporal dynamics of *A l'ami*, see L. Hill (1995), 'Ecrire – la maladie', *Nottingham French Studies*, vol. 34, pp. 89–99.

11. Edmund Smyth notes that Guibert was already drawing on insights offered in *Surveiller et punir* in *Des Aveugles* (1985). See E. Smyth (1995), '*Des Aveugles*: modes d'articulation', *Nottingham French Studies*, vol. 34, pp. 8–14, p. 10.

12. In *Alcibiades* (cf. pp. 174–5), Schehr glosses *A l'ami*'s play with doctors' names illuminatingly.

13. 'fait de chaque individu un "cas": [. . .] un objet pour une connaissance et une prise pour un pouvoir' (SP, p. 224).

14. Kafka was a preferred author of Foucault's, as well as Guibert's.

15. '[pour] les transformer en matière désactivée d'un vaccin qui sauvera les autres après ma mort, d'une gammaglobuline, ou pour en infecter un singe de laboratoire' (ALA, p. 52).

16. For a summary of these aspects of Foucault's text, see Ransom, *Foucault's Discipline*, pp. 54–7.

17. 'l'unique cellule éclairée qui continuait de bourdonner derrière ses verres dépolies' (ALA, p. 56).

18. For a compelling discussion of Guibert's account of the visibilization of the AIDS sufferer, and of the resistance his hospital diary *Cytomégalovirus* mounts against it, see Murray Pratt (1998), '"A Walk Along the Side of the Motorway": AIDS and the Spectacular Body of Hervé Guibert', in O. Heathcote, A. Hughes and J. S. Williams (eds), *Gay Signatures: Gay and Lesbian Theory, Fiction and Film in France, 1945–1995*, Oxford and New York, pp. 151–72. This essay draws, as I draw here, on *Surveiller et punir*, and recognizes Guibert's debt to it.

19. 'Trois infirmières se tassaient [. . .] en compulsant frénétiquement les pages d'un classeur et en criant des noms, c'est alors qu'elles ont crié le mien, mais il est un stade de la maladie où l'on n'a que faire du secret, où il devient même odieux' (ALA, p. 57).

20. Schehr has interesting things to say about the polymorphous, unclassifiable character of AIDS, and its consequences for the narrative act. See *Alcibiades*, p. 157 and *passim*.

21. M. Foucault (1976), *La Volonté de savoir: Histoire de la sexualité I*, Paris, translated as *The History of Sexuality I: An Introduction*, trans. R. Hurley, London, 1990. For a reading of Foucault's analyses of the connections between confession, power and self-individualization/decipherment/formation, see Diprose, *The Bodies of Women*, pp. 23–4.

22. See 'De la métastase', p. 256.

23. See *Alcibiades*, p. 183, p. 186.

24. AIDS features in Guibert's *L'Incognito* (1989) and *Fou de Vincent* (1989), but less centrally than in *A l'ami*.

25. See 'Hervé Guibert: Foucault a été mon maître, je devais écrire sa mort . . .', p. 84. A reference made by Guibert, here, to the fact that, when they first met, he had not read Foucault's books, suggests that he did so later.

26. On the outcry provoked by the betraying aspect of *A l'ami*, see 'Hervé Guibert: Foucault a été mon maître: je devais écrire sa mort . . .' (this records Guibert's contention that he never claimed to tell/hold the truth of Foucault/Muzil's death) and 'Les écrivains peuvent-ils tout dire', *L'Evénement du jeudi*, 1–7 March 1990, pp. 86–7. For a sensitive discussion of this phenomenon, and of Guibert's reasons for staging Foucault's death in his text, see Sarkonak, 'De la métastase', pp. 244–51.

27. See 'Autobiographie/vérité/psychanalyse', pp. 73, 77; 'Autobiography/Truth/ Psychoanalysis', pp. 37, 41. I shall refocus on insights provided by this essay in Chapter 5, and provide citations from the original there.

28. See 'Autobiographie/vérité/psychanalyse', p. 77; 'Autobiography/Truth/ Psychoanalysis', p. 40.

29. 'L'Autofiction, un genre pas sérieux', pp. 377–8.

30. Ibid., p. 375.

31. In *La Volonté de savoir* (VDS, p. 80/HOSI, p. 59), Foucault associates confessional literature with the emergence and proliferation, in the disciplinary era, of power-compelled processes of individualizing avowal. He also casts domination as located not in the subject of the confession, but in its *recipient/ reader* (VDS, p. 83/HOSI, p. 62).

32. See 'L'Autofiction, un genre pas sérieux', pp. 377–8.

33. See Lecarme and Lecarme-Tabone, *L'Autobiographie*, p. 278.

34. See Darrieussecq, 'De l'autobiographie à l'autofiction: *Mes parents*, roman?', in Sarkonak (ed.) *Le corps textuel d'Hervé Guibert*, pp. 115–30, 115. This piece (cf. pp. 126–8) comments helpfully on the reader-response *autofiction* engenders.

35. Ibid., pp. 126, 130. Pertinent here, also, is her comment in 'L'Autofiction, un genre pas sérieux' (cf. p. 378) that Guibert 'inoculates' his AIDS-fiction with a 'true/false' virus. On the true/false (con)fusion of *A l'ami*, see also Sarkonak, 'De la métastase', pp. 231, 238–9, 247. On the 'disidentificatory' character of earlier Guibertian writings, and their relation to Guibert's rejection of institutional autobiographical models that serve heterosexism's need for a 'readable' gay subject, see Pratt, 'De la désidentification', pp. 70–2.

36. This is missing from the cover of the 'folio' edition of *A l'ami* referenced here.

37. H. Guibert (1991), *Le Protocole compassionnel*, Paris, translated as *The Compassion Protocol*, trans. by J. Kirkup, London, 1993.

38. Remarks made by Guibert in an interview with Antoine de Gaudemar (cf. 'La Vie sida', *Libération*, 1 March 1990, pp. 19–21, p. 19) also stress the fictive character of the 'personnage' Hervé Guibert.

39. Published in 1986, *Mes parents*, unlike *A l'ami*, is given no generic label, and

is readable as squarely biographically-located. That said, as Darrieussecq argues (cf. 'De l'autobiographie à l'autofiction'), it is a text that seems to pull towards 'l'espace autofictif'.

40. It is obviously possible to view the name-changes/name-playing included in *A l'ami* as no more than protective. Given, however, the consistent manner in which, within his AIDS-narrative, Guibert manipulates the referential/real, I prefer to view his onomastic jugglings as textual 'clues' to its ambiguous, autofictional generic status.

41. See Sarkonak, 'De la métastase', pp. 237–8.

42. 'Ce jour où j'entreprends ce livre, le 26 décembre 1988' (ALA, p. 10).

43. 'Hervé Guibert's' text enjoys, clearly, a complex relationship with *A l'ami*. This relationship is signalled as one of identity by Guibert's narrator's use of phrases such as 'ce livre' and 'As I write these lines'/'A l'heure où j'écris ces lignes' (cf. tableau 55). However, its identitarian basis is simultaneously *undermined* by virtue of the fact that 'Hervé Guibert's' text is (i) flagged as imbricated in a self-revelatory 'projet du dévoilement de soi' (ALA, p. 264/ TTF, p. 228) that *A l'ami* does not in my view promote and (ii) covers events whose temporal end-point seems to be 20 March 1989 (*A l'ami* itself addresses, it appears, events occuring as late as October 1989). Consequently, I would suggest, we cannot read it *unproblematically* as the autofictional *A l'ami*'s narrative 'twin', or read observations pertaining to it as (necessarily always) relevant to, or as a meta-commentary on, *A l'ami*.

44. This unwillingness is addressed in Guibert's interview with de Gaudemar, when he states that, in terms of telling the truth in his AIDS-text, he 'clouded the issue' ('a brouillé les pistes'). See 'La Vie sida', p. 19. My sense of the central role 'untruthfulness' plays in *A l'ami* means that I am reluctant to detect in Guibert's *opus*, or, at least, to detect unproblematically, the 'contrat de trans-parence' that Jean-Pierre Boulé isolates as a hallmark of Guibert's work. See Boulé (1997), 'Guibert ou la radicalisation du projet sartrien d'écriture existen-tielle', in Sarkonak, *Le Corps textuel de Hervé Guibert*, pp. 25–42, p. 30.

45. Darrieussecq describes this as voyeurism. See 'L'Autofiction, un genre pas sérieux', p. 378.

46. Ibid.

47. Ibid.

48. On Foucault and resistance-as-resistance-to-imposed-individualization, see P. Rabinow (1984), 'Introduction', in *The Foucault Reader*, New York, pp. 3–29, p. 22. On resistance as power's product, see Susan Bordo (1993), 'Feminism, Foucault and the Politics of the Body', in C. Ramazanoglu (ed.), *Up Against Foucault*, London and New York, pp. 179–202, pp. 192–3.

49. In a recent essay, Brad Epps argues that in *A l'ami*, the complexity of his self-representational enterprise notwithstanding, Guibert pursues a practice of

self-revelation significantly dissimilar to the self-effacing writerly 'déprise de soi' advocated by Foucault/Muzil. See B. Epps (1997), 'Le Corps "techno-ascétique": Guibert, le sida et l'art de la maîtrise de soi', in Sarkonak, *Le Corps textuel de Hervé Guibert*, pp. 43–62. I do not find his reading convincing, although I do accept that Guibert and Foucault – as, at least, he is textually represented in *A l'ami* – relate differently to the act of self-nomination. I also recognize that a 'projet de dévoilement de soi' (ALA, p. 264) *is* pursued by Guibert's autofictional persona, 'Hervé Guibert'.

50. On the nature/function of the *mise-en-abyme*, see L. Dällenbach (1977), *Le Récit spéculaire*, Paris and (1986), *Mirrors and After: Five Essays on Literary Theory and Criticism*, New York. The former defines the textual *mise-en-abyme* as a (meta)narrative element that, as a 'métaphore emblématique du texte', reflects the 'signifying organization' of the work containing it and, in a gesture of readerly 'direction', draws it to the reader's attention (cf. *Le Récit spéculaire*, pp. 123–5). The Guibertian *mises-en-abyme* discussed here are all 'textual'.

51. 'visage inidentifiable comme celui d'un escrimeur' (ALA, p. 59).

52. The fact that these texts are both – albeit differently – unmarked with Foucault's real name makes them, we should note, *A l'ami*'s counterfoil as well as its *mise-en-abyme*.

53. In 'L'Autofiction, un genre pas sérieux' (cf. p. 378), Darrieussecq establishes a pertinent parallel between Guibert's autofictional writing and the decoy aspect of the AIDS virus.

54. 'Une fois que le docteur Nacier fut parti, [Muzil] me dit: "C'est ce que je lui ai conseillé, à ton petit copain, son truc ça ne devrait pas être une institution où l'on vient mourir, mais où l'on vient faire semblant de mourir. Tout y serait [. . .] seulement pour mieux dissimuler le pot aux roses, car il y aurait une petite porte dérobée tout au fond de cette clinique [. . .], dans la mélodie engour-dissante du nirvana d'une piqûre, on se glisserait derrière [un] tableau, et hop, on disparaîtrait, on serait mort aux yeux de tous, et on réapparaîtrait sans témoin de l'autre côté du mur, dans l'arrière-cour, sans bagage, sans rien dans les mains, sans nom, devant inventer sa nouvelle identité"' (ALA, pp. 24–5).

55. On mirroring in Guibert's work, see A.-C. Guilbard (1995), 'De la pratique du narcissisme à la recherche de l'image vraie', *Nottingham French Studies*, vol. 34, pp. 42–8.

56. On the relationship between these segments of *A l'ami*, see F. Reymondet (1997), 'La fin: issue fatale, issue narrative', *Dalhousie French Studies*, vol. 39/40, pp. 181–91, p. 188.

57. Published in the inaugural issue of *Gai pied* (1 April 1979, pp. 1, 10), 'Un plaisir si simple' is reproduced in M. Foucault (1994), *Dits et écrits 1954–88*, Paris, pp. 777–9.

58. 'Une entreprise', pp. 122–4.
59. One of the focuses of Schehr's 'Cippus: Guibert' is *A l'ami*'s status as a site of philosophical exchange between Guibert and Foucault.
60. On the nature and proliferation of such paradigms – which *are* echoed in *A l'ami*'s accounts of the 'Hervé'/Jules relation – see Edelman, 'The Mirror and the Tank', in *Homographesis*, pp. 93–117. The arguments offered in this last section of my reading of *A l'ami* owe much to Edelman's essay.
61. Ibid., pp. 104–9. In 'The Mirror' (cf. pp. 115–16) Edelman seeks *inter alia* to isolate the transgressive, politically resistant nature of the narcissism that *A l'ami* reveals 'Hervé Guibert' to hold fast to in the face of AIDS.
62. On the nature and implications of Beauvoir's other-oriented, biographical/autobiographical discourse, see N. K. Miller (1992), 'Autobiographical Deaths', *The Massachusetts Review*, vol. 33, pp. 19–47, p. 46; Elaine Marks (1998), 'Encounters with Death in *A Very Easy Death*', in E. Fallaize (ed.), *Simone de Beauvoir: A Critical Reader*, London and New York, pp. 132–42, pp. 133–4; U. Tidd, *Simone de Beauvoir, Gender and Testimony* (Cambridge, forthcoming). Chapter 7 of this last work includes a compelling discussion of *Une mort très douce* as the site of a corporeal encounter with embodied alterity, and as an instance of intersubjective, 'testimonial' autobiography.
63. As my discussion has already signalled, imaginary relations are relations in which the self and the other coexist in a dyadic bond that is unmediated and turns on self–other reflexivity/imbrication. Countless works of psychoanalytic theory and literary analysis published in the 1970s and after address the 'imaginary' dynamic subtending the mother–daughter tie. Particularly pertinent, although conceptually at odds, are the writings of Nancy Chodorow and Luce Irigaray. Insights offered by these theorists and by analysts of their work inform the reading offered here, notably its latter stages.
64. We should not forget that Beauvoir's text also makes reference to a state hospital where Françoise spends a single night. Primarily, however, *Une mort* is concerned with private clinical space (and, amongst other things, with its class-related aspect).
65. 'Autobiographical Deaths', p. 34.
66. On Foucault's vision of 'identifying', codifying space, see Diprose, *The Bodies of Women*, pp. 23, 27.
67. Clearly, this latter body is *not* 'docile' in the (Foucauldian) sense of productive and publicly viable/useful. For summaries of how the female (post)menopausal body is designated in cultural and medical discourse as non-productive, see D. Lupton (1994), *Medicine as Culture*, London, pp. 145–6; Emily Martin (1997), 'Medical Metaphors of Women's Bodies: Menstruation and Menopause', in K. Conboy, N. Medina and S. Stanbury (eds), *Writing on the Body: Female Embodiment and Feminist Theory*, New York, pp. 15–41, pp. 27–9.
68. See Marks, 'Encounters', p. 133.

69. 'ivre de technique' (MTD, p. 73).
70. 'Et je lui ai dit: "Tu n'as qu'à te soulager sans bassin: elles changeront tes draps, ce n'est pas compliqué." – "Oui", m'a-t-elle dit; les sourcils froncés, un air de détermination sur le visage, elle a lancé comme un défi: "Les morts font bien dans leurs draps." [. . .] Et maman, qui avait vécu hérissée d'orgueilleuses susceptibilités, n'éprouvait aucune honte. C'était aussi une forme de courage, chez cette spiritualiste guindée, que d'assumer avec tant de décision notre animalité' (MTD, p. 77).
71. On cultural conceptualizations of the aged (post)menopausal female body as emblematic of lack of production, and as a kind of disused factory, idle machine and failed business, see Martin, 'Medical Metaphors', p. 29. On the imbrication of gender issues in the ageing process, and on the female aged body as the target *par excellence* of cultural attitudes that combine sexism and ageism, see S. Arber and J. Ginn (eds), (1995), *Connecting Gender and Ageing: A Sociological Approach*, Buckingham and Philadelphia.
72. For an extensive reading of this phenomenon, see Sawicki, 'Disciplining Mothers: Feminism and the New Reproductive Technologies', in *Disciplining Foucault*, pp. 67–94. See also M. Shildrick (1997), 'Fabrica(tions)', in *Leaky Bodies and Boundaries*, London and New York, pp. 13–61.
73. On disciplinary space as space that assigns to the individual his/her 'true' place, body and name, and obliges him/her to perform accordingly, see Ransom, *Foucault's Discipline*, p. 43.
74. On the disciplined female body as one that polices itself against such norms, and testifies to its own failure to meet normalcy-standards, see Shildrick, *Leaky Bodies*, p. 49.
75. 'La kinésithérapeute s'approcha du lit, rabattit le drap, empoigna la jambe gauche de maman: sa chemise de nuit ouverte, celle-ci exhibait avec indifférence son ventre froissé, plissé de rides minuscules, et son pubis chauve. "Je n'ai plus aucune pudeur", a-t-elle dit d'un air surpris' (MTD, p. 26).
76. '[J]e me détournai et je m'absorbai dans la contemplation du jardin. Voir le sexe de ma mère: ça m'avait fait un choc. [. . .] Le consentement insouciant de ma mère l'aggravait' (MTD, p. 27). In 'Autobiographical Deaths' (cf. p. 36), Miller argues that what shocks Beauvoir, as she observes her mother's desiccated sexed body/genitalia, is the spectacle of her mother's female embodiment: an embodiment that 'ruptures any conventional bonds of female continuity'. More convincingly, Alice Jardine reads Beauvoir's narratively-reported horror as a function of her lifelong fear of a dangerous maternal body that threatens her (writerly and subjective) autonomy. See Alice Jardine (1985), 'Death Sentences: Writing Couples and Ideology', in S. Suleiman (ed.), *The Female Body in Western Culture*, pp. 84–96, p. 94. I shall return to Beauvoir's inability to look at her mother's body below, offering an alternative reading of it.

77. See Martin, 'Medical Metaphors', p. 29.
78. As Sawicki indicates (cf. *Disciplining Foucault*, pp. 67–8), disciplinary power – a power over the individual – is but one facet of biopower, which also targets and regulates populations and their (re)productivity.
79. '[Maman] s'est appuyée contre ses oreillers, elle m'a regardée dans les yeux et elle m'a dit avec décision: "Vois-tu, j'ai abusé; je me suis trop fatiguée; j'ai été au bout de mon rouleau. Je ne voulais pas admettre que j'étais vieille. Mais il faut savoir regarder les choses en face [. . .]"' (MTD, p. 23).
80. See S. de Beauvoir (1949), *Le Deuxième Sexe II*, Paris, p. 467. The vision of the post-menopausal female subject as a free subject outlined here coincides with positive notions of women's post-menopausal existence that prevailed in some nineteenth-century medical writings (cf. Martin, 'Medical Metaphors', p. 21), and with contemporary research into the independence and gender-role emancipation enjoyed by older woman (cf. Ginn and Arber, '"Only Connect": Gender Relations and Ageing', in *Connecting Gender and Ageing*, pp. 1–14, pp. 8–9). However, this vision, echoed in Beauvoir's *La Vieillesse* (1970), is by no means consistently sustained in Beauvoir's seminal feminist essay.
81. Miller is right to argue that what Beauvoir's text charts is 'that violence [. . .] across bodies that no longer know their own story'. See 'Autobiographical Deaths', p. 41.
82. See 'Encounters with Death', p. 136.
83. See Tidd, *Simone de Beauvoir*, forthcoming.
84. On Beauvoir's experience of a guilt engendered by her own silences and choices, see L. Corbin (1996), 'Complicity and Silence', in *The Mother Mirror: Self-Representation and the Mother–Daughter Relation in Colette, Simone de Beauvoir, and Marguerite Duras*, New York and Washington DC, pp. 45–70, p. 62.
85. On the emotional journey Beauvoir embarks on as a result of her mother's illness and on *Une mort* as a tale of rediscovered mother-love, see C. Montfort (1996), '"La Vieille Née": Simone de Beauvoir, *Une mort très douce*, and Annie Ernaux, *Une femme*', *French Forum*, vol. 41, pp. 349–64. On the absence/occlusion of the mother's voice within what seems to be a deeply sincere daughterly exercise in truth-telling, and its relation to Beauvoir's ongoing ambivalence towards mother–daughter relationality, see Corbin, *The Mother Mirror*, pp. 63–4.
86. S. de Beauvoir (1958), *Mémoires d'une jeune fille rangée*, Paris, translated as *Memoirs of a Dutiful Daughter*, trans. J. Kirkup, Harmondsworth, 1987.
87. '[Q]uand des amis, des cousins l'invitaient à la campagne ou en province, rien ne l'arrêtait: elle n'hésitait pas à se faire hisser dans le train par le contrôleur' (MTD, pp. 25–6).

88. Doris Kadish argues that a feminist celebration of her mother's defiant, independent elderly existence and her chosen, belated emancipation from certain kinds of gender-constraint and existential convention is central to Beauvoir's project in *Une mort*. See D. Kadish (1989), 'Simone de Beauvoir's *Une Mort très douce*: Existential and Feminist Perspectives on Old Age', *The French Review*, vol. 62, pp. 631–9. Kadish's reading, while powerful, neglects to address the ambiguity towards her mother's aged 'indocility' to which Beauvoir's narrative attests.

89. These elements are offset by parts of *Une mort*'s second chapter that both deplore Françoise's 'docile' acceptance of roles and conventions relating to her status as wife and mother and signal Beauvoir's adult understanding of her mother's situation. They are, nonetheless, detectable within it, and come as no small surprise to readers of Beauvoir's *Mémoires*, a text where maternal nurturance/conventionality is posited as a threat to the subjective autonomy of the young Beauvoir. On this aspect of the *Mémoires*, see Alex Hughes (1998), 'Murdering the Mother in *Memoirs of a Dutiful Daughter*', in Fallaize, *Simone de Beauvoir: A Critical Reader*, pp. 120–31.

90. On the *Mémoires* as a chronicle of mother–daughter (dis)entanglement and an epic of daughterly emancipation, see ibid. On Beauvoir's 'pathologization' of mother–daughter intersubjective (con)fusion, see ibid., p. 123. My essay chimes with the account of Beauvoir's use in her later autobiographical works (including *Une mort*) of 'matricidal' narrative strategies offered by Alice Jardine, in 'Death Sentences' (an account I am 'writing against' in my own reading of *Une mort*). It also signals key works of psychoanalytic theory that address the phenomenon of mother–daughter 'indifference'.

91. On this aspect of *Une mort*, see for example Kadish, 'Simone de Beauvoir's *Une mort très douce*', p. 638. The 'move towards the mother' that Beauvoir's text effects/records is a key focus of Kadish's essay: however, her account of the treatment which, she claims, *Une mort* offers of Beauvoir's 'progression' out of the symbolic and into the (maternal) space of the imaginary fails properly to address the problematic nature of such a move.

92. 'Autobiographical Deaths', p. 39.

93. Alice Jardine and Toril Moi both argue that Beauvoir's first, autobiographically-inflected novel *L'Invitée* (1943) stages a struggle for subjective independence in which Beauvoir is personally implicated, and which is fundamentally mother-oriented. See 'Death Sentences', p. 95; T. Moi (1994), *Simone de Beauvoir: The Making of an Intellectual Woman*, Oxford, pp. 95–124, esp. 121, 124.

94. 'Je parlai à Sartre de la bouche de ma mère, telle que je l'avais vue le matin [. . .]. Et ma propre bouche, m-a-t-il dit, ne m'obéissait plus: j'avais posé celle de maman sur mon visage' (MTD, pp. 43–4).

95. See my 'Murdering the Mother', p. 123.

–5–

Queer Articulations

In my last chapter, I highlighted the inscription, in *A l'ami* and *Une mort*, of identity-performances that we can read as abjecting, as imposed in disciplinary spaces whose norms of bodily viability the ailing subjects who effect them have infringed, and as docilely assumed/accepted by these narratively-invoked individuals (Guibert's self-denotingly serocompromised 'Hervé'; Beauvoir's self-identifyingly obsolete Françoise), if not by the authors of the texts in which they feature. In the present chapter, I shall take as my focus a set of performances that are likewise 'deviant', or extranormal, and the narratives where these performances are displayed. However, the performances I want to examine, here, are more patently performances of sex/gender than those evoked in Chapter 4. What is more, we can view them less as 'docile' than as transgressive of the heterosexual norm that requires sex, gender and sexuality to cohere 'logically' and 'properly'.

The notion that gender constitutes a form of enactment – an enactment that is produced by a constructive Law of sexual identity, and involves a regulated, imitative, bodily citation of it – is privileged in the radical analyses of Judith Butler, most notably in her seminal essay *Gender Trouble* (1990).[1] Gender performances, Butler affirms, in no way reflect a 'voluntarism which presumes a subject intact, prior to its gendering', but are expressive of constraint.[2] Born out of a disciplinary regulation of the flesh – Butler is nothing if not resolutely Foucauldian – they are 'mimes', which are inscribed on the surface of the body, but appear as the effects of an *inner essence*. Because they are compelled and contoured by the dominant sexual regime, gender performances mostly approximate, moreover, the 'intelligible grids of an idealized, compulsory heterosexuality': that is, they respect the limits of a binarized either/or paradigm imposed by the 'naturally' binarized material phenomenon of sex.[3] The disciplinary production of gendered 'doing' effects in other words what Butler construes as a false stabilization of gender, that works in the 'interests of the heterosexual construction and regulation of sexuality within the reproductive domain'.[4] This stabilization shores up a binary, heteropolarized system wherein, generally, sexual practices, gender identities and anatomical sex mesh together 'cohesively'.

Gender performances can, of course, succumb to 'incoherence'. That this is so is evidenced, says Butler, by those (troubling) 'discontinuities that run rampant within heterosexual, bisexual, and gay and lesbian contexts where gender does not necessarily follow from sex, and desire, or sexuality generally, does not seem to follow from gender – indeed where none of these dimensions of significant corpo-reality express or reflect one another'.[5] For Butler, 'queer' disorganizations within the gendered field of bodies potentially denaturalize and disrupt the regulatory model of (hetero)sexual coherence, exposing it as a constructive norm and as a fiction destined to promote the 'obligatory frame of reproductive heterosexuality'.[6] However, the strategic performance, on the part of the collectivity, of 'coherent' gender acts serves to marginalize such disorganizations. It serves also to produce the appearance of fixed, primary, naturally binarized gender cores.

The narratives scrutinized in detail here in Chapter 5 are Violette Leduc's *La Bâtarde* (1964) – an autobiography inaugurated by the establishment of an exem-plary autobiographical 'pact',[7] but one that combines classically referential writing techniques with forays into avant-garde experimentation and narrative procedures that manifestly flag up the (self-) constructive function of autobiographical discourse – and Serge Doubrovsky's autofictional *Un amour de soi* (1982). The readings that I make of them, and of the gendered/sexual performances they invoke, are indebted to Butler's accounts of gender performativity (accounts that we can read in counterpoint to, and as vehicling a reaction against, the essentialist identity politics privileged in some feminist discourses of the 1970s). And their focus, as my opening paragraph indicated, is the articulation, in *La Bâtarde* and *Un amour de soi*, of queer gender enactments: that is, of modes of being and doing that bear the stamp of sexed 'incoherence' and trouble the normative requirement that gender performances should not exceed boundaries instituted by (the duality that is) biological sex. Like the texts that they address, and by virtue, no doubt, of the dissimilarities that divide them, my readings differ from each other somewhat in their tenor, for all that they foreground parallel phenomena. If I have brought them together in this final chapter of *Heterographies* it is because, counterposed, they encourage us to reflect on the 'locational' factors that incite autobiographical authors to accord 'gender trouble' representational space.

Violette Leduc's Homotextualities[8]

That Leduc's writings concern themselves, generally, less with the production of an *écriture féminine* predicated on the inscription of feminine specificity than with the representation of gendered doing in all its proliferating, normative *and* queer modalities is intimated by comments contained in René de Ceccatty's *Eloge de la bâtarde*. De Ceccatty remarks that in Leduc's texts there is, 'in spite of [a] stubborn repetition of sexual labels', a negation of the notion of *tendance sexuelle*.[9] This negation, he suggests, turns on the fact that, 'neither lesbian nor heterosexual nor bisexual by nature or by education [. . .], [Leduc] is an unspecified, label-free subject of pleasure and desire'.[10] De Ceccatty's observations are interesting in so far as they endorse the argument – a cornerstone of the discussion offered here – that Leduc's narratives emphasize, centrally and *denaturalizingly*, the absence of an abiding, essential gender core, as well as the potentially fluid character of gendered and sexual performance. That this is the case is evinced by Leduc's manifold metamorphoses of her textual/sexual self: metamorphoses that characterize both her directly autobiographical *récits* and her autobiographical fictions. The following sections of this chapter will focus on these metamorphoses, specifically in their homosexual mode and most especially as they are invoked in *La Bâtarde*, a text 'covering' the formative, emotionally-fraught years of Leduc's illegitimate child-hood, adolescence and early adulthood. Tracing their manifestations will allow me to situate them in terms of that phenomenon of 'discontinuous' gender performa-tivity whose contestatory potential Judith Butler, amongst others, pertinently dissects.

If, in the late twentieth century, Leduc is 'known' as any particular kind of writer it is, doubtless, as a lesbian writer. Her status reflects the primary place that female same-sex love occupies in her narrative recreations of her past. Her second auto-biographical novel, *L'Affamée* (1948), transcribes a lesbian epiphany inspired by her infatuation with Simone de Beauvoir. Violette, the autobiographical persona Leduc creates in *La Bâtarde*, has two female lovers: her initiatrix, the luminous Isabelle, and the more prosaic Hermine, who seeks to enclose Violette in a stultifying union in which she must play the 'petite femme'. The 'real-life' Violette–Hermine and Violette–Isabelle relationships reproduced in *La Bâtarde* mirror lesbian bonds chronicled in Leduc's third autobiographical fiction *Ravages* (1955) and her novella *Thérèse et Isabelle* (1966). This last work, in particular, invokes lesbian eroticism with a lyrical violence attenuated but not obliterated by the censoring cuts Gallimard compelled its author to introduce.[11]

Within the baroque world of her own writing, and by virtue of the concerns it addresses, Leduc 'performs', then, as lesbian autobiographical creatrix and as lesbian protagonist. Hence, to classify her as an exemplary feminine homoerotic literary voice would seem to be entirely appropriate. The innovatory nature of Leduc's narrative treatment of female homosexuality, conveyed by parallels binding elements of the original version of *Thérèse et Isabelle* with Monique Wittig's *Le Corps lesbien* (1973), reinforces the validity of such a categorization. So, too, does Elaine Marks's comment, in her essay 'Lesbian Intertextuality', that in Leduc's autobiographies, for the first time in French literature, 'the lesbian is no longer the object of literary discourse seen from an outside point of view. She is her own heroine.'[12] But Leduc herself – for all her sense of belonging to a continuum of women writers bent on achieving a 'necessary opening up of a [female] sexuality too long concealed'[13] – would probably not have appreciated being categorized in this delimiting fashion. Her account, in the autobiographical *La Chasse à l'amour* (1973), of her awkward encounter with a pair of lesbian readers – readers impassioned by the passion of *L'Affamée* – fuels our feeling that this is so. Confronted with these women's enthusiasm for her lesbian writing, and with their determined sexual openness, Leduc's narrator Violette is left to wonder to herself whether, in fact, she actually dislikes lesbians ('Est-ce que, par hasard, je détesterais les lesbiennes?').[14]

This unexpected observation hints, amongst other things, at the fact that the sexual practice that, in Leduc's creative universe, is valorized above any other is not lesbianism at all, but, rather, *male* homosexuality. Leduc's narcissistic narrative productions reveal a marked predilection for gay males on the part of their author and her textually inscribed counterparts. Evidence of it is provided by the cohort of homosexual love objects – starting with Maurice Sachs – who provoke a destructive devotion in Leduc's autobiographical *sosie*. The lengthy disquisition on male homoeroticism contained in her *récit de voyage Trésors à prendre* (TAP) (1960) – beginning as it does with a categorical 'I am for male homosexuality' ('Je suis pour l'homosexualité masculine')[15] – leaves us in no doubt as to Leduc's idealization of gay masculinity: an idealization that, amongst other things, leads her to 'homosexualize' the heterosexual men who feature in her novels and *récits*.

Various factors explain the privileged position that male homosexuals occupy in Leduc's life-writings. In their company, her self-creation Violette feels immune to pregnancy, the dread of which her unwed mother dunned into her. The outsider status that is hers within their erotic space means that the lack of desire gay men manifest towards her – unlike that displayed by their heterosexual counterparts – need in no way prove humiliating. It even, in fact, allows Violette to give free rein to her craving for the unattainable. Most importantly, homosexual men appeal because, astonishingly, they recall her adored grandmother Fidéline, who cared for her in her childhood:

> Fearful of my mother [. . .], I turned to a woman who resembled neither a man nor a woman. Her face, captured on the one old photograph I have of her, isn't beautiful. It is virile. I've thought hard about what I am about to write: my grandmother (who got married, had two children) will have been the first homosexual with whom I fell passionately in love as I took refuge in the skirts of her secular cassock [*soutane de laïque*]. She was a man in a dress [*homme en robe*], who protected me when she shielded me from my mother and showed no fear of her.[16]

This extraordinary excerpt from *Trésors à prendre* intimates that the passion for male homosexuality that Leduc's solipsistic *oeuvre* bespeaks has as its particular focus the 'grandmotherly' or 'priestly' homosexual; the 'homme en robe'. Avatars of this cross-gendered being who people Leduc's autobiographical world are, variously, Maurice Sachs – portrayed in *La Bâtarde* as possessed of 'pudgy prelate hands' ('mains potelées de prélat'), day-robes, mules, silken socks and belongings whose odour is that of its heroine's grandmother's sacerdotal skirts – and the seemingly interchangeable, camp figures of the *folle* (queen) and the *travesti* (drag queen).[17] Leduc's last autobiographical *récit*, *La Chasse à l'amour* (CAL), documents the pitying detachment she feels with regard to the 'dames affligées de ne pas l'être' who parade nightly at the Carrousel, a Parisian transvestite nightclub (CAL, p. 121). But other elements within her autobiographical corpus signal that she is profoundly alive to similarities that tie her own situation to that of the *folle*, the self-feminizing queen.

Folles, asserts Leduc in *Trésors à prendre*, are the filial progeny of authoritarian mothers: mothers whose consorts' role in the reproductive process remained minimal. Having taken Woman as their patron saint, they are the reincarnation of their masculinized progenitrixes, who were not, and could not be, attractive to men. Caught, like their mothers before them, between the 'weaker' and the 'stronger' sex, *les folles* occupy a kind of limbo gender-identified state.[18] Consequently, Leduc unsettlingly suggests, their lot involves a hell on earth, an *enfer sur terre* (TAP, pp. 120–1). Diverse facets of Leduc's depiction, in *Trésors*, of the traits of the *folle* resonate with the autobiographical representations of her text-self Violette furnished by *La Bâtarde* and its sequels. Violette, too, is the child (and the reflection/ projection) of an authoritarian woman and single, 'phallic' mother who, on every level save the biological, produced her offspring all by herself. She too lives out an *enfer sur terre*, not least by virtue of her physical unattractiveness. We sense, therefore, that if, as she unquestionably is, the self-projective protagonist of Leduc's *récits autobiographiques* is drawn not only towards male homosexuals in general but also, specifically, towards *les folles*, this is because these last not only remind her of her beloved 'good' grandmother but also stand in some sort of cognate relation to herself.

In Leduc's narrative universe, empathy regularly leads to identification. So the fact that Leduc's autobiographies record episodes during which her narrative duplicate effects a kind of (bodily) 'self-homosexualization' should come as no surprise. In *La Bâtarde* (LB), recalling how she obliged Gabriel, her future husband, to penetrate her anally (LB, p. 287/B [trans.], p. 289), Leduc's narrator explains that she was motivated not by a fear of pregnancy, ultimately, but by the desire to have in her bed a male homosexual couple/coupling ('le souhait d'un couple d'homosexuels sur ma couche'). In *La Chasse à l'amour*, in an erotic exchange with another lover, René, Violette – having deliberated as to whether or not she wishes René to sodomize her – opts to adopt a more active, penetrative 'homosexual' stance, creating a reversed reiteration of the homosexual couple scenario of *La Bâtarde* (CAL, pp. 213–14, p. 289). This latter encounter is not only imagined by Leduc as a male–male meeting but is also cast as the antithesis of – and as an improvement upon – lesbian sexual congress. In the same *récit*, after her brush with her lesbian readers, Violette comments 'lesbians make me gloomy. They aren't gay, but rather frenetic',[19] endorsing a (denigratory) judgement that, in *Trésors à prendre*, Leduc signals as typically proffered about lesbians by male homosexuals (TAP, p. 121).

Violette's male-homosexualizing self-metamorphoses may be taken to constitute so many performative gender acts: acts that, if they are rendered dissonant and 'incoherent' by her biological femininity, nonetheless acquire their own logic and impetus in the realm of sexual flexibility and illegitimacy adumbrated in Leduc's life-writings. Inevitably, perhaps, her variform gender performances transport Leduc's narrative self-creation into the camp universe of the *folle/travesti*; the cross-gendered, cross-dressed male homosexual. The process whereby this incursion occurs is complex, and merits careful delineation.

In *La Bâtarde*'s central chapters (LB, pp. 119–353/B, pp. 119–355), the dynamics of Leduc's autobiographical avatar's post-adolescent liaisons with a man, Gabriel, and a woman, Hermine, provide a key object of scrutiny. These liaisons, which are equally emotionally draining and which, for a while, overlap, induce Violette to pursue a panoply of contradictory gender enactments. With Gabriel, in the earliest phase of their dealings, Violette – suited, booted and sporting a cravat – plays heterosexual man to the 'woman' she intermittently wishes him to play (LB, pp. 125–6, 166–7/B, pp. 126, 167), pitting her 'manliness' against the delicate femininity she discerns in him. As her lesbian relationship with the exigent Hermine develops, however, she (apparently) trades mannishness for an intense feminization, effecting one of the many gender-crossings chronicled in Leduc's *récit*. The following extract, in which Violette narrates herself through the routine of physical transmogrification she follows before going to parade around the boulevards of Paris clad in the designer finery Hermine has offered her, records a typical, if extreme, manifestation of this phenomenon:

> It is pleasant, drums, to hear you catch exactly the right tone. I am playing too: I am patting the dark-toned makeup on my Nordic-skinned face. I pat, I slap the makeup on, I slap my skin. Those are the instructions. [. . .] Imagine a tiny porthole of pink lacquer, a circle of pink swooning with its own pallor, inside which there lies a disc of paste, a concentrate of timidity. [. . .] Several circles on the left cheek, several circles on the right cheek, for it must be patted in before you spread it out, that is the secret of a natural base, of perfect makeup, the saleslady told me so quite clearly. [. . .] You know you're getting ready for your circus act, smudged clown in the glass. Drums, into training, all fatigue forbidden. I am about to do my circus act, and my ring is to be the wide boulevards of Paris (B, p. 202).[20]

The process that Violette submits to in episodes such as this has been read in a variety of ways by Leducian critics.[21] Shirley Neuman, for instance, interprets it as evidence of her inability to resist the constraining force of patriarchy's 'cultural script of femininity': an inability signalled by her involvement in a 'series of invitations and losses each of which stages her body as spectacle'.[22] Neuman's reading of the compelled nature of Violette's womanly masquerade – a masquerade that she views as 'produced' by Hermine's normative demands and as 'sewn into [Violette's] flesh'[23] – is not unconvincing. However, it obscures the highly ambivalent nature of the 'feminine' gender-state Violette actually slips into in those parts of *La Bâtarde* typified by the excerpt cited above.

In these narrative sections, Violette does not achieve, by means of the vestimentary and bodily modifictions she effects, a gender identity performance properly consonant with what Neuman terms 'the ideology of femininity/heterosexuality'.[24] She is propelled, rather, into a form of theatrical display that, if anything, recalls the monstrous semiosis of the feminine intrinsic in camp performativity, and gives birth to something close to the hyperbolic femininity of male drag.[25] Violette's flirtation with feminization, then, which is short-circuited when she is mocked for her ugliness by a woman passer-by encountered on the Pont de la Concorde (LB, p. 221/B, p. 222), incorporates and disguises a flirtation with a quite other type of gender performance: the melancholic performance of the (gay) male drag artist who, Butler suggests, forever grieves, and endlessly pursues, the uninhabitable Feminine.[26]

The masculine/feminine, ersatz nature of Violette's 'circus act' is implied by comments proffered by the men who observe her Parisian parade: comments that draw attention to her not-so-very-feminine 'half-boyish femininity' (*féminité d'androgyne*), her 'sculptured bullfighter's buttocks' (*fesses sculptées de toréro*) and the Dietrich-like huskiness of her voice (LB, pp. 203–9/B, pp. 204–10). Its homosexualized dimension is highlighted by the connections binding the account offered in *La Bâtarde* of Violette's engagement with beautification to Leduc's dissection, in *Trésors à prendre*, of the activities and practices of *les folles*. *Folles*, suggests *Trésors*, crave and covet all the dresses they see models wearing; all the fur-wraps glimpsed in theatre foyers; all the silky underwear spotted in mail-order catalogues – so desirous are they of access to an iconic Womanhood that permanently eludes them (TAP, p. 121). In the central segments of *La Bâtarde*, Leduc's Violette – as she remoulds her face and figure, doggedly accumulating the emblems of femininity (these include a Joan Crawford coiffure) – manifests markedly similar tendencies (LB, pp. 210–11/B, pp. 212–13). This parallel helps to confirm our sense that, in this particular phase of her sexual/textual trajectory, the identity category into which Violette is inserted is not (at least, not entirely) that of normative, culturally-conscripted femininity, but pertains rather to that cross-gendered, 'paradigmatic' enclave within male homosexuality adulated by her autobiographical creatrix. Violette may be taken, in other words, to be 'performing' here in tandem with, not to say as, the doubly sexed, highly ambiguous figure of the gay male cross-dresser: a figure that Leduc, in *La Chasse à l'amour* and *Trésors à prendre*, associates with martyred saintliness. We can read her, in short, as accessing a gendered performance for which the compellingly ambivalent gender model presented by her 'priestly' grandmother had, perhaps, always already destined her.

In *La Bâtarde*, then, Leduc constructs her autobiographical self-creation in such a way that Violette can be seen to 'inhabit' (i) (a mime of) straight masculinity; (ii) a lesbian identity incorporating the femininity of the domestic concubine, or 'little woman' (LB, p.187/B, p. 187)); (iii) the passive sexuality/masculinity of the submissive gay male; and (iv) the theatrical, ambiguous gender comportment of the *travesti/folle*; as well as (v) the normative category of heterosexual femininity. Clearly, some of these variant modalities of gendered doing – which offer ample confirmation of Butler's contention that the inner truth of gender is (in both senses of the word) a fabrication[27] – are negotiated by Violette more seriously and more enduringly than others. That said, in the light of their combined textual articulation, it is hard to concur with de Ceccatty's contention that, in the work of Violette Leduc, male and female homosexual modalities remain distinct and discrete.[28] In fact, male and female homosexuality, together with the male (homosexual) practice of drag, are connected in Leduc's writing by virtue of the gender peripeteia of her protean autobiographical avatar. What, though, are we to make of Violette's sexed metamorphoses? Can we, more particularly, interpret her shift into the parodic, *overdone* (non)femininity of drag – a femininity that, Butler notes, has been viewed as degrading to women[29] – as anything other than a problematic appropriation of what may be a misogynistic, ridiculizing masculine practice? In order to address these questions, I want to return to Butler's analyses of gender-as-performance, in the specific context of drag, and to gloss them in more detail.

In the fourth chapter of *Bodies that Matter*, 'Gender is Burning', Butler theorizes gender as the result of a normalizing interpellation. She suggests that gendered being/doing involves us in repeated acts of performative obedience to the call of the symbolic, heterosexual 'law': an obedience generated by our fear of punishment. She goes on to point out, however, that the Law of Gender 'calls up' not only gender states and acts that are loyally expressive of reproductive heterosexuality, but also 'pathologizing practices' or 'sites of ambivalence'.[30] Produced 'at the limits of legitimacy' and characterized by a failure to respect that unity of sex, sexuality, gender and desire required by and for heterosexual coherence, these illegitimacies serve to consecrate the status of heterosexual performativity as originary and proper.[31] Butler's contention, in sum, is that hegemonic heterosexuality needs and negotiates a space of gender otherness – a space constituted by 'abject' gender performances, whose status within the terms of heterosexual sociality is degraded and outlawed[32] – in order to establish itself as that which is natural, normal and 'right'.

The 'pathologizing' activity on which Butler focuses in 'Gender is Burning' is drag. Her specific point of reference is the cross-dressing practised by the black and latino homosexuals and transsexuals who feature in Jennie Livingston's documentary *Paris is Burning* (1991). On the one hand, Butler's reading of Livingston's film-text illuminates the extent to which drag can be seen as supportive of the heterosexual order, and its gender ideology. It does so by signalling the ways in which drag performances involve an exaggerated reconsolidation and reidealization of that order's 'natural', normative gender categories.[33] But Butler's discussion also suggests that drag – resting as it does on an equation of gender and mime – possesses the potential to 'unmask' and *denaturalize* the gender performances of hegemonic, heterosexual 'normality'. Her account construes it as offering clues to the fact that these 'coherent' performances are neither essential nor originary but constitute, rather, constructed and compelled acts of *mimicry*. And her analysis persuades us to concede that the (hyperbolic, theatrical) approximations of 'real', 'natural' gender that drag produces intimate that 'natural' gender itself rests always on a 'constant and repeated effort to imitate its own idealizations':[34] an effort that betrays its actual, fabricated unnaturalness. If, in other words, in the Butlerian optic, drag is viewed as a practice that somehow idealizes dominant heterosexuality and its norms, it is also recognized as one that 'reveals the imitative structure of [heterosexual] gender itself – as well as its contingency'.[35] Acknowledged as steeped in ambivalence, it is conceived by Butler as much as a phenomenon that betrays the 'mundane impersonations by which heterosexually ideal genders are performed and naturalized', thereby sapping their power, as an activity that shores hetero-sexualized gender up.[36]

How, to come back to the focus of my own analysis, does all this relate to Violette Leduc? Can we use Butlerian insights to interpret, 'politically', the performative gender shifts mobilized in *La Bâtarde*? If we transpose the gender acts performed by Leduc's autobiographical heroine onto a Butlerian grid, we can in fact construe them as possessing a denaturalizing impact that is analogous to that effected by the cross-dressers discussed by Butler but that, I would suggest, is actually more contestatory. Like the mimicries of Butler's/Livingston's drag queens, Violette's identity performances can be taken implicitly to expose the contingent, non-natural character of hegemonic gender enactments. They do not, however, I want to propose, ultimately function in the service of heterosexual norms and in the service of their consolidation, or idealization.

The particular drag artist who 'stars' as the heroine of Livingston's film and Butler's reading of it is Venus Xtravaganza, a homosexual transvestite and pre-operative transsexual. In his/her hyperbolic miming of a 'real' woman, Venus certainly – on one level – contests binary gender norms, by reworking their 'natural' cohesion of anatomical sex, gender identity and gender performance. However, as Butler indicates, Venus's imitative acting out of 'whole womanhood' clearly cannot be viewed as entirely disruptive. The end point of his/her trajectory is, after all, a sort of heterosexually ideal gender performance. S/he may denaturalize that (sanctioned, 'natural', normative) performance by intimating, through ambiguous mimicry, its own inevitably fabricated foundation; but his/her imitative activities also involve an adulatory reinforcement of it, manifest in the desire to 'be Woman' (and nothing but) that they bespeak.[37] Leduc's Violette, on the other hand, incarnates a limit-case of gender denaturalization. Her crossings of gender and sexual boundaries are transgressive, or disloyal, in a way that Venus's are not. This is because, instead of moving from the margins towards the hegemonic, Violette does the opposite. She transmutes herself not towards conformism, or normativity, but towards the modalities of what Butler terms 'abjection'. The gender-crossings that she enacts in *La Bâtarde* take her, intermittently, out of a womanhood (whether heterosexual or lesbian) on which her purchase is always less than secure, and into a mime of maleness that incorporates not only the heterosexual and the homosexual Masculine but also, on occasion, a feminized, illegitimate, wholly *un*natural masculinity: the masculinity of the cross-identified *folle*.[38] If, in other words, Livingston's Venus cites heterosexually consecrated gender norms in such a way that they are ultimately validated, Violette's proliferating and misplaced gender acts cannot possibly be said to support – even by working in 'abject' and 'naturalizing' contradistinction to them – the gender ideals of what Butler designates as the heterosexual project.

Confronted with the autobiographical textual space that is *La Bâtarde*, the reader encounters some remarkable – and mutating – chroniclings of sexual/gender possibilities. Their inclusion in Leduc's first and best-known *récit autobiographique* allows us to view it as a narrative in which 'queer' identitarian practice – which we may define not as a practice of exclusive homosexuality but, rather, as any practice that deviates from and disturbs sanctioned norms of sexuality and gender[39] – is represented powerfully and originally. Their textual inscription troubles, moreover, a number of 'truths' about, or conceptualizations of, gender, all of which are addressed if not endorsed by Judith Butler in her theoretical writings. It troubles, first, the notion that gender in any way constitutes, or is immutably tied to, a core, primary, either/or phenomenon such as anatomical sex. Likewise, it troubles our willingness to conceive gender as a static modality of identificatory being or fixed substance, compelling us to regard it instead in the manner in which Butler incites us to regard it: that is, as a 'kind of becoming or activity'.[40] Finally, Leduc's articulations of Violette's queering, 'disloyal' self-metamorphoses trouble our faith in the proposition – entertained by Butler, in *Bodies that Matter* – that gender performances of an 'illegitimate' or 'pathological' stripe are called up and function finally to consecrate heterosexual gender ideals/norms.

By virtue of its accounts of gender deviation, and by virtue of the conceptual 'trouble' that they provoke, *La Bâtarde* must be acknowledged as a text that not only gives queerness a voice, but also takes a queer delight in challenging normative notions of what gender is and should be.[41] The same cannot be said of *Un amour de soi*, the autofictional *opus* I want to examine next. In its refusal 'properly' to affirm the (total, unproblematic) identifiability of its author and narrator/protagonist, its self-designation as a *roman* and its sustained play with aesthetic strategies usually associated with avant-garde fiction,[42] *Un amour de soi* is deliberately and self-consciously autobiographically unorthodox in ways that *La Bâtarde* is not. Yet, with regard to the 'gender trouble' or queer enactments that it likewise transcribes, Doubrovsky's text adopts what seems to be a far more orthodox – in other words, critical – stance than its Leducian predecessor. But at the same time, and paradoxically, *Un amour* also, as I shall demonstrate in what follows, bespeaks a certain investment in a specific sort of (male homo)sexual 'deviance'. This investment, though, is made much less apparent in Doubrovsky's self-history than it is in *La Bâtarde* and other Leducian writings. It is obscured by virtue of the fact that, in *Un amour*, (the lure of) male homosexuality is narratively occulted. And we can take its elision to signal that Doubrovsky's *autofiction* can be situated – up to a point – in the same autobiographical enclave as Sartre's sexually occlusive *Les Mots* – a text that has long fascinated the author of *Un amour de soi*.

Serge Doubrovsky's Gender Trouble: Writing the (Homo)textual Self [43]

In the back-page blurb of *Fils* (1977), the first of a series of self-denotingly auto-fictional works published in the 1970s–1990s, in his seminal essay 'Autobiographie/vérité/psychanalyse' and in other critical pieces, Serge Doubrovsky devotes a great deal of time to dissecting the autofictional project. Moreover, in his metanarrative exegeses, he is at pains to establish that in his own autofictional productions – productions he presents as 'fake' fictions that tell the story of a real life[44] – he maintains a firm, not to say 'umbilical' grip on the facts of his lived existence.[45] He also, however, makes it clear that his autofictional self-narrations, like the retrospective self-(re)readings produced by analysands, constitute *reconstructions* of moments of being that tend to the fictive, the phantasmatic.[46] He posits his *autofictions* as offering 'working' reworkings of the self/selves of his past that privilege the creative and the salutary over the documentary. We do not, though, need to regard this as militating against the *personal* truth that they articulate, because, for Doubrovsky, as my discussions in Chapter 4 affirmed, the truthful meaning of a life never exists in a pregiven or immutable or extra-narrative form. It is not 'something to be discovered but something to be invented, not from scratch but from a multiplicity of traces; it is something to be [narratively] *constructed*'.[47]

Doubrovsky's contention, in sum, is that the (re)constructed self-truth invoked in his autofictional writing, while it is in no way 'objective', is potentially more truthful than the 'truth' proffered by the *autoportrait classique* (that is, by the type of text that claims to be imbued with an authorial self-awareness that allows for the authentic depiction of its author's *vérité*).[48] The textual, 'truer' self-truth in question – a truth that, as my last chapter indicated, Doubrovsky conceives as the 'fiction that I have decided, as a writer, to make of myself and for myself'[49] – is clearly, moreover, a willed, elected truth. The notion that *autofiction* constitutes the site of a textual truth of the writing self that is not only invented but is also *desired* provides a frame of reference for the reading I wish to offer here of Doubrovsky's *Un amour de soi*.[50] Like *La Bâtarde*, this particular autofictional work – Doubrovsky's second – provides us with an extraordinarily convoluted chronicle of the peripeteia of love. From within its textual web we can, if we read with care, unearth oblique – and unexpected – 'clues' that point up the homoerotic desires of 'Serge', Doubrovsky's autofictional narrator/protagonist and narrative self-construct.[51] 'Serge's' sexual truth is, indubitably, a disguised truth. It runs counter to the normative Law of heterosexual Desire that Doubrovsky's *roman* appears to defend. It is, nonetheless, a truth that is hinted at interstitially in his text. Its 'markers' form part of the 'fiction que [Doubrovsky a] décidé de [se] donner de [lui]-même', of the *implant fictif*[52] he autofictionally grafts onto himself. And its occluded articulation allows us to view *Un amour de soi*, finally, not simply as the vehicle for a vilification of female 'Gender Trouble' – which, as we shall see, is what Doubrovsky's text superficially constitutes – but also as a tale of male sexual 'abjection'[53] and, more precisely, as the tale of a homosexuality that Doubrovsky narratively invents and enjoys for himself, even as he seems to disown it.

In 'prélude', the opening segment of *Un amour de soi* (UA), Doubrovsky's autofictional persona, 'Serge', a professor of French literature in New York and would-be author, encounters Rachel, a young colleague whose academic career is in its infancy. As the text's Proustian epigraph announces ('To think that I've wasted years of my life, that I've longed to die, that I've experienced my greatest love, for a woman who didn't appeal to me, who wasn't even my type!'),[54] Rachel does not conform to 'Serge's' ideal of feminine desirability. After, however, she instigates a sexual liaison, he falls in love with her, succumbing to an *amour-maladie*[55] comparable to the unhealthy passion recounted in Proust's *Un amour de Swann*.[56] In the course of the rest of Doubrovsky's narrative – composed of subsections entitled *spirales* – we witness the decomposition of the 'Serge'–Rachel affair. This process, whose backdrop is the world of academia where 'Serge' has his established place and Rachel is seeking hers, is rendered almost inevitable by 'Serge's' inability to commit to his mistress. It is accompanied by increasingly damaging confrontations and by increasingly rare *retours d'amour*. Finally, 'Serge' must recognize that the woman for whom he eventually divorces no longer desires him, that she loves someone else and that she proves, ultimately and always, to have been a stranger (UA, p. 379). Doubrovsky's *récit* closes *in cauda venenum*, with a Coda that transcribes 'revealing' missives Rachel has received, and concludes with a 'happy ending': the initiation of his self-construct's courtship of a new, more suitable mistress.

As in Leduc's *L'Asphyxie*, a key feature of *Un amour de soi* is its hermeneutic element. As every good Barthesian knows, the hermeneutic pertains to that narrative dimension comprising 'the various (formal) terms by which an enigma can be distinguished, suggested, formulated, held in suspense, and finally disclosed'.[57] Its relevance to Doubrovsky's own text, and to our understanding of its workings, is mooted in *Un amour*'s first *spirale*, in which Rachel, rewriting her thesis on Balzac, alerts 'Serge's' attention – and ours – to Barthes's account of it (UA, p. 76). Her reiteration of the Barthesian notion of narrative as the site of mystery/disclosure leads us to reflect on and seek out the secrets hidden in the autofictional tale in which she herself is a primary player.

Not one but two *énigmes* are, in fact, profiled within *Un amour de soi*. This allows the reader who opts to approach Doubrovsky's text in detective guise to treat it as a bipolar *polar*, or dually-focused mystery novel. It appears, initially, that the conundrum we must solve is that communicated by *Un amour*'s epigraph. It seems, in other words, that our task is to unravel the riddle of how it is that 'Serge', Doubrovsky's autofictional narrator, can love a woman 'qui n'est pas son genre' and who is increasingly rejecting of him. 'Serge's' authorial creator/double seems keen to keep this particular mystery – which, for simplicity's sake, I shall call 'mystery 1' – at the forefront of his story and his reader's consciousness. His apparent desire to do so is reflected in his transcription of conversations between 'Serge' and his Anglophone analyst Akeret, who interrogates 'Serge' about his inexplicable desire for Rachel: 'Why do you cling to her so? [. . .] You told me she is not even your type' (UA, p. 208). However, Doubrovsky's determination to foreground 'mystery 1' is no more than illusory. Manipulatively, and without appearing deliberately to do so, he contrives to lure our interpretative antennae elsewhere, by creating within his text a further, extensively adumbrated puzzle. The existence of this second, 'decoy' enigma can lead us, unless we are careful, to lose sight of our efforts to make sense of 'mystery 1'. I shall highlight the motivation subtending Doubrovsky's hermeneutic shift below. For the moment, though, I want to establish what 'mystery 2' is, and how Doubrovsky works to resolve it.

If 'mystery 1' is 'Serge's' mystery, and turns on the mystery of his damaging desire, then 'mystery 2', centred around Rachel, is constituted by the enigma of what she is and seeks to achieve. This conundrum is only posed as such, explicitly, in the last of 'Serge's' conversations with Akeret, by 'Serge' himself: 'Robert, Robert, I can't understand what's happening' (UA, p. 312). However, its signals are set up in *Un amour*'s prelude, in part through the inclusion of a cluster of motifs that recur subsequently and frequently. Here, Rachel is introduced to the reader and to Doubrovsky's narrator/protagonist. By the end of the prelude, the two of them have made love, 'Serge' has dissected the episode with Akeret and has established various 'facts' about his new lover. These facts – which illuminate Rachel, implicitly, as a locus of 'oddness'/puzzlement – may be summarized as follows:

(i)   She displays an unsettling strangeness, conveyed in her voice, whose French accent is barely foreign, yet is alien as well as familiar to 'Serge' (UA, p. 16).

(ii) She is nevertheless a potential double for 'Serge', because she, like him, is Jewish, intellectual and has Eastern European antecedents (UA, p. 18).

(iii) She possesses a bizarrely masculine aspect, evinced by the 'fur' 'Serge' finds on her upper lip (UA, p. 18); the curious hairiness (*villosité filandreuse*) he discovers, with horror, when he kisses her breasts ('biting into female teats, suddenly I'm sucking a man');[58] and the glasses she favours: glasses that 'steal women's femininity away, passing it on to men'.[59] Her 'masculinity' provokes in 'Serge' a primitive castration anxiety that intensifies as he penetrates her (UA, p. 28). Since it appears to have as its concomitant his own feminization (her hairiness, for instance, forces him to recall the feminine hairlessness that was for years his portion (UA, p. 30)), her 'maleness' likewise instils in 'Serge' a fleeting sense of obliteration.

The portrait of Rachel inaugurated here is consolidated in ensuing chapters of *Un amour*. In the main, Doubrovsky is careful, in the body of his text, not to 'explain' Rachel definitively or prematurely, by resorting to overstatement. However, in certain *spirales* he is prepared to be quite explicitly elucidatory in what he conveys about her. In these sections, he chronicles incidents that constitute catalytic moments in his story, providing us with further 'illumination' as to the nature and motivations of his sexually unsettling heroine and preparing the ground for the 'revelations' contained in the Coda of his tale.

Spirale VII, for instance, invokes the analytical activities 'Serge' and Rachel embark on after each has dreamt dramatically. In 'Serge's' dream, we discover, he sees himself in Florida, dressed in bright mauve clothing (UA, p. 203). He finds his oneiric apparel inexplicable: Rachel, however, observes that mauve is *her* colour, the colour she wore when they first met. Rachel's dream turns on a visit she makes to a museum in Israel, where she expects to find paintings by her artist father, discovers they are missing and leaves feeling content (UA, p. 213). The two dreams, and the lovers' interpretations of them, are reconstructed in Doubrovsky's text in such a way as to imply several things about Rachel. A first is that she is bent on effecting a sexual reversal that 'Serge' fears because it castrates/violates him: 'Mauve, a deadly colour, she's contaminated me like a dose of clap. Violet, violated. If I'm dressed like a chick, like a man in drag, maybe I'm the girl. Rachel the guy. The bearded lady.'[60] A second is that this reversal masks a desire on Rachel's part to liquidate a paternal figure who is less her biological father than her pseudo-father and intellectual mentor, 'Serge' himself.

The twin motifs of castration and paternal liquidation are invoked elsewhere, in sections of *Un amour* focused on Rachel's relations with her lover. In *spirale X*, she almost succeeds in replacing/displacing 'Serge', at an MLA meeting he is loath to attend and at which he asks her to give, in his stead, his paper on Sartre. In *spirale XII* – an extended chronicle of the death of an affair – Rachel informs 'Serge' of the unoriginality of his recent critical work (UA, p. 325), before flaunting, at the fiftieth birthday party she organizes to fête the decline of his youth (UA, p. 345), her emasculatory infidelity with John, a younger colleague: 'no crown, no throne, I've no longer a sceptre, a sex, she's taken it from me, there on the sofa, in front of everyone, it's capital punishment, she's castrating me [. . .] Rachel's the guy, I'm the girl, I'm the one with the pallid, pasty chicken's chest, she's the one with the hairy breasts, like a priapic monkey'.[61]

Confronted with depictions such as the above, which repeatedly invoke Rachel's penchant for clothes, hairstyles, accessories and practices of bodily presentation/ performance that 'unsuitably' accentuate her virile aspect, the reader cannot help but wonder, as Doubrovsky certainly intends us to wonder, what it is, exactly, that Rachel 'means' and wants. Her creator ensures that our questions are answered, finally and fully, in his venomous Coda, which, in the manner of the classic dénouement of detective fiction, offers a 'conclusive' solution to the 'puzzle' Rachel incarnates. Much of *Un amour*'s Coda is composed of letters, written to Rachel by her friend Annie and discovered belatedly by Doubrovsky's self-construct 'Serge'. These documents are employed, vengefully, against their recipient in order to 'elucidate' – and to criminalize – her. Rachel's narrative criminalization is twofold. It proceeds in part from a highly Lacanian observation proffered by Annie in the seventh of her letters: 'I recall what you used to say, that you didn't so much want to HAVE Serge as to BE Serge.'[62] This remark foregrounds, retroactively, all the references to Rachel's masculine/castratory demeanour and activities and all the evocations of her (deliberately) phallicized physical appearance that constellate *Un amour*. Echoing as it does the having/being binary subtending Lacan's account of male/female sexualization, Annie's comment illegalizes Rachel by revealing her to have sought out a 'place' not hers by biological right: that of the phallic, masculine subject.[63] If the intention behind its original articulation is benign, its narrative reproduction ensures that Rachel is conclusively condemned: condemned for having aspired to obliterate her ageing lover, in order to assume the male, paternal intellectual mastery that is his at their liaison's inception, and condemned for having pursued a 'monstrous ascent into phallicism'.[64] The parricidal nature of Rachel's usurpatory, gender-crossing enterprise is illuminated, further, by Annie's 'humorous' observation that 'Serge' should have written an *autofiction* entitled not *Fils* but *Père* (UA, p. 377).[65] The other dimension of Rachel's culpa-bility established in Doubrovsky's criminalizing Coda is signalled in Annie's disquisitions on lesbianism, most notably by her description of herself and Rachel as *homosexuelles rentrées* (UA, p. 371). Annie's letters parallel Rachel's sexuality with her own burgeoning homoeroticism. Her suggestion that Rachel, like herself, is sexually susceptible to what are clearly sister-selves – women with 'phallic' cunts ('des femmes dont les cons sont phalliques' UA, p. 371) – indicts 'Serge's' ex-lover further and definitively, and in spite of her affair with John Rubin, as a phallic lesbian castratrix whose sexual 'unsuitability', because he has never really known her, does not implicate 'Serge' in any significant way.

The Coda of *Un amour* abjects Rachel, in a gesture whose terms of reference reflect and reinforce the gender ideology of heterosexism. It explicates her in the context of, and consigns her to, that 'illegitimate' domain of gender/sexual perform-ance – likewise inhabited by Leduc's Violette, and the *folles* she is identified with – in which 'all the wrong identifications are pursued; men wishing to "be" the phallus for other men, women wishing to "have" the phallus for other women, [. . .] women wishing to "have it" for a man who "is" it'.[66] It subjects Rachel to a symbolic assassination more violent than those occasionally contemplated by 'Serge' in the course of his stormy relationship with her. Concomitantly, Doubrovsky's Coda confirms in his reader's mind the centrality of 'enigma 2', the Rachel mystery. It sets the seal on a process whereby *Un amour* becomes a sort of palimpsest, in which 'mystery 1', the mystery of why 'Serge' wants Rachel so lastingly, comes to be covered up. It consolidates Rachel's role as a narrative riddle that is eventually unravelled and, in securing her enigmatization *and* resolving the enigma she represents, functions to incite us to forget about the puzzle of her lover's 'inexplic-able' love. But the de-enigmatization of 'Serge's' desire, because it is engineered so skilfully by Doubrovsky, suggests that there may be elements of his text-self's desiring investments that he seeks to obscure.

If, undeterred by the palimpsestic layering effected in *Un amour*, we refuse to abandon our efforts to resolve the riddle of 'Serge's' passion for 'une femme qui n'était pas son genre', then we find that Doubrovsky's *autofiction* does, in fact, furnish (at least) three solutions to it. Two of these solutions to 'mystery 1', as I have argued elsewhere, are narratively intimated quite explicitly – and may be deemed, therefore, also to be narratively 'licensed'. They are brought to our attention by 'clues' planted deliberately and overtly in *Un amour*. They enucleate 'Serge's' need for Rachel in terms of (i) her status as a mirror-self whose specular aspect satisfies 'Serge's' overwhelming narcissism ('See myself through her eyes, in her eyes. Suddenly I forget to see *her*. The thing I can't resist about her is me')[67] and (ii) the 'maternal' nurturance with which, intermittently, she gratifies his primitive oral impulses.[68] At the same time, they somehow desexualize 'Serge's' attraction to his lover, and, more significantly, distance it from the perverse queerness she is shown to embody and emblematize. The third solution, however, is neither extra-sexual nor openly signalled in Doubrovsky's *opus*. Instead of being flagged up in or 'sanctioned' by the narrative fabric of *Un amour*, it is encrypted beneath its surface. It meshes, moreover, with that dimension of Doubrovsky's *roman* character-ized by 'gender trouble'. And it provides the focus of the rest of this discussion.

As my remarks so far have established, the source of *Un amour*'s 'gender trouble' is Rachel. There are, in fact, two ways in which we can read her. On the one hand, we can opt for the reductive interpretation that *Un amour*'s queering Coda encourages us to elaborate. We can position Rachel, in other words, as a phallicized, castratory, 'misidentified' dyke, complete with moustache, hairy chest, *côté mec et al.* (UA, p. 380). If we do so, then we seal her fate as a figure of abjection. We constitute her, as the climax of Doubrovsky's text certainly constitutes her, as a cipher of sexual and gender irregularity. We turn her into a spectre of outcast, minatory otherness of the kind, Butler asserts, the heterosexual sociosymbolic order produces so that its hegemony may continue to prevail.[69]

On the other hand, and more radically, we can interpret Rachel – whose desire is depicted in Doubrovsky's narrative as feminine and masculine, as heterosexual and lesbian (UA, p. 217), as maternal and infantile, as male-homosexualized even (like Violette, she enjoys the 'homosexual' activity of anal sex (UA, p. 31, p. 313)) – as incarnating a profound *subversion* of the normalizing heterosexual Law of gender/sex. We can read her as exemplifying 'precisely the kind of complex crossings of identification and desire which exceed and contest the [heterosexual gender-]binary frame'.[70] We can see her, in sum, not as a symbol of abject illegitimacy but as the site of a stirring destabilization/denaturalization of fixed, polarized gender categories, and as a figure of sexual resignification with and via whom *all sorts of desiring relations* become possible. This second version of what Rachel may be taken to signify has major implications for the mystery of 'Serge's' long-term attachment to his 'troubling' Dulcinea.

We are left in no doubt that 'Serge' relates to Rachel as if to a double, whose similarity is deeply appealing. And, as I indicated above, we may take his investment in the parallelism subtending their connection as symptomatic, simply, of his overweening *self*-love. Because, however, Rachel's gendered and sexual identificatory crossings take her, as *Un amour* endlessly intimates, into a 'deviant' domain of phallicity/'maleness', it is possible – and indeed tempting – to read 'Serge's' double-oriented desire for her not, as we are invited and incited to read it, as a solipsistic *amour de soi*, but, rather, as an eroticized desire for the male *same*, the fundamentally homosexual nature of which, because its object is biologically a woman, remains hidden.[71]

As early as the prelude of *Un amour*, as well as elsewhere (cf. UA, p. 168), 'Serge's' intolerance of gender ambiguity and his own acute sexual/gender conformism are made insistently explicit, in a manner that discourages us from 'homosexualizing' his desiring habits: 'An obsession, maybe, at least that shows I have my rules. There's an absolute one, etched in stone, instilled at my birth, when I was in the womb, even. THE SEPARATION OF THE SEXES. [. . .] Each in his place, each has his sex. Each sex in its place.'[72] But other facets of Doubrovsky's narrative and of the story 'Serge' tells within it, for all that that story recounts a male–female coupling, hint that homoerotic gratification and male–male relationality *are* what he ultimately pursues, phantasmically, in and through his dealings with the sexually slippery, (ever more) 'masculine' Rachel. There is the fact that she, by virtue of her social *entrées* into the male homosexual world, is construed not only as a part of that world but also as 'Serge's' passport into it: 'Thanks to Rachel, I'm penetrating queer circles. She has an 'in'. Don't know why, a fag hag, as they call them here.'[73] There is the telling discussion, reiterated in *Un amour*'s prelude, in which 'Serge' reports to Akeret Rachel's account of her anal, 'homosexual' defloration by a Brazilian lover, Paulo, conveying as he does so the arousal *he* felt on hearing it (UA, pp. 31–2). There are the personal sexual recollections of episodes of anal penetration that *Un amour* includes: recollections that imply that what 'Serge' seeks to enjoy with his mannish inamorata may indeed be what Leduc's Violette likewise tries to perform with Gabriel; that is, an ersatz gay male connection. Finally, Doubrovsky's narrative documents incidents that suggest that 'Serge's' interaction with Rachel offers him a means to access displaced homoerotic bonds with individual male others, and that he exploits and enjoys the mediatory dimension of their affair, even as he appears to misperceive or resent it. These incidents involve Paolo (UA, p. 28), who telephones while 'Serge' is making love with Rachel, leaving him 'breathless', and John, 'Serge's' cuckolding competitor for Rachel's affections: 'I'm the one he's fucking through her, I'm the target, [. . .] I've been buggered'.[74]

Un amour is studded with elements that defuse or inter the appeal that homosexuality holds for 'Serge', and occult the homosexualized foundation of his desire for Rachel. It presents, for instance, the homoerotic realm into which Rachel initiates 'Serge' as a territory that is profoundly unpalatable and alien to him: 'At the Ecole Normale, I only knew normal guys. [. . .] Here, perversion's on parade, tastes get talked about, their colours nailed to the mast. There's the clan in black, the leather-clones, SS caps, jackets striped with zippers, belts with giant buckles, studded flies.'[75] Likewise, Doubrovsky's narrative incorporates 'confessional' components whose function is, in fact, deflectional. In these textual segments, 'Serge' admits belatedly that his liaison with his multisexed, multi-identified mistress has allowed him, from time to time, to love as a *tante* (nance) or as a *gouine* (dyke) (UA, p. 217) and to take a little (homo)sexual trip that suited his 'fairy side', his *côté tapette* (UA, p. 380). His (dis)avowals serve, essentially, a decoy purpose, and thus cohere with the other narrative lures that Doubrovsky introduces into *Un amour*. Grounded in a camp lexicon, all that they actually reveal, in the end, is that 'Serge' has flirted briefly, in the course of his lengthy affair, with a transitory feminization, and with a sort of playful sexual polymorphosity. They tell us effectively nothing about – and hence help to occlude – the homoerotic, androcentric desire for male–male relationality that we can take to be a primary but unacknowledged motivating force behind his pursuit of the self-phallicizing/virilizing Rachel.[76] The hom(m)osexual thrust of the bond of sameness that 'Serge' and Rachel share is further elided by 'Serge's' insistence on the *familial* status of their identificatory tie ('Brother and sister, [. . .] a pinch of incest, that peps things up, makes them spicy'),[77] and on the unexpectedly *feminine* charms of the wo/manly rump he enjoys breaching when he makes love to his mirror-self (UA, p. 313). Homosexual desire, then, remains the repressed element of Doubrovsky's autofictional text. As with all instances of repression, however, there are moments at which it narratively 'returns'.

The first of these punctuates 'Serge's' account of a trip he makes to Spain (*spirale X*), on which Rachel does not accompany him and during which he finds himself, for once, in exclusively male company, in a *bistrot pour hommes* in Salamanca (UA, p. 260). Rachel is not present to mediate his suppressed homosexual desire: her absence, however, means that there is also nothing to block its actualization. Free of her constraining physical presence, 'Serge' offers himself to his male companions, in whom he discerns Rachel's manly silhouette, by proffering the synecdochical gift of his money/penis.[78] His gesture is fruitless. Rebuffed by what is presented as an act of kindness – the men of the men's bar refuse to let a visiting stranger pay (UA, p. 261) – he can only stare disconsolately at the phallic emblem of his thwarted homosexual need: 'the raw ham hanging on the meat hook the bone-end covered with a hairy tuft of black bristles'.[79] The second narrative moment at which sexual/textual repression is overturned occurs at the end of *Un amour de soi*, in a narrative fragment that highlights 'Serge''s pleasure at having replaced Rachel with a more appropriate – because highly feminine – lover. Observing this woman, delighting in her charms, he is excited by her blue velvet sheath-dress, noting that its sleeves shimmer with shiny zips, *fermetures Eclair* (UA, p. 381). In his essay on Sartre's *La Nausée*, Doubrovsky remarks that a primary concern of psychoanalytic criticism is the 'production in the text of an insignificant detail' that cannot be explained.[80] The zips evoked in the Coda of his *autofiction* furnish the reader with such a detail, recalling as they do that *fermetures Eclair* – the focus, here, of 'Serge's' fetishizing admiration – are an emblem of that universe of homosexual 'perversion' that, once Rachel is gone, should no longer attract or taint his desire.

Clearly, in the last analysis, we can read 'Serge', Serge Doubrovsky's auto-fictional self-construct, as no less normatively deviant than his moustachioed, gender-boundary crossing consort. ''Serge's' infringement of sexual normativity (that is, his crossing of the heterosexual line) is occulted, however, in *Un amour de soi* in a way that the 'gender trouble' that Rachel incarnates is not. Crucially, 'Serge's' elided extranormal sexual aspect enhances our understanding of the narrative project pursued by his authorial counterpart in his second self-inventive *opus*, and of the delights it potentially affords him. In 'Autobiographie/vérité/psychanalyse', Doubrovsky observes that within the textual space that is *autofiction*, writing – that 'supplementary inscription of sexuality'[81] – 'furnishes fantasy with the successful realization that it is always denied in reality'.[82] The (re)construction of a textual, elected truth of the self permitted by the autofictional enterprise opens up to the autofictional practioner, in other words, the 'space of a new and forbidden pleasure'.[83] In *Fils*, autofictional self-manipulation affords the existentially conventional Doubrovsky a textual purchase on the holistic pleasures of bisexedness. In its sequel, I would suggest, his autofictional self-(re)configuration as 'Serge-lover-of-Rachel' enables him to access and to derive gratification from a textually inscribed homosexuality that is not a feature of his lived reality,[84] and is both disguised and delightful, *jouissif*. Male same-sex desire constitutes at once *the* key unspoken element of *Un amour de soi* and a key component of the self-truth its creator elaborates within it. Articulated, assumed and above all occluded by Doubrovsky, deep in the dazzling fabric of his self-fiction, we cannot help but read the play of that desire as a narrative facet that must constitute no less an object of private authorial delectation than the hidden gynosexual episodes of *Les Mots*.

La *Bâtarde* is a text whose language has frequently been qualified as visceral (not least by critics keen to foreground its 'feminine' tenor), and whose concerns include unhappy and thwarted affective relationships, a life constellated with frustrations and a coming to life-writing that facilitated what Beauvoir chose to conceive as the 'reworking of a destiny by a freedom' (B, preface, p. 6).[85] In contrast, *Un amour de soi* is a narrative whose account of its protagonist's destructive, frustrating love affair, professionally fruitful mid-life trajectory and *venue à l'écriture autofictive* is couched in a discourse whose semiotic intricacies owe much to its author's formation as an intellectual, linguist and literary exegete. In these very different autobiographical essays, Violette Leduc and Serge Doubrovsky likewise posit male homosexuality as somehow alluring and likewise illuminate a 'monstrous' female queerness centred less in lesbianism than in a radical performative disruption/denaturalization of heterosexual gender-binaries and gender-norms: they do so, however, in manifestly disparate ways. Leduc presents these sexed phenomena with the defiant, self-exposing *sincérité intrépide* for which her autobiographical writing is fêted by Beauvoir (LB, p. 8/B, p. 6), and in a fashion that confronts her readers' potential prejudices head on. Doubrovsky, on the other hand, writes female gender transgression in a manner that panders, misogynistically, to such prejudices and fuels our awareness of the gynocidal dimension of his textual productions, whilst transcribing male homoerotic desire in a masking, self-reinventive mode that, we sense, puts self-gratification within his reach.[86]

It is by no means surprising, given their individual experiental 'baggage' and the dissimilarity of their narrative projects, that the autobiographers I have focused on in the readings elaborated in Chapter 5 imagine and invoke 'gender trouble' – more especially, female 'gender trouble' – distinctly differently. If, however, we look beyond the evident disparities inherent in their queer articulations, can we regard the visions of sexed deviation, or mobility, that are mobilized in *La Bâtarde* and *Un amour* as in any way stimulated by cognate causal factors? Do Leduc and Doubrovsky, in other words, have things in common that allow us not to be all that astonished by their parallel production of autobiographical self-histories within whose discursive boundaries gender, sexual and desiring borders and identity-categories are traversed so strikingly?

If Leduc and Doubrovsky share any sort of essential 'likeness', it is a 'likeness' generated by the fact that both are writers possessed of an intense awareness of their own lack of a fixed place, their own existential non- or multi-sitedness. Both give voice to this phenomenon time and again, not only in their *récits de vie* but also elsewhere. Leduc, for instance, addresses her lifelong dislocatedness in a 'Radioscopie' interview accorded to Jacques Chancel on 28 April 1970. Here, invoking the social, sexual and literary marginality she knows to be her portion, she poignantly articulates a litany of the milieux and the communities – 'le monde des respectables'; 'le monde des bandits'; 'le monde des intellectuels'; 'le monde des artistes'; 'le monde des femmes de ménage' and so on – to which she has some right of access but in which, ultimately, she has no secure standing or acceptance. Similarly, in an interview with John Ireland included in the 'Doubrovsky special issue' of the literary journal *Genre*, Doubrovsky confirms himself as a 'homeless' subject. Further, he confirms his homelessness as grounded in the liminal, oscillatory existence that, as a (well-established) literary analyst and ('minor') literary practi-tioner, a teacher in two continents and a bilingual subject, he leads between 'two professions, writer and critic; two languages, English and French; two cities, Paris and New York'.[87] It is my sense, finally, that if Doubrovsky and Leduc are equally able, as autobiographical practitioners, to fashion narrative artefacts that construct their primary/self-projective and secondary players as subject to and as the subjects of gender and sexual border-crossings that are not, by and large, charted in other life-writings evoked in my study, this is a function less of their personal sexual or desiring histories than of their fundamental – and enduring – rootlessness, and of their resultant acute sensitivity to the multi-identifiedness that subjectivity admits. Equally, without doubt, it is their individual, unique immersion in unplaceability and deracination that makes these autobiographical authors compelling creative artisans.

Notes

1. See J. Butler (1990), *Gender Trouble: Feminism and the Subversion of Identity*, London and New York. Also crucial to an understanding of Butler's work on gender/sexed identity, and the relationship between gender and sex, is Butler's 1993 study *Bodies that Matter*. On the evolution of Butler's thinking around

the latter relationship, see A. Hughes and A. Witz (1997), 'Feminism and the Matter of Bodies: From de Beauvoir to Butler', *Body and Society*, vol. 3, pp. 47–60.

2. J. Butler (1993), 'Critically Queer', *GLQ: Journal of Gay and Lesbian Studies*, vol. 1, pp. 17–32, p. 21.

3. See *Gender Trouble*, p. 135, p. 112. In *Bodies that Matter*, we should note, Butler comes to construe the very materiality of the sexed body as constituted through discourses and matrices of power. See Hughes and Witz, 'Feminism and the Matter of Bodies', p. 55.

4. *Gender Trouble*, p. 135.

5. Ibid., pp. 135–6. As the citations taken from Butler's work in this introductory section indicate, one of its most interesting aspects is that it reassociates the categories of gender and sex (and, indeed, sexuality) – categories that much feminist theory seeks to keep separate. It does so, *inter alia*, via the notion that gender constitutes a mode of bodily performativity or corporeal stylization, i.e. constitutes something that is enacted at the level of the anatomical as opposed to something that society and culture overlay on beings possessed of particular kinds of sexed anatomy. However, as Anne Witz and I have argued in 'Feminism and the Matter of Bodies' (cf. p. 56), Butler's development of this notion in *Bodies that Matter* leads her in the end to occult gender – the key analytical concept of *Gender Trouble*, and one that is productively theorized as a bodily enactment – by causing it to 'disappear' behind sex (a category conceived, primarily, as a cultural norm governing the materialization of bodies).

6. *Gender Trouble*, p. 136.

7. On *La Bâtarde* as the first instance of Leduc's engagement with the name-based activity of 'proper' autobiographical self-identification, and on the strategies adopted in autobiographical novels such as *L'Asphyxie* to elude (self-) nomination, see Marson, *Le Temps de l'autobiographie: Violette Leduc*, pp. 183–4.

8. The following discussion returns to and expands upon material published in A. Hughes (1998), 'Commodifying Queer: Violette Leduc's Autobiographical Homotextualities', in Heathcote, Hughes and Williams, *Gay Signatures*, pp. 113–29.

9. 'malgré la répétition obstinée de ses désignations sexuelles'. See *Eloge de la Bâtarde*, p. 79 (my trans.).

10. 'Ni lesbienne, ni hétérosexuelle, ni bisexuelle de nature ou d'éducation [. . .], elle est sujet non spécifié et non désigné de plaisir et d'amour'. Ibid.

11. On the chequered history of *Thérèse et Isabelle*, which began life as the prologue to *Ravages* but was removed by Gallimard and then censored further, see C. Jansiti (1994), 'Ils ont refusé le début de *Ravages*', *nord'*, vol. 23, pp. 77–89.

12. Elaine Marks (1990), 'Lesbian Intertextuality', in G. Stambolian and E. Marks (eds), *Homosexualities and French Literature*, Ithaca and London, pp. 353–77, p. 373.

13. 'la mise à jour nécessaire d'une sexualité trop longtemps maintenue discrète'. Interview with P. Descargues, *Tribune de Lausanne*, 18 Oct. 1964, p. 8.

14. See V. Leduc (1973), *La Chasse à l'amour*, Paris, p. 303. Beauvoir published this final volume of Leduc's autobiographical corpus after Leduc's death from breast cancer in 1972. No English translation of it exists.

15. V. Leduc (1960), *Trésors à prendre*, Paris, p. 113. This text has not been translated into English; all translations are mine.

16. 'Craignant ma mère [. . .] je me suis tournée vers celle qui ne ressemblait ni à un homme, ni à une femme. [. . .] Son visage que je revois sur l'unique et vieille photographie n'est pas beau. Il est viril. [. . .] Je réfléchis à ce que je vais écrire: ma grand-mère (qui se maria, eut deux enfants) aura été le premier homosexuel auquel je me sois attachée avec passion pendant que je me réfugiais dans les plis de sa soutane de laïque. C'était un homme en robe qui me protégeait lorsqu'elle m'enlevait à ma mère et qu'elle n'avait pas peur d'elle' (TAP, p. 116).

17. It is important to note that *folles* and *travestis* should not automatically be placed on a continuum that elides significant differences between them. Leduc, however, tends to do so, perhaps because camp, as Daniel Harris explains, given its status as 'something that can be donned like formal wear for occasions of state and similarly doffed when the situations demands', implies always a kind of 'cross-dressing'. See D. Harris (1991), 'Effeminacy', *Michigan Quarterly Review*, vol. 30, pp. 72–81, p. 78. In *Trésors à prendre* (pp. 120–1), for instance, Leduc makes it clear that she considers *les folles* ('children who have taken Woman as their patron Saint'/'des petits enfants qui ont choisi la femme pour sainte patronne') to possess transvestite tendencies. Further, she perceives both *folles* and *travestis* to be haunted by a sense of exile from their 'enrobed' sexual organs (cf. *Trésors* p. 121; *Chasse* p. 121) – a fact that reinforces our sense that she views them as somehow identical. Consequently, the terms *folle* and *travesti* will be used interchangeably in the rest of this discussion. We need also to take note of the politically fraught character of Leduc's generalizing equation of homosexuality and (the desire for) *travestissement*. In fact, as Butler points out, 'cross-gendered identification is not the exemplary paradigm for thinking about homosexuality, although it may be one. [. . .] Not only are a vast number of drag performers straight, but it would be a mistake to think that homosexuality is best explained through the performativity that is drag'. See 'Critically Queer', p. 25.

18. A 'folle' suggests Leduc, is the fruit of 'une femme autoritaire qui a fait toute seule le fils, mais comme il lui manquait le sperme personnel, ce fils est

encore elle-même, exacerbée, écartelée entre le sexe faible et le sexe fort' (TAP, p. 120).

19. 'Les lesbiennes [. . .] m'attristent. Elles ne sont pas gaies: elles sont frénétiques' (CAL, p. 303).

20. 'Tambours, c'est plaisant, avec vous c'est le ton juste. Moi aussi, je joue: je tapote la crème rachel sur mon visage de Nordique. Je tapote, je gifle le produit, je gifle l'épiderme. C'est recommandé. [. . .] Imagine un hublot miniscule de laque rose, d'un rose éperdu de pâleur à l'intérieur duquel se trouve un disque de pâte, un concentré de timidité. [. . .] Plusieurs pastilles [de fard] sur la joue gauche, plusieurs pastilles sur la joue droite puisqu'il faut tapoter avant d'étaler, c'est le secret d'un maquillage naturel, parfait, précisait la vendeuse. [. . .] Tu le sais, tu te prépares pour un cirque, clown effacé. Tambours, à l'entraînment, défense de se fatiguer, je vais entrer dans le cirque, ma piste sera les grands boulevards' (LB, p. 201).

21. These include Martha Noel Evans who, in her essay on gendered writing and language-strategies in *La Bâtarde*, has interesting things to say about Leduc's gender shifts. See M. Evans (1987), 'Violette Leduc: The Bastard', in *Masks of Tradition*, Ithaca and London, pp. 102–22.

22. S. Neuman (1989), '"An appearance walking in a forest the sexes burn": Autobiography and the Construction of the Feminine Body', *Signature*, vol. 2, pp. 1–26, 11, 15. This excellent piece of Foucauldian/Butlerian analysis explores Leduc's autobiographical transcriptions of obligatory gender-construction. A complement to it – which also exploits Butlerian insights, albeit less intuitively – is Sabine Schrader's recently published discussion of Leduc's gender masquerades. See Schrader (1998), 'Le Bonheur était une façade', in P. Renard and M. Hecquet (eds), *Violette Leduc*, Lille, pp. 37–50.

23. Ibid., p. 19. Neuman is privileging, here, the equation of femininity and masquerade favoured by psychoanalysis, and invoked, briefly, in my reading of Duras in Chapter 2.

24. Ibid., p. 17.

25. The notion that gay male camp involves a 'monstrous semiosis' of the feminine is mooted by Kim Michasiw. Michasiw takes camp to involve acts of identification with those elements of the masculine construction of femininity that betray the way in which 'masculine desire shades over into terror'. He argues, in other words, that camp incorporates an 'increasingly panicked defense against what the female might signify [that] produces monsters of semiosis'. See K. Michasiw (1994), 'Camp, Masculinity, Masquerade', *Differences*, vol. 6, pp. 146–73, p. 162.

26. In 'Critically Queer', Butler convincingly connects drag with melancholia, defining melancholia as 'the effect of an ungrieved loss (a sustaining of the lost object/Other as a psychic figure with the consequence of a heightened

identification with that Other, self-beratement, and the acting out of unresolved anger and love)'. Her point is that drag issues from an introjection by the male subject of an insufficiently mourned maternal object, who becomes a focus for identification. See 'Critically Queer', pp. 24–5.

27. See *Gender Trouble*, p. 136.

28. See *Eloge*, p. 162.

29. See *Gender Trouble*, p. 137; *Bodies that Matter*, pp. 126–7.

30. *Bodies that Matter*, pp. 124–5.

31. Ibid., p. 124.

32. Ibid., p. 243.

33. Ibid., pp. 125, 130.

34. Ibid., p. 125.

35. *Gender Trouble*, p. 137.

36. *Bodies that Matter*, p. 231.

37. In a fascinating essay that offers, amongst other things, a compelling analysis of Butler's theoretical work on sex and gender, Biddy Martin argues that in seeking to 'pass' as a woman, Venus passes, if anything, too successfully. Martin's reading of Venus's gender identity performance usefully illuminates its 'idealizing', normatively-produced aspect. See Biddy Martin (1998), 'Sexualities without Genders', in Merck, Segal and Wright, *Coming out of Feminism?*, pp. 11–35, p. 21.

38. Although I do not, myself, wish so to read it here, it would not be impossible/illogical to construe the 'dragged', feminized masculinity or masculine performance I am foregrounding in this discussion and attributing to Leduc's Violette as a performance of *lesbian* 'femmeness' that is routed through gay camp maleness and back again. In 'Sexualities without Genders', Martin works to think through femmeness in such terms, and to view it as a gay-routed female performance that 'makes the crossings [inherent] in all forms of identification more evident' (ibid., p. 22).

39. For an overview of what queer signifies, as a conceptual category and as a reading practice, see Owen Heathcote, Alex Hughes and James S. Williams (1998), 'Introduction: Reading Gay Signatures', in Heathcote, Hughes and Williams, *Gay Signatures*, pp. 1–25, pp. 6–7. For an excellent account of queerness that, refusing to privilege a restrictive definition of it, categorizes it as a state that embraces sexual and gender diversity/deviance in all its forms, see J. Eadie (1994), 'Queer', *Paragraph*, vol. 17, pp. 244–51. On queer as that which defines itself not so much against the heterosexual as against the normal and against the normatively grounded identities it deconstructs, see Michael Warner (1993), 'Introduction', in M. Warner (ed.), *Fear of a Queer Planet: Queer Politics and Social Theory*, Minneapolis, pp. vii–xxxi.

40. *Gender Trouble*, p. 112.

41. Obviously, as she wrote *La Bâtarde* in the early 1960s, Leduc had no way of knowing how conceptual thinking around, and social norms of, gender would evolve in the later decades of the twentieth century. She had certainly, however, already read Beauvoir's *Deuxième Sexe* — a work that both sets gender up as a crucial and productive category for feminist analysis and shrinks from viewing it, as Butler and Leduc herself both readily and radically view it, as an 'action that can potentially proliferate beyond the binary limits imposed by the [. . .] binary of sex' (cf. *Gender Trouble*, p. 112).

42. On Doubrovskian *autofiction* as a life-writing practice of a self-recreative stripe, which turns on an aesthetic response to its author's existential neuroses that produces narratives that are minutely crafted, characterized by dazzling admixtures of sound and sense and imbricated in textual, literary and semiotic experimentation and plenitude, see J. Ireland (1993), 'Introduction: Monstrous Writing', *Genre*, vol. XXVI, pp. 1–11, especially pp. 4–5. It is, I would argue, fair to say that Doubrovskian *autofictions* such as *Un amour de soi* or the earlier *Fils* are far more textually innovative, experimental and readable as works whose very form 'dereferentializes' their content than Guibertian autofictional texts such as *A l'ami* or its sequel *Le Protocole compassionnel*. The fact that Guibert and Doubrovsky practice *autofiction* in different ways explains, perhaps, why Guibert's autofictional writings, as my last chapter indicated, are more productively illuminated by Darrieussecq's analyses of *autofiction* than by those exegeses produced by Doubrovsky himself, in his incarnation as literary theorist.

43. The following discussion includes and develops material that first appeared in A. Hughes (1995), 'Serge Doubrovsky's "Gender Trouble": Writing the (Homo)textual Self in *Un amour de soi*', *French Forum*, vol. 20, pp. 315–31.

44. See 'Autobiographie/vérité/psychanalyse', p. 69; 'Autobiography/Truth/ Psychoanalysis', p. 34.

45. See Serge Doubrovsky (1993), 'Textes en main', in S. Doubrovsky, J. Lecarme and P. Lejeune (eds), *Autofictions et Cie*, Paris, pp. 207–17, p. 212. Doubrovsky's self-confessed attachment to the data of his *vécu* leads Lecarme to allege that Doubrovskian *autofiction* is only minimally distinguishable from autobiography 'proper', and differs from more radically autofictional writing that works to fictionalize, dramatically, the substance of lived being. See J. Lecarme (1993), 'L'Autofiction: un mauvais genre?', *Autofictions et Cie*, pp. 227–49, p. 228. My own sense is that Doubrovsky's *autofictions* are more radical in their relation to the 'real', and its transcription, than Lecarme allows.

46. See 'Autobiographie/vérité/psychanalyse', p. 77; 'Autobiography/Truth/ Psychoanalysis', p. 40. Doubrovsky signals, here, that his production of *autofiction* is indebted to his experience of analysis and to the kind of narrative activity it impelled him into.

47. 'le sens d'une vie n'existe nulle part, n'existe pas. Il n'est pas à découvrir,

mais à inventer, non de toutes pièces, mais de toutes traces: il est à *construire*. See 'Autobiographie/vérité/psychanalyse', p. 77; 'Autobiography/Truth/ Psychoanalysis', p. 40.

48. For Doubrovsky's conceptualization of the *autoportrait classique* and of the flawed, 'foolish' project that subtends its production, see 'Autobiographie/vérité/ psychanalyse', pp. 61–3; 'Autobiography/Truth/Psychoanalysis', pp. 27–9.

49. 'la fiction que j'ai décidé, en tant qu'écrivain, de me donner de moi-même et par moi-même'. See 'Autobiographie/vérité/psychanalyse', p. 77; 'Autobiography/Truth/Psychoanalysis', p. 41.

50. S. Doubrovsky (1982), *Un amour de soi*, Paris. This text, like *Fils*, flags its referential foundation up by giving its narrator/protagonist and his analyst names that are those of its author and his real-life analyst. Further, it includes in its 'Coda' letters that are, apparently, authentic documents. However, as Hélène Jaccomard argues, it can be taken to privilege, more determinedly than *Fils*, its 'composante fictive'. See Jaccomard, *Lecteur et lecture dans l'autobiographie française contemporaine*, pp. 98–9. While it includes passages in English, *Un amour de soi* has no Anglophone translation, so translations are my own. As these may, I fear, reveal, Doubrovsky's text resists translation, not least because of its endless punning. This phenomenon attests to Doubrovsky's will to abandon 'transparent', (purely) 'referential', 'objective' autobiographical discourse in favour of a discourse whose vertiginous manipulation of linguistic 'stuff' takes itself – and imposes itself on the reader – as a primary object of attention, and illuminates Doubrovskian *autofiction* as a self-inscriptive practice that belongs in the realm of the creative/experimental rather than the descriptive or documentary.

51. Because the gap between *Un amour*'s moment of narration and the 'slice of life' it transcribes is sometimes elided, it is not, in fact, meaningful always to distinguish between its protagonistic and narrating personae. I have chosen to cast Doubrovsky's autofictional avatar as 'Serge' in order to signal his ambiguously referential status.

52. 'Autobiographie/vérité/psychanalyse', p. 77.

53. As I indicated above, the notion of the abject, as used by Butler, denotes a realm comprising those individuals/bodies whose sexuality transgresses the norms of the heterosexual symbolic/social order. Abjection at once 'designates a degraded or cast out status within the terms of [heterosexual, reproductive] sociality' and constitutes, potentially, the site of a contestation of the sociosexual order. See *Bodies that Matter*, p. 243.

54. 'Dire que j'ai gâché des années de ma vie, que j'ai voulu mourir, que j'ai eu mon plus grand amour, pour une femme qui ne me plaisait pas, qui n'était pas mon genre!' These remarks form the closing lines of Proust's *Un amour de Swann* (1913). See M. Proust (1954), *Du côté de chez Swann*, Paris, p. 441;

M. Proust (1981), *Remembrance of Things Past*, vol. I, trans. C. K. Scott Moncrief and T. Kilmartin, London, p. 415.

55. See M. Miguet (1992), '*Un amour de so*i: Doubrovsky et Proust et le père profané', *Lettres Romanes*, vol. 46, pp. 69–87, p. 80 and *passim*.

56. The Proustian dimension of *Un Amour de soi*, and its relationship to *Un Amour de Swann*, are dissected by Miguet (cf. '*Un amour de soi*: Doubrovsky et Proust'). A variant reading of the Proustian aspect of Doubrovsky's *autofiction*, whose points of reference are the Combray episode of *Du côté de chez Swann* and Doubrovsky's own exegesis of it in *La Place de la Madeleine* (Paris, 1974) is offered in my 'Serge Doubrovsky's "Gender Trouble"', pp. 322–6.

57. 'l'ensemble des unités qui ont pour fonction d'articuler, de diverses manières, une question, sa réponse et les accidents variés qui peuvent préparer ou retarder la réponse; ou encore: de formuler une énigme et d'amener son déchiffrement'. See *S/Z*, p. 24; R. Barthes (1974), *S/Z*, trans. R. Miller, New York, p. 19.

58. 'je mords mammes de femme soudain suce un mec' (UA, p. 27).

59. 'enlèvent leur féminité aux femmes, la refilent aux hommes' (UA, p. 24).

60. 'Mauve, couleur mortelle, elle m'a contaminé comme un chtouille. Violet, violé. Si je suis habillé comme une gonzesse, un homme travesti, peut-être que la nana, c'est moi. Rachel le mec. La femme à barbe' (UA, p. 204). Doubrovsky's play with the signifier 'violet' echoes the way in which he considers Sartre to employ it: that is, as the 'emblem of a lethal female sexuality' and as part of a chain of signifiers (including rape/*viol* and violated/ *violé*) relating to male castration anxiety. See Serge Doubrovsky (1990), 'Sartre's *La nausée*: Fragment of an Analytic Reading', in Stambolian and Marks, *Homosexualities and French Literature*, pp. 330–40, p. 337.

61. 'plus de couronne, plus de trône, je n'ai plus de sceptre, plus de sexe, elle me l'ôte, là, sur le canapé public, exécution capitale, elle me castre [. . .] Rachel le mec, moi la gonzesse, moi qui ai la poitrine blanche, fade comme une chair de poulet, elle les seins velus comme un singe en érection, [. . .] elle qui les a' (UA, p. 348).

62. 'je me rappelle ce que tu disais, que tu ne voulais pas tellement AVOIR Serge qu'ETRE Serge' (UA, p. 367).

63. For Lacan, sexual identity issues from an imaginary – and imperfect – identification with the position either of having the phallus (= masculinity) or of being it (= femininity). Revealed here as wanting to be rather than have 'Serge', Rachel is shown simultaneously to have wanted to have (cf. to be) the phallus: that is, to have wanted to be masculine, transgressing gender norms.

64. See Butler, *Bodies that Matter*, p. 103.

65. Like *La Bâtarde*, which charts Leduc's creation of *L'Asphyxie*, *Un amour* chronicles a *venue à l'ecriture*. Within its pages, 'Serge' writes and finally publishes an inceptive autofictional *roman* entitled *Fils*.

66. Butler, *Bodies that Matter*, p. 103.
67. 'Me vois par ses yeux, dans ses yeux. Du coup, j'oublie de la voir, elle. Ce qu'il y a d'irrésistible en elle: je ne peux pas me résister, à moi' (UA, p. 46).
68. For a detailed reading of these solutions and the manner in which Doubrovsky's text proffers them for our scrutiny, see my 'Serge Doubrovsky's "Gender Trouble"', pp. 321–5.
69. See *Bodies that Matter*, p. 104. Butler argues here that the two key figures of 'abjected' homosexuality, the feminized fag and the phallicized dyke, symbolize the 'constraining force of gendered punishment' that subtends the sociosymbolic order. She likewise asserts that 'the terror over occupying either of these positions is what compels the assumption of a sexed position [. . .] assumed through a move that excludes and abjects gay and lesbian possibilities' (ibid., p. 96).
70. Ibid., p. 103.
71. We should note that, if we read his desire in this way, we are engaging to a degree with notions of male-homosexuality-as-narcissism that are privileged in psychoanalytic thought (cf. S. Freud (1905/1977), 'The Sexual Aberrations', in *On Sexuality*, *Penguin Freud Library*, vol. 7, pp. 45–87, p. 56) but are critiqued by queer theorists such as Edelman.
72. 'Une obsession, ça montre au moins que j'ai mes règles. D'or, absolue, il y en a une, inculquée dès ma naissance, dès avant même. LA SEPARATION DES SEXES. [. . .] Chacun à sa place, chacun son sexe. Chaque sexe à sa place' (UA, pp. 24–5).
73. 'Grâce à Rachel, je pénètre dans le monde de la pédale. Elle a ses entrées. Aucune idée pourquoi, *fag hag*, comme on les appelle ici' (UA, p. 180).
74. 'moi qu'il baise à travers elle, moi qu'on vise, [. . .] moi l'enculé' (UA, p. 348).
75. 'A Normale, connu que des gars normaux. [. . .] Ici, l'illicite s'affiche, les goûts se discutent, on annonce la couleur. Il y a la secte du noir, les tenants de la tenue cuir, casquette SS, blousons zébrés de fermetures Eclair, ceinturons à boucles massives, braguettes cloutées' (UA, pp. 180–1).
76. My sense of the decoy function of 'Serge''s (dis)avowals is reinforced by the fact that, in the segment of *Un amour*'s Coda where he 'confesses' to the 'petite excursion homosexuelle' he took with Rachel, he also states that she was never his 'type'. In so doing, he not only signals, once again, that she was not his kind of woman but also, in yet another gesture of sexual denial, makes it clear that, for all her polysexuality, she was in no way his 'guy'/homosexual love object. We can, of course, read all the textual sections where 'Serge' insists, endlessly, that his lover was not his 'type' or his 'genre' (in English 'genre' translates as 'sort' but also as 'gender') as pointers to the fact that she constitutes on one level, precisely, the focus of a same-sex desire he is determined to disown.

77. 'Frère et soeur, [. . .] un zeste d'inceste, ça corse, ça pimente un peu les rapports' (UA, p. 175).
78. Freud symbolically equates money with the penis (and with faeces and the (male) baby). See S. Freud (1917/1977), 'On Transformations of Instinct as Exemplified in Anal Erotism', in *On Sexuality, Penguin Freud Library*, vol. 7, pp. 293–302.
79. 'le jambon cru pendu au croc l'os orné au bout de sa corne d'une touffe de poils noirs' (UA, p. 261).
80. See 'Fragment of an Analytic Reading', p. 331.
81. 'inscription supplémentaire de la sexualité'. See 'Autobiographie/vérité/psych-analyse', p. 71; 'Autobiography/Truth/Psychoanalysis', p. 35.
82. 'l'écriture fournit au fantasme, par la fiction qu'elle instaure, l'accomplissement sans cesse dénié par la réalité'. See 'Autobiographie/vérité/psychanalyse', p. 70; 'Autobiography/Truth/Psychoanalysis', p. 35.
83. 'l'espace d'une jouissance interdite et inédite'. See 'Autobiographie/vérité/psychanalyse', p. 70; 'Autobiography/Truth/Psychoanalysis', p. 35.
84. In the correspondence we exchanged after I first published the arguments reprised here, Doubrovsky was categorical in his assertion of this fact, whilst generously cognizant of the validity of – and, indeed, the 'Doubrovskian' tenor of – the reading I have performed on *Un amour*. His refutation of homosexuality as in any way appealing to him is reiterated, forcefully, in his latest autofictional essay, *Laissé pour conte*. See S. Doubrovsky (1999), *Laissé pour conte*, Paris, pp. 293–307. Useful comments regarding the fundamentally *textual* character of the sexed 'deviations' his writings ascribe to Doubrovsky and their centrality to the Doubrovskian autofictional enterprise are offered by Ireland, in 'Introduction: Monstrous Writing', p. 7.
85. 'la reprise d'un destin par une liberté' (LB, préface, p. 8).
86. In a number of his *autofictions*, Doubrovsky confirms that his writings somehow 'kill off' women with whom he has been involved. See for example *Laissé pour conte*, p. 47.
87. J. Ireland (1993), '"The fact is that writing is a profoundly immoral act": An Interview with Serge Doubrovsky', *Genre*, vol. XXVI, pp. 43–9, p. 45.

Afterword

In putting *Heterographies* together, I wished amongst other things to provide a snapshot of the discursive space constituted by modern and contemporary French life-writing. The narratives that make up my corpus, produced as they were at different moments of the twentieth century, offer us an enhanced awareness of the multifaceted nature and breadth of the space in question and permit us, moreover, to intuit the centrality of autobiographical practice to the wider French literary-cultural field.

Clearly, the texts I selected for study embrace the life-writing endeavour in variant ways. However, all of them bear out my founding premise that questions of sexuality, gender and difference are fundamental to the autobiographical discourse of both sexes. In working to illuminate the ways in which they do so, I chose to follow a particular constellation of critical pathways, carving up my corpus in a manner determined by my personal – and present – reading concerns. But it would have been equally possible to produce other gender-oriented explications of the narratives I elected to scrutinize, grounded in different narrative pairings or encounters. As I indicated in my Introduction, the autobiographical works with which *Heterographies* engages can be taken to be multiply connected, and to form a discursive body characterized by a marked degree of cohesiveness.

It was not my purpose, here, to think through and about sexual and auto-biographical difference in a monolithic fashion. Certainly, the readings elaborated in *Heterographies* turn primarily on the diverse ways in which the texts of my corpus incorporate discursive strategies that repress, reveal, revisit or resolve the sexual and emotional motivations and impulses of the sexed autobiographical narrative subject. However, I sought wherever possible to construct these readings in a manner intended to signal how the writing of sexual difference inevitably intersects with other discursive and political phenomena such as colonial/post-colonial narrative practice, visual representation, philosophical auto-theorization, the representation of the culturally- and discursively-contoured body and so forth. I sought, in other words, not to lose sight of the fact that gendered and sexed subjectivity, and its narrative expression, does not exist in a vacuum uninflected by broader issues of subjective positioning, portrayal and politics. In the final analysis, though, I willingly acknowledge that the critical exegeses that make *Heterographies* up – exegeses that invoke the narrative inscription of sexuality, desire and sexed identity – speak above all of questions of gender. That they do so seems to me to be entirely legitimate. I argued, in my Introduction, for an expansion of the gender agenda, an expansion predicated on the need to move the activity of gender-focused literary interpretation beyond the purely gynocentric. *Heterographies* seeks to contribute to that necessary and vital expansion, participating in an evolving, dynamic reading enterprise that cannot fail to open up the literary-critical terrain.

Alex Hughes,
University of Birmingham

Select Bibliography

Primary Texts

Beauvoir, S. de (1964), *Une mort très douce*, Paris: Gallimard.

Beauvoir, S. de (1969), *A Very Easy Death*, trans. P. O'Brian, Harmondsworth: Penguin.

Cardinal, M. (1975), *Les Mots pour le dire*, Paris: Grasset and Fasquelle.

Cardinal, M. (1993), *The Words to Say It*, trans. P. Goodheart, London: The Women's Press.

Doubrovsky, S. (1982), *Un amour de soi*, Paris: Hachette.

Duras, M. (1984), *L'Amant*, Paris: Minuit.

Duras, M. (1986), *The Lover*, trans. B. Bray, London: Flamingo.

Gide, A. (1955), *Si le grain ne meurt*, Paris: Gallimard.

Gide, A. (1977), *If It Die . . .*, trans. D. Bussy, Harmondsworth: Penguin.

Guibert, H. (1981), *L'Image fantôme*, Paris: Minuit.

Guibert, H. (1990), *A l'ami qui ne m'a pas sauvé la vie*, Paris: Gallimard.

Guibert, H. (1995), *To the Friend Who Did Not Save My Life*, trans. L. Coverdale, London: Quartet.

Leduc, V. (1946), *L'Asphyxie*, Paris: Gallimard.

Leduc, V. (1964), *La Bâtarde*, Paris: Gallimard.

Leduc, V. (1965), *La Bâtarde*, trans. D. Coltman, London: Peter Owen.

Sartre, J.-P. (1964), *Les Mots*, Paris: Gallimard.

Sartre, J.-P. (1967), *Words*, trans. I. Clephane, Harmondsworth: Penguin.

Critical Studies Relating to Authors Discussed

Beauvoir

Corbin, L. (1996), 'Complicity and Silence', in *The Mother Mirror: Self-Representation and the Mother–Daughter Relation in Colette, Simone de Beauvoir, and Marguerite Duras*, New York and Washington, DC: Peter Lang, pp. 45–70.

Hughes, A. (1998), 'Murdering the Mother in *Memoirs of a Dutiful Daughter*', in E. Fallaize (ed.), *Simone de Beauvoir: A Critical Reader*, London and New York: Routledge, pp. 120–31.

Jardine. A. (1985), 'Death Sentences: Writing Couples and Ideology', in S. Suleiman (ed.), *The Female Body in Western Culture*, Cambridge, MA and London: Harvard University Press, pp. 84–96.

Kadish, D. (1989), 'Simone de Beauvoir's *Une Mort très douce*: Existential and Feminist Perspectives on Old Age', *The French Review*, vol. 62, pp. 631–9.

Marks, E. (1998), 'Encounters with Death in *A Very Easy Death*', in E. Fallaize (ed.), *Simone de Beauvoir: A Critical Reader*, London and New York: Routledge, pp. 132–42.

Miller, N. K. (1992), 'Autobiographical Deaths', *The Massachusetts Review*, vol. 33, pp. 19–47.

Montfort, C. (1996), '"La Vieille Née": Simone de Beauvoir, *Une mort très douce*, and Annie Ernaux, *Une femme*', *French Forum*, vol. 41, pp. 349–64.

Tidd, U. (forthcoming), *Simone de Beauvoir, Gender and Testimony*, Cambridge: Cambridge University Press.

Cardinal

Cairns, L. (1993), 'Roots and Alienation in Marie Cardinal's *Au pays de mes racines*', *Forum for Modern Language Studies*, vol. XXIX, pp. 346–58.

Durham, C. (1992), *The Contexture of Feminism: Marie Cardinal and Multicultural Literacy*, Urbana, IL and Chicago: University of Illinois Press.

Ha, M.-P. (1995), 'Outre-Mer/Autre Mère: Cardinal and Algeria', *Romance Notes*, vol. XXXVI, pp. 315–23.

Haigh, S. (1994), 'Between Irigaray and Cardinal: Reinventing Maternal Genealogies', *Modern Language Review*, vol. 89, pp. 61–70.

Hall, C. (1994), *Marie Cardinal*, Amsterdam: Rodopi.

Le Clézio, M. (1981), 'Mother and Motherland: the Daughter's Quest for Origins', *Stanford French Review*, vol. V, pp. 381–9.

Lionnet, F. (1989), 'Privileged Difference and the Possibility of Emancipation', in *Autobiographical Voices: Race, Gender, Self-Portraiture*, Ithaca, NY and London: Cornell University Press, pp. 191–206.

Powrie, P. (1990), 'Reading for pleasure: Marie Cardinal's *Les Mots pour le dire* and the text as (re)play of Oedipal Configurations', in M. Atack and P. Powrie (eds), *Contemporary French Fiction by Women*, Manchester: Manchester University Press, pp. 163–76.

Woodhull, W. (1993), 'Out of France', in *Transfigurations of the Maghreb: Feminism, Decolonization and Literatures*, Minneapolis, MN and London: University of Minnesota Press, pp. 154–71.

Select Bibliography

Doubrovsky

Darrieussecq, M. (1996), 'L'Autofiction, un genre pas sérieux', *Poétique*, no. 107, pp. 369–80.

Hughes, A. (1995), 'Serge Doubrovsky's "Gender Trouble": Writing the (Homo)textual Self in *Un amour de soi*', *French Forum*, vol. 20, pp. 315–31.

Ireland, J. (1993), 'Introduction: Monstrous Writing', *Genre* (Doubrovsky special issue), vol. XXVI, pp. 1–11.

Ireland, J. (1993), '"The fact is that writing is a profoundly immoral act": An Interview with Serge Doubrovsky', *Genre*, vol. XXVI, pp. 43–9.

Kingcaid, R. (1993), 'Romancing the Tome: the Seduction of Intertext in Doubrovsky's *Un amour de soi*', *SubStance*, vol. 22, pp. 25–40.

Miguet, M. (1992), '*Un amour de soi*: Doubrovsky, Proust et le père profané', *Lettres romanes*, vol. 46, pp. 69–87.

Turcanu, R. (1996), 'Le Désir d'être auteur: Doubrovsky et Sartre en intertexte', *Dalhousie French Studies*, vol. 35, pp. 79–94.

Duras

Armel, A. (1990), 'Le Jeu autobiographique', *Magazine Littéraire*, no. 278, pp. 28–31.

Beaujour, D.(1990), 'L'Oubli de la photographie', *Magazine Littéraire*, no. 278, pp. 49–51.

Cohen, S.D. (1990), 'Fiction and the Photographic Image in Duras' *The Lover*', *L'Esprit Créateur*, vol. XXX, pp. 56–68.

Fauvel, M. (1993), 'Photographie et autobiographie: *Roland Barthes* par Roland Barthes et *L'Amant* de Marguerite Duras', *Romance Notes*, vol. XXXIV, pp. 193–202.

Ferrières-Pestureau, S. (1997), *Une étude psychanalytique de la figure du ravissement dans l'oeuvre de M. Duras*, Paris: L'Harmattan.

Hellerstein, N. (1991), '"Image" and Absence in Marguerite Duras' *L'Amant*, *Modern Language Studies*, vol. 21, pp. 45–56.

Kristeva, J. (1987), 'La maladie de la douleur: Duras', in *Soleil noir: dépression et mélancolie*, Paris: Gallimard, pp. 227–65.

Saint-Amand, P. (1994), 'La Photographie de famille dans *L'Amant*', in A. Vircondelet (ed.), *Marguerite Duras: Rencontres de Cerisy*, Paris: Ecriture, pp. 225–40.

Selous, T. (1988), *The Other Woman: Feminism and Femininity in the Work of Marguerite Duras*, New Haven, CT and London: Yale University Press.

Gide

Apter, E. (1987), *André Gide and the Codes of Homotextuality*, Stanford: Anma Libri.

Bersani, L. (1995), 'The Gay Outlaw', in *Homos*, Cambridge, MA and London: Harvard University Press, pp. 113–81.

Boone, J. (1995), 'Vacation Cruises; or, The Homoerotics of Orientalism', *PMLA*, vol. 110, no. 1, pp. 95–107.

Delay, J. (1956/7), *La Jeunesse d'André Gide*, 2 vols, Paris: Gallimard.

Dollimore, J. (1991), *Sexual Dissidence: Augustine to Wilde, Freud to Foucault*, Oxford: Clarendon Press.

Kopelson, K. (1994), 'Pederastic Trappings: Gide and Firbank', in *Love's Litany: The Writing of Modern Homoerotics*, Stanford, CA: Stanford University Press, pp. 49–73.

Lejeune, P. (1975), 'Gide et l'espace autobiographique', in *Le Pacte autobiographique*, Paris: Seuil, pp. 165–96.

Lucey, M. (1995), *Gide's Bent: Sexuality, Politics, Writing*, New York and Oxford: Oxford University Press.

Marty, E. (1994), 'Le Poète sans livre', *Bulletin des amis d'André Gide*, vol. XXII, pp. 219–26.

Millot, C. (1996), 'Un hybride de bacchante et de Saint-Esprit', in *Gide Genet Mishima: Intelligence de la perversion*, Paris: Gallimard, pp. 19–79.

Pratt, M. L. (1981), 'Mapping Ideology: Gide, Camus and Algeria', *College Literature*, vol. 8, pp. 158–74.

Saegert, M. (1994), 'Exotisme, métissage et écriture', *Bulletin des amis d'André Gide*, Vol. XXII, pp. 173–87.

Schehr, L. (1995), 'On Vacation with Gide and Barthes', in *Alcibiades at the Door: Gay Discourses in French Literature*, Stanford, CA: Stanford University Press, pp. 113–54.

Segal, N. (1998), *André Gide: Pedagogy and Pederasty*, Oxford: Clarendon Press.

Segal, N. (1998), 'André Gide and the Niece's Seduction', in M. Merck, N. Segal and E. Wright (eds), *Coming Out of Feminism?*, Oxford: Blackwell, pp. 194–213.

Guibert

'Hervé Guibert: Foucault a été mon maître, je devais écrire sa mort . . .', *L'Evénement du jeudi*, 1–7 March 1990, pp. 82–5 (interview).

Apter, E. (1993), 'Fantom Images: Hervé Guibert and the Writing of "sida" in France', in T. F. Murphy and S. Poirier (eds), *Writing AIDS: Gay Literature, Language, and Analysis*, New York: Columbia University Press, pp. 83–97.

Bellour, R. (1995), 'Une entreprise qui n'eut jamais d'exemple . . .', *Nottingham French Studies* (Guibert special issue), vol. 34, pp. 121–30.

Boulé, J.-P. (1995), *Hervé Guibert: 'A l'ami qui ne m'a pas sauvé la vie'* and *Other Writings*, Glasgow: Glasgow Critical Guides.

Buisine, A. (1995), 'Le Photographique plutôt que la photographie', *Nottingham French Studies*, vol. 34, pp. 32–41.

Guilbard, A.-C. (1995), 'De la pratique du narcissisme à la recherche de l'image vraie', *Nottingham French Studies*, vol. 34, pp. 42–8.

Hill, L. (1995), 'Ecrire – la maladie', *Nottingham French Studies*, vol. 34, pp. 89–99.

Hughes, A. (1998), 'Reading Guibert's *L'Image fantôme*/Reading Desire', *Modern and Contemporary France*, vol. 6, pp. 203–14.

Pratt, M. (1995), 'De la désidentification à l'incognito: à la recherche d'une autobiographie homosexuelle', *Nottingham French Studies*, vol. 34, pp. 70–81.

Pratt, M. (1998), '"A Walk Along the Side of the Motorway": AIDS and the Spectacular Body of Hervé Guibert', in O. Heathcote, A. Hughes and J. S. Williams (eds), *Gay Signatures: Gay and Lesbian Theory, Fiction and Film in France, 1945–1995*, Oxford and New York: Berg, pp. 151–72.

Reymondet, F. (1997), 'La fin: issue fatale, issue narrative', *Dalhousie French Studies*, vol. 39/40, pp. 181–91

Sarkonak, R. (1994), 'De la métastase au métatexte: Hervé Guibert', *Texte*, vol. 15/16, pp. 229–59

Sarkonak, R. (1997), 'Traces and Shadows: Fragments of Hervé Guibert', *Yale French Studies*, vol. 90, pp. 172–202.

Sarkonak, R. (ed.) (1997), *Le Corps textuel d'Hervé Guibert*, Paris: Minard.

Schehr, L. (1995), 'Guibert: Cippus', in *Alcibiades at the Door: Gay Discourses in French Literature*, Stanford, CA: Stanford University Press, pp. 155–96.

Smyth, E. (1995), '*Des Aveugles*: modes d'articulation', *Nottingham French Studies*, vol. 34, pp. 8–14.

Wilkerson, D. (1995), 'Hervé Guibert: Writing the Spectral Image', *Studies in Twentieth Century Literature*, vol. 19, pp. 269–88.

Leduc

Ceccatty, R. de (1994), *Eloge de la Bâtarde*, Paris: Stock.

Courtivron, I. de (1985), *Violette Leduc*, Boston: Twayne.

Evans. M. (1987), 'Violette Leduc: The Bastard', in *Masks of Tradition*, Ithaca, NY and London: Cornell University Press, pp. 102–22.

Girard, P. (1986), *Œdipe masqué*, Paris: des femmes.

Hall, C. (1988),'*L'Ecriture féminine* and the Search for the Mother in the Works of Violette Leduc and Marie Cardinal', in M. Guggenheim (ed.), *Women in French Literature*, Saratoga: Anma Libri, pp. 231–8.

Hughes, A. (1994), *Violette Leduc: Mothers, Lovers, and Language*, London: MHRA.

Hughes, A. (1998), 'Commodifying Queer: Violette Leduc's Autobiographical Homotextualities', in O. Heathcote, A. Hughes and J. S. Williams (eds), *Gay Signatures: Gay and Lesbian Theory, Fiction and Film in France, 1945–1995*, Oxford and New York: Berg, pp. 113–29.

Jansiti, C. (1994), 'Ils ont refusé le début de *Ravages*', *nord'*, vol. 23, pp. 77–89.

Marks, E. (1990), 'Lesbian Intertextuality', in G. Stambolian and E. Marks (eds), *Homosexualities and French Literature*, Ithaca, NY and London: Cornell University Press, pp. 353–77.

Marson, S. (1995), 'Au bord de *L'Asphyxie*, *Littérature*, no. 98, pp. 45–58.

Marson, S. (1998), *Le Temps de l'autobiographie: Violette Leduc*, Saint-Denis: Presses Universitaires de Vincennes.

Neuman, S. (1989), '"An appearance walking in a forest the sexes burn": Autobiography and the Construction of the Feminine Body', *Signature*, vol. 2, pp. 1–26.

Schrader, S. (1998), 'Le Bonheur était une façade', in P. Renard and M. Hecquet (eds), *Violette Leduc*, Lille: UL3, pp. 37–50.

Sartre

Beauvoir, S. de (1981), *La Cérémonie des adieux, suivi de Entretiens avec Jean-Paul Sartre août–septembre 1974*, Paris: Gallimard.

Beauvoir, S. de (1986), *Adieux: A Farewell to Sartre*, trans. P. O'Brian, Harmondsworth: Penguin.

Burgelin, C (ed.), (1986), *Lectures de Sartre*, Lyons: Presses Universitaires de Lyon.

Chiantaretto, J.-F. (1995), '*Les Mots*, une lecture psychanalytique', in *De l'acte autobiographique: Le Psychanalyste et l'écriture autobiographique*, Seyssel: Champ Vallon, pp. 181–236.

Contat, M. (ed.) (1996), *Pourquoi et comment Sartre a écrit "Les Mots"*, Paris: Presses Universitaires de France.

Doubrovsky, S. (1989), *Le Livre brisé*, Paris: Grasset.

Doubrovsky, S. (1991), 'Sartre: autobiographie/autofiction', *Revue des Sciences Humaines*, vol. 98, pp. 17–26.

Green, A. (1992), 'Des *Mouches* aux *Mots*', in *La Déliaison*, Paris: Les Belles Lettres, pp. 340–70.

Idt, G. (1982) 'Des *Mots* à *L'Enfance d'un chef*: autobiographie et psychanalyse', in M. Issacharoff and J.-C. Vilquin (eds), *Sartre et la mise en signe*, Paris: Klincksieck, pp. 11–30.

Leak, A. (1989), *The Perverted Consciousness*, Basingstoke and London: Macmillan.

Lejeune, P. (1975), 'L'Ordre du récit dans les *Mots* de Sartre', in *Le Pacte auto-biographique*, Paris: Seuil, pp. 197–243.

Lejeune, P. (1989), 'The Order of Narrative in Sartre's *Les Mots*', in *On Auto-biography*, trans. K. Leary, pref. P. J. Eakin, Minneapolis, MN: University of Minnesota Press, pp. 70–107.

Mehlman, J. (1974), 'Sartre and His Other', in *A Structural Study of Autobiography: Proust, Leiris, Sartre, Lévi-Strauss*, Ithaca, NY and London: Cornell University Press, pp. 151–67.

Murat, M. (1988), 'Jean-Paul Sartre, un enfant séquestré', *Les Temps modernes*, vol. 498, pp. 128–49.

Pacaly, J. (1980), *Sartre au miroir*, Paris: Klincksieck.

Smyth, E. (1995), 'Autobiography, Contingency, Selfhood: A Reading of *Les Mots*', in T. Keefe and E. Smyth (eds), *Autobiography and the Existential Self*, Liverpool: Liverpool University Press, pp. 25–37.

Walling, J. (1996), 'Repression and Denial: The Absent Childhood Self in Sartre's *Les Mots*', *Romance Studies*, no. 27, pp. 49–61.

Secondary and Further Reading

Anzieu, D. (1965), 'Le Discours de l'obsessionnel dans les romans de Robbe-Grillet', *Les Temps Modernes*, vol. 21, pp. 608–37.

Apter, E. (1991), *Feminizing the Fetish: Psychoanalysis and Narrative Obsession in Turn-of-the-Century France*, Ithaca, NY and London: Cornell University Press.

Arber, S. and Ginn, J. (eds) (1995), *Connecting Gender and Ageing: A Sociological Approach*, Buckingham and Philadelphia, PA: Open University Press.

Ashcroft, B., Griffiths, G. and Tiffin, H. (eds) (1995), *The Post-Colonial Studies Reader*, Routledge: London and New York.

Barthes, R. (1970), *S/Z*, Paris: Seuil.

Barthes, R. (1975), *S/Z*, trans. R. Miller, New York: Hill and Wang.

Barthes, R. (1977), *Fragments d'un discours amoureux*, Paris: Seuil.

Barthes, R. (1979), *A Lover's Discourse: Fragments*, trans. R. Howard, London: Cape.

Barthes, R. (1980), *La Chambre claire: Note sur la photographie*, Paris: Gallimard Seuil.

Barthes, R. (1984), *Camera Lucida: Reflections on Photography*, trans. R. Howard, London: Fontana.

Beauvoir, S. de (1949), *Le Deuxième Sexe*, Paris: Gallimard.

Beauvoir, S. de (1988), *The Second Sex*, trans. H. Parshley, Picador: London.

Beauvoir, S. de (1958), *Mémoires d'une jeune fille rangée*, Paris: Gallimard.

Beauvoir, S. de (1987), *Memoirs of a Dutiful Daughter*, trans. J. Kirkup, Harmondsworth: Penguin.

Beauvoir, S. de (1990), *Lettres à Sartre 1940–1963*, Paris: Gallimard.

Beauvoir, S. de (1991), *Letters to Sartre*, trans. Q. Hoare, London: Radius.

Benstock, S. (ed.), (1988), *The Private Self: Theory and Practice of Women's Autobiographical Writings*, London and New York: Routledge.

Bergner, G. (1995), 'Who is that Masked Woman?, or, The Role of Gender in Fanon's *Black Skin, White Masks*', *PMLA*, vol. 110, pp. 75–88.

Bonnet, G. (1981), *Voir Etre vu, I*, Paris: Presses Universitaires de France.

Brodzki, B. and Schenck, C. (eds), (1988), *Life/Lines: Theorizing Women's Autobiography*, Ithaca, NY and London: Cornell University Press.

Brooks, P. (1984), *Reading for the Plot*, New York: Knopf.

Buisine, A. (1988), 'Tel Orphée', *Revue des Sciences Humaines*, vol. 81, pp. 124–49.

Burgin, V. (1986), 'Re-reading *Camera Lucida*', in *The End of Art Theory*, Basingstoke: Macmillan, pp. 71–92.

Butler, J. (1986), 'Sex and Gender in Simone de Beauvoir's *Second Sex*', *Yale French Studies*, no. 72, pp. 35–49.

Butler, J. (1990), *Gender Trouble: Feminism and the Subversion of Identity*, London and New York: Routledge.

Butler, J. (1993), 'Critically Queer', *GLQ: Journal of Gay and Lesbian Studies*, vol. 1, pp. 17–32.

Butler, J. (1993), *Bodies that Matter: On the Discursive Limits of Sex*, London and New York: Routledge.

Cardinal, M. (1977), *Autrement dit*, Paris: Grasset.

Cardinal, M. (1980), *Au pays de mes racines*, Paris: Grasset.

Chauduri, N. and Strobel, M. (eds) (1992), *Western Women and Imperialism: Complicity and Resistance*, Bloomington, IN and Indianapolis, IN: Indiana University Press.

Colomina, B. (ed.) (1992), *Sexuality and Space*, Princeton, NJ: Princeton Papers on Architecture.

Cowie, E. (1997), *Representing the Woman: Cinema and Psychoanalysis*, London: Macmillan.

Dällenbach, L. (1977), *Le Récit spéculaire*, Paris: Seuil.

Dällenbach, L. (1986), *Mirrors and After: Five Essays on Literary Theory and Criticism*, New York: Pro Helvetia.

Danahy, M. (1991), *The Feminization of the Novel*, Gainesville, FL: University of Florida Press.

Darian-Smith, K., Gunner, G. and Nuttall, S. (eds) (1996), *text, theory, space*, London and New York: Routledge.

Darrieussecq, M. (1996), 'L'Autofiction, un genre pas sérieux', *Poétique*, no. 107, pp. 369–80.

Diprose, R. (1994), *The Bodies of Women: Ethics, Embodiment and Sexual Difference*, London and New York: Routledge.

Doubrovsky, S. (1974), *La Place de la Madeleine*, Paris: Mercure de France.

Doubrovsky, S. (1977), *Fils*, Paris: Galilée.

Doubrovsky, S. (1988), *Autobiographiques: de Corneille à Sartre*, Paris: Presses Universitaires de France.

Doubrovsky, S. (1990), 'Sartre's *La nausée*: Fragment of an Analytic Reading', in G. Stambolian and E. Marks (eds), *Homosexualities and French Literature*, Ithaca, NY and London: Cornell University Press, pp. 330–40.

Doubrovsky, S. (1993), 'Autobiography/Truth/Psychoanalysis', trans. L. Whalen and J. Ireland, *Genre*, vol. XXVI, pp. 27–42 (originally published as 'Autobiographie/vérité/psychanalyse', in *Autobiographiques*, pp. 61–79).

Doubrovsky, S. (1999), *Laissé pour conte*, Paris: Grasset.

Doubrovsky, S., Lecarme, J. and Lejeune, P. (eds) (1993), *Autofictions et Cie*, Paris: Cahiers RITM.

Duncan, J. and Ley, D. (eds) (1993), *place/culture/representation*, London and New York: Routledge.

Eadie, J. (1994), 'Queer', *Paragraph*, vol. 17, pp. 244–51.

Edelman, L. (1994), *Homographesis: Essays in Gay Literary and Cultural Theory*, New York and London: Routledge.

Foucault, M. (1975), *Surveiller et punir: naissance de la prison*, Paris: Gallimard.

Foucault, M. (1977), *Discipline and Punish: The Birth of The Prison*, trans. A. Sheridan, London: Allen Lane, Penguin.

Foucault, M. (1976), *La Volonté de savoir: Histoire de la sexualité I*, Paris: Gallimard.

Foucault, M. (1990), *The History of Sexuality I: An Introduction*, trans. R. Hurley, London: Penguin.

Foucault, M. (1994), *Dits et écrits 1954–88*, Paris: Gallimard.

Freud, S. (1905/1977), 'The Sexual Aberrations', in *On Sexuality*, *Penguin Freud Library*, vol. 7, Harmondsworth: Penguin, pp. 45–87.

Freud, S. (1912/1977), 'On the Universal Tendency to Debasement in the Sphere of Love', in *On Sexuality*, *Penguin Freud Library*, vol. 7, pp. 243–60.

Freud, S. (1920/1922), *Beyond the Pleasure Principle*, London: The International Psychoanalytic Library.

Freud, S. (1923), 'The Ego and the Id', Chapter III, *Standard Edition*, vol. 19, pp. 28–39.

Freud, S. (1917/1977), 'On Transformations of Instinct as Exemplified in Anal Erotism', in *On Sexuality*, *Penguin Freud Library*, vol. 7, pp. 293–302.

Freud, S. (1924/1977), 'The Dissolution of the Oedipus Complex', in *On Sexuality*, *Penguin Freud Library*, vol. 7, pp. 313–22.

Freud, S. (1927/1977), 'Fetishism', in *On Sexuality*, *Penguin Freud Library*, vol. 7, pp. 344–57.

Freud, S. (1933/1973), 'Femininity', in *New Introductory Lectures On Psycho-analysis*, *Penguin Freud Library*, vol. 2, pp. 145–69.

Gilmore, L. (1994), *Autobiographics: A Feminist Theory of Women's Self-Representation*, Ithaca, NY and London: Cornell University Press.

Gittings, C. E. (ed.) (1996), *Imperialism and Gender: Constructions of Masculinity*, New Lambton and Hebden Bridge: Dangaroo Press.

Grosz, E. (1995), *space, time and perversion*, New York and London: Routledge.

Guibert, H. (1984), *Le Seul Visage*, Paris: Minuit.

Guibert, H. (1986), *Mes Parents*, Paris: Gallimard.

Guibert, H. (1992), *Cytomégalovirus*, Paris: Seuil.

Hornung, A. and Ruhe, E. (eds) (1992), *Autobiographie et Avant-garde*, Tübingen: Narr.

Hughes, A. and Witz, A. (1997), 'Feminism and the Matter of Bodies: From de Beauvoir to Butler', *Body and Society*, vol. 3, pp. 47–60.

Jaccomard, H. (1993), *Lecteur et lecture dans l'autobiographie française contemporaine*, Geneva: Droz.

JanMohamed, A. (1985), 'The Economy of Manichean Allegory: The Function of Racial Difference in Colonialist Literature', *Critical Inquiry*, vol. 12, pp. 59–85.

Kristeva, J. (1980), *Pouvoirs de l'horreur: Essai sur l'abjection*, Paris: Seuil.

Kristeva, J. (1982), *Powers of Horror: An Essay on Abjection*, trans. L. Roudiez, New York: Columbia University Press.

Kristeva, J. (1987), *Soleil noir: dépression et mélancolie*, Paris: Gallimard.

Kristeva, J. (1989), *Black Sun: Depression and Melancholia*, trans. L. Roudiez, New York: Columbia University Press.

Kristeva, J. (1993), *Les Nouvelles Maladies de l'âme*, Paris: Fayard.

Lacan, J. (1971), *Ecrits II*, Paris: Seuil.

Lecarme, J. and Lecarme-Tabone, E. (1997), *L'Autobiographie*, Paris: Colin.

Leduc, V. (1948), *L'Affamée*, Paris: Gallimard.

Leduc, V. (1960), *Trésors à prendre*, Paris: Gallimard.

Leduc, V. (1973), *La Chasse à l'amour*, Paris: Gallimard.

Lejeune, P. (1975), *Le Pacte autobiographique*, Paris: Seuil.

Lejeune, P. (1989), *On Autobiography*, trans. K. Leary, pref. P. J. Eakin, Minneapolis, MN: University of Minnesota Press.

Lupton, D. (1994), *Medicine as Culture*, London: Sage.

MacCabe, C. (1997), 'Barthes and Bazin: The Ontology of the Image', in J.-M. Rabaté (ed.), *Writing the Image After Roland Barthes*, Philadelphia, PA: University of Pennsylvania Press, pp. 71–6.

McClintock, A. (1995), *Imperial Leather: Race, Gender and Sexuality in the Colonial Contest*, London and New York: Routledge.

Martin, B. (1998), 'Sexualities without Genders', in M. Merck, N. Segal and E. Wright (eds), *Coming out of Feminism?*, Oxford: Blackwell, pp. 11–35.

Martin, E. (1997), 'Medical Metaphors of Women's Bodies: Menstruation and Menopause', in K. Conboy, N. Medina and S. Stanbury (eds), *Writing on the Body: Female Embodiment and Feminist Theory*, New York: Columbia University Press, pp. 15–41.

Metz, C. (1990), 'Photography and Fetish', in C. Squiers (ed.), *The Critical Image: Essays in Contemporary Photography*, Seattle: Bay Press, pp. 154–66.

Michasiw, K. (1994), 'Camp, Masculinity, Masquerade', *Differences*, vol. 6, pp. 146–73.

Mills, S. (1994), 'Knowledge, Gender and Empire', in A. Blunt and G. Rose (eds), *Writing Women and Space: Colonial and Postcolonial Geographies*, New York and London: The Guilford Press, pp. 29–50.

Mitchell, J. (ed.) (1986), *The Selected Melanie Klein*, Harmondsworth: Penguin.

Mitchell, J. and Rose, J. (eds) (1982), *Feminine Sexuality: Jacques Lacan and the Ecole Freudienne*, Basingstoke and London: Macmillan.

Moi, T. (1994), *Simone de Beauvoir: The Making of an Intellectual Woman*, Oxford: Blackwell.

Mulvey, L. (1996), *Fetishism and Curiosity*, Bloomington, IN and Indianapolis, IN: Indiana University Press.

Neuman, S. (ed.) (1991), *Autobiography and Questions of Gender*, London and Portland, OR: Frank Cass.

Rabinow, P. (ed.) (1984), *The Foucault Reader*, New York: Pantheon.

Ramazanoglu, C (ed.) (1993), *Up Against Foucault*, London and New York: Routledge.

Ransom, J. (1997), *Foucault's Discipline: The Politics of Subjectivity*, Durham, NC and London: Duke University Press.

Said, E. (1993), *Culture and Imperialism*, London: Vintage.

Said, E. (1995), *Orientalism*, London: Penguin.

Sawicki, J. (1991), *Disciplining Foucault: Feminism, Power and the Body*, London and New York: Routledge.

Schehr, L. (1996), 'Body/Antibody', *Studies in Twentieth Century Literature*, vol. 20, pp. 405–30.

Schor, N. (1986), 'Female Fetishism: the Case of George Sand', in S. Suleiman (ed.), *The Female Body in Western Culture*, Cambridge, MA and London: Harvard University Press, pp. 363–72.

Sheringham, M. (1993), *French Autobiography: Devices and Desires*, Oxford: Clarendon Press.

Sheringham, M. (1998), 'Invisible Presences: Fiction, Autobiography and Women's

Lives – Virginia Woolf to Annie Ernaux', *Sites*, vol. 2, pp. 5–24.

Shildrick, M. (1997), *Leaky Bodies and Boundaries*, London and New York: Routledge.

Showalter, E. (ed.) (1989), *Speaking of Gender*, London and New York: Routledge.

Smart, B. (1985), *Michel Foucault*, Chichester: Ellis Horwood Limited.

Smith, S. and Watson, J. (eds) (1992), *De/Colonizing the Subject: The Politics of Gender in Women's Autobiography*, Minneapolis, MN: University of Minnesota Press.

Stanley, L. (1992), *The Auto/biographical I: The Theory and Practice of Feminist Auto/biography*, Manchester and New York: Manchester University Press.

Stanton, D. (ed.) (1984), *The Female Autograph: Theory and Practice of Auto-biography from the 10th to the 20th Century*, Chicago, IL and London: University of Chicago Press.

Index

Index

Index

Index

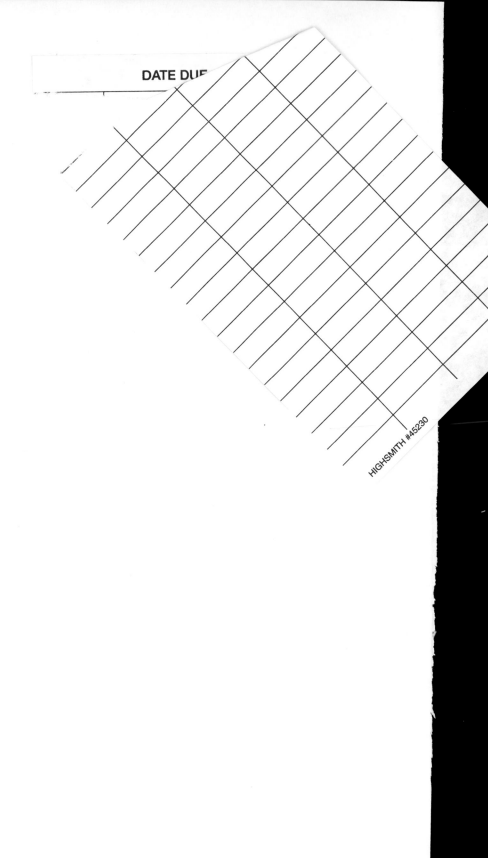

DATE DUE

HIGHSMITH #45230

Printed in USA